DEVICES

Architectural Press is an imprint of Elsevier
Linacre House, Jordan Hill, Oxford OX2 8DP
30 Corporate Drive, Suite 400, Burlington, MA 01803

First published 2006

British Library Cataloguing in Publication Data
A catalogue record for this book is available from the British Library

Library of Congress Cataloguing in Publication Data
A catalogue record for this book is available from the Library of Congress

ISBN-13: 978-0-7506-6384-7
ISBN-10: 0-7506-6384-7

Design by Studio 8
Printed and bound in Italy

06 07 08 09 10 10 9 8 7 6 5 4 3 2 1

DEVICES

a manual of architectural + spatial machines

cj Lim

AMSTERDAM • BOSTON • HEIDELBERG • LONDON • NEW YORK • OXFORD
PARIS • SAN DIEGO • SAN FRANCISCO • SINGAPORE • SYDNEY • TOKYO
Architectural Press is an imprint of Elsevier

Introduction
cj Lim, architectural inventor

Device: an instrument or tool designed for a specific task.

Devices have shared a long and complex history with architecture. The machines of Vitruvius and Leonardo da Vinci were devised in times of peace and war for both the construction and destruction of the built form. Today, kinetic intelligent systems are incorporated into building facades for environmental and aesthetic control. The device, however, has simultaneously followed a parallel trajectory - the Victorians invented a proliferation of devices, often ingenious, rarely of much practical use; Heath Robinson's contraptions displayed the absurd lengths to which devices were invented to satisfy our convenience and curiosity; his illustrations, sometimes carrying satirical and political overtones, are best remembered for their humour. Similarly, many of today's devices no longer perform quotidian practical tasks but are the results of artistic endeavour and are housed in galleries and museums. The works of artists such as Rebecca Horn and Jean Tinguely are choreographed to sing, dance and even interact with the audiences.

'Devices' is a manual celebrating architectural and spatial machines. The selection of works contained herein vary in scale, function and technological complexity. They are fun and theatrical. They are intelligent and thought-provoking (the device-maker's toolkit often includes metaphor, irony and lyricism, along with the usual staple of screws, pivots, motors, cam plates and armatures). Most significantly, however, they stimulate the human need for invention.

For the most part, the devices eschew function in the most conventional sense. The notion of an abstract device, distilling the mannerisms and characteristics of a machine, but freed of purpose and servitude, is clearly a paradox. Perhaps the *function* of these devices is instead to manipulate phenomena in the same way that architecture does - using space, time, sound and materiality to interact with its audience in a performative relationship. The diminished physical and financial scale, coupled with disconnection from purpose, makes device-making a breeding ground for invention and spatial possibility.

A number of devices in this manual appear to revel in a

nostalgia for Victorian technologies and quaint romantic iconography. 'The Star Gazer', 'Through the Looking Lens' and the 'Anticipation Navigator' might well be objects from the curio cabinet of a 19th Century inventor. Reconstituted from found objects and chemistry apparatus, their technologies are delightfully reminiscent of antiquated sewing machines. Another work, 'The Dry Stone Waller' appropriates steampunk sensibilities to brand new levels, being a piece of computer software written with clock springs, cogs and an old Victorian weighing scale amongst its components.

The muse of the 19th Century is not finished there – 'The Smoking Stool' employs a sequence of over-the-top mechanisms and gadgetry to light a solitary cigarette while the 'Spud-master 204' fires cooked potatoes at high speed to make mash, invoking the wit and daftness of Heath Robinson at his most outlandish. Theatre is the order of the day; practicality and sense have been mashed, incinerated and consigned to the scrapheap!

Then there are the narrative-inspired pieces such as 'The Shipping Forecast', 'Climatic Threat Assembly' and 'Mealtimes'. The poetically entitled 'Nostalgia' marks the landscape leaving behind memories of the past and thoughts of the present. Embedded with multi-layered metaphors and meaning, these devices are abstract representations in search of poetic spatial possibility. Also included in the book, however, are devices whose singular purpose is to record, measure, alter or perform spatial research.

Why can't we just use a computer chip instead? Not all the devices are stylised Victorian contraptions. 'I See What You Hear' is an interactive installation where users interact through sound and movement, its intelligence relying upon ingenuity with computer circuitry and programming. The power of new technology is also elegantly displayed in 'The Litmus' and 'Daycaster', which both respond to a variety of environmental inputs. How much science do we need to know before we can start conducting such experiments of our own at home? The answer varies, but to construct the 'Light Fibre Field', it appears one would need a degree in electronics at the very least!

'The Light-Space Modulator can be put to use in various optical experiments, and I find it reasonable that such experiments be carried on systematically, for they lead us towards new possibilities of optical and kinetic creations.'

Moholy-Nagy, 'Lichtrequisit einer elektrischen Bühne' 1930

From the romanticised machine to the minimal language of the electronic gismo microchip, aesthetic language is determined by the fabrication techniques and materials used. Conversely, the construction process sometimes leads to the discovery of new technological principles, unconventional techniques and surprising materials. Can a technological or abstract understanding of these devices and their construction influence and redefine the potential of architecture and spatial thinking?

The Light-Space Modulator: A device for demonstrating light and kinetic phenomena. Bulbs flash to a set of predetermined points, illuminating a continuously moving mechanism consisting of translucent, transparent and perforated material. Magical configurations of light appear.

By day, Toyo Ito's Tower of Winds stands an elegant 21m tall, opaque and unreadable, in front of the bustling Yokohama station. By night, it becomes magically insubstantial and ephemeral - a stunning display of ever-evolving light patterns, colour and transparencies. How is this achieved? Sheets of multi-layered perforated aluminium, acrylic mirror plates, 1,280 lamps and 12 white rings of neon, are all programmed to respond to the incidental music of the city.

Camera: An optical device consisting of a variable size aperture and a shutter to let in the correct amount of light, a series of lenses to focus the light, and light-sensitive film that records the image in a lightproof construct.

The southern façade of the Institut du Monde Arabe in Paris is made entirely of camera aperture diaphragms. 25,000 metal-bladed apertures, configured into Islamic patterns and sandwiched between two layers of glass, are controlled by 250 motors linked to a central computer system, which choreographs the metal irises depending on the intensity and level of daylight entering the building. The filtered light brings a decorative and distinctly Middle-Eastern atmosphere to what would otherwise be an elegant but soulless glass and steel edifice. According to its architect, Jean Nouvel, the client expressed concerns during the façade's developmental stages, questioning whether Venetian blinds would have the same effect!

Umbrella: A portable device used for protection against rain and consisting of a light canopy supported on a collapsible metal frame mounted on a central rod.

Allan Wexler's Umbrella Raincatcher is a collaborative project with the Bedouin community in the Negev Desert, Israel. A dozen umbrellas are grouped upside down on the ground, held in place by large stones. At night, the sun-warmed stones cause water to condense into the umbrellas, ready for morning collection.

Atomiser: A device for reducing a liquid to a fine spray, such as the nozzle used to feed oil into a furnace or an enclosed bottle with a fine outlet used to spray perfumes.

Diller + Scofidio's arteplage for the Swiss Expo takes the form of a huge cloud of mist on the lakeshore. The mist is not an illusion; a metal construct sprays millions of tiny water droplets of 4 to 10 microns in diameter from 31,400 steel jets. High-pressure spraying at 80 bars forces the water through atomisers of 120 microns in diameter. The water droplets have to be small enough to remain suspended, saturating the air with moisture and creating a cloud at a seemingly impossible altitude.

Nostalgic, metaphorical, analytical and even the downright daft, each of the illustrated pieces demonstrates the potential for spatial occupation, leading to new territories in architectural design. What is common to all is the ambition to refute the constraining prejudices of scale, materiality and construction in service of the imagination. The hope is that, like the camera, umbrella and the atomiser, the works in this book will inspire future developments and the evolution of architectural and spatial tectonics.

Designer: Jimmy Hung

Device: Sound Diary

Function: Tracing daily activities

Concept:
The device picks up different sounds created by the user's journey and produces certain patterns that record the user's everyday life. There is no longer an untouched piece of land on earth. We are shaping the landscape through everyday activities. The new landscape is a constantly changing surface between the wheel, the rubber and the wing. Land becomes the canvas of the various patterns we create through activities. The device attempts to trace these activities by collecting sounds.

Dimensions: 300 x 150 x 230mm

Fabrication time: 9 days

Assembly time: 15 minutes

Materials:
1no airbrush
1no sound responsive toy
1no bottle of acetone
1no amplifier
1no aluminium funnel (8cm diameter)
1no power pack gas can
1no aluminium strip (45 x 1cm)
1no aluminium strip (30 x 1cm)
1no polystyrene sheet (10 x 10 x 1cm)
1no headphones
1no piece of MDF board (30 x 15 x 1cm)
2no metal fastening belts
5no L-shaped metal joint
2no plastic circular clips (4cm diameter)
3no plastic wire clips (0.5cm diameter)
18no nuts and bolts
13no screws
2no triangular metal plates
1no metal plate (12 x 3cm)
1no 20cm threaded aluminium rod
1no 12cm threaded aluminium rod
1no 21cm threaded aluminium rod
1no 8cm threaded aluminium rod

Fabrication:
- Gather all metal components from hardware store according to the indicated dimensions.
- Cut the aluminium strips and threaded aluminium rods according to the indicated dimensions.
- Extract sound responsive component from sound responsive toy.

Assembly:
- Cut out a piece of MDF board.
- Drill holes to MDF board to which components are bolted.
- Screw two triangular metal plates to the MDF board according to the size of the sound responsive component.
- Screw the sound responsive component to the angular plates.
- Nut and bolt the 12cm threaded aluminium rods to a plastic circular clip and the MDF board.
- Fit the air brush into the circular plastic clip.
- Bend the 45cm aluminium strip to a clip-shape.
- Screw it to the sound responsive component and the MDF board.
- Drill a hole at the tip of the 12cm x 3cm metal plate.
- Screw the 12cm x 3cm metal plate on the side of the MDF board in order to fasten the position of the airbrush.
- Nut and bolt two L-shaped metal joints to the 21cm threaded aluminium rods and to the MDF board.
- Screw the polystyrene sheet to the L-shaped metal joints.
- Screw three L-shaped metal joints to the MDF board according to the position of the amplifier.
- Nut and bolt the 8cm threaded aluminium rods to a plastic circular clip and the MDF board.
- Fit the aluminium funnel to the plastic circular clip.
- Nut and bolt the funnel to the sound amplifier.
- Bend the 30cm aluminium strips to required shape.
- Fasten gas can to bent aluminium strip using fastening belts.
- Nut and bolt the 20cm threaded aluminium rod to the bent aluminium strip and screw to side of MDF board.
- Screw three x plastic wire clips (0.5cm diameter) to required position to secure headphones and airbrush feeding tube.
- Plug in the headphone to the amplifier.
- Fasten both ends of the airbrush feeding tube.
- Switch on the amplifier and the sound responsive component.

Additional notes:
- Adjust gas pressure carefully.

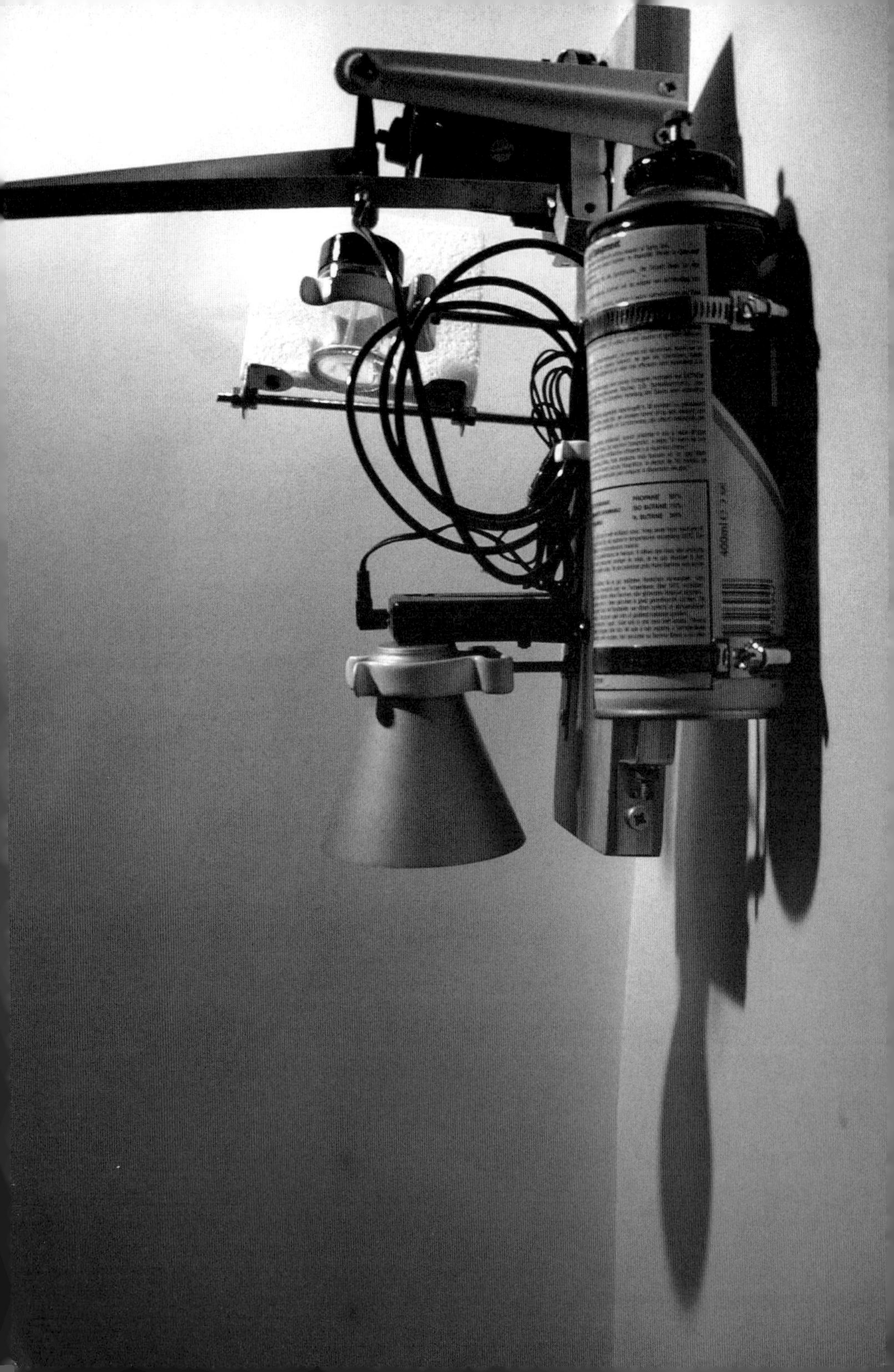

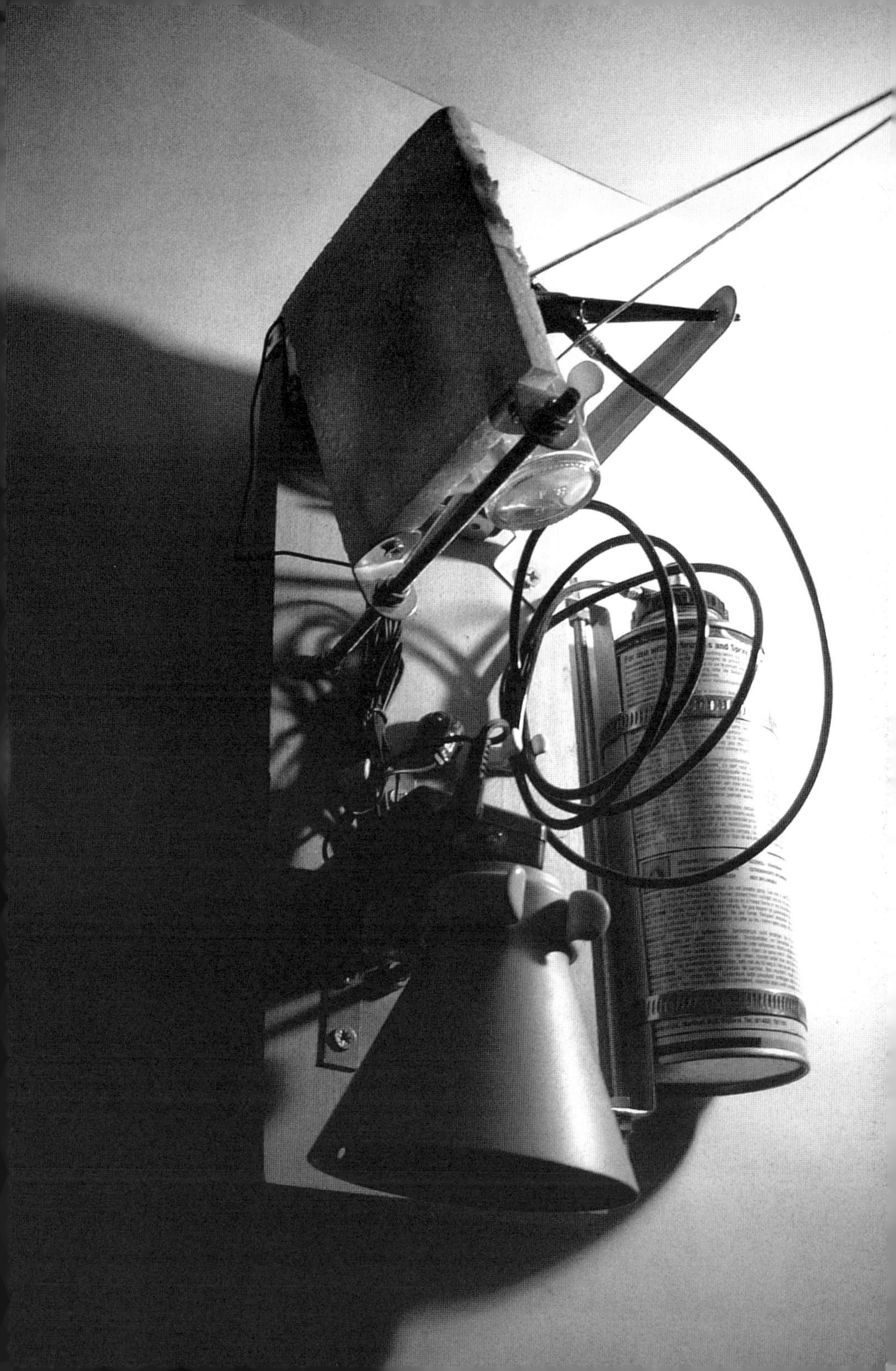

Designer: Nick Westby

Device: An Instrument of Pilgrimage

Function: A portable traveller's companion for the collection and burning of olive oils

Concept:
Playing on ideas of a cultural pilgrimage the device takes olive oil as being synonymous with refinement. By entwining memories of places with the collection of oils the subsequent burning becomes an act of reminiscence; the evocative smell and glow providing comfort to a weary traveller.

Dimensions: 270 x 160 x 60mm

Fabrication time: 200 hours

Assembly time: 10 hours

Materials: Wood, Brass, Leather, Glass

Fabrication:
- Mould a form from MDF and use to fashion the curved laminated frame.
- Glue the twin hardwood braces into routed slots forming a rigid frame.
- The vials are blown 15mm glass tube with two puncturing 6mm capillaries such that each vial has a filler and a vent pipe.
- The sides protect and cocoon the vials within, opening up to allow the burning of oils.

Leather side: molded laminated leather.
Other: wooden ribs with leather cushions on sprung brass hinges.

Assembly:
The vials are supported on 1mm brass rod, held with tiny leather straps to dampen vibrations.
All brass/metal joints are a transition fit.
Where brass sheet meets wood, peened rod ends puncture the surface clamping the sheet to the wood.

Additional notes:
Put your shoes on, put straps on the device, pack it on your back and head for Italy!

Designers: Jon Ashmore, Grace Craddock + Tom Holberton

Device: Anticipation, Deluge + Erosion

Function: Demonstrating the anticipation associated with imminent downpour

Concept:
A ticking clock is attached to a wall mounted box. As the second hand of the clock brushes over the minute hand, an electrical connection is made and a motor within the box whirrs for a split second. Unbeknown to the observer, the motor is turning an axle within the box which is studded with dress pins. With each whirr of the motor, these pins are pushed further into balloons containing salt water. Suddenly, the silence of the room and intermittent grumble of the motor is shattered by the explosion of a balloon. As the 'monsoon rain' falls onto the surface below, electrical connections are formed between adjacent lengths of charged wire and light bulbs are lit. As the landscape surface dries out post downpour, the extent of material erosion can be seen.

Dimensions: 1000 x 1200 x 600mm

Fabrication time: 1 day

Assembly time: 2 days

Materials:
Water balloon box (800 x 200 x 250mm):
1msq 15mm MDF
0.2 litre white paint
1no small battery operated clock
1no 200/1 motor
2no AA batteries
0.3m electrical wire
0.8m 6mm dia. metal tube
15no dress pins
1no 70mm long 12mm dia wooden dowel
10no white balloons
5 litre salt water
1 x 0.25m mesh

Landscape surface:
1 x 1.5m thick white cartridge paper
20no 0.8m long steel wires

10no light bulbs and connectors
5m electrical wire
0.8 x 0.2m 15mm MDF sheet painted white
5no AC/DC adapters

Fabrication:
- Construct MDF box without a top or bottom face.
- Drill 7mm holes at either end of the box.
- Glue a piece of MDF (internal dim of bottom of box but only 150mm of it's length) into the bottom of the box at one end so that it is flush with the bottom edges of the MDF uprights.
- Insert wire mesh sheet into the remaining open portion of the bottom of box.
- Paint box white.
- Drill 15 1.5mm holes at random through the 0.8m length of metal tube.
- Take a 70mm long section of 12mm dowel and drill a 6mm hole through its length.
- Slide the metal tube halfway into the wooden dowel sleeve and glue in place.

Assembly:
White box:
- Take punctured metal tube and thread dress pins through the holes so that their points stick out perpendicular to the tube. Glue these in place.
- Within the box, mount the motor horizontally on the MDF shelf.
- At the other end of the box, position the end of the spiked axle into the pre-drilled hole and slip the wooden sleeve on the other end of the axle onto turning element of the motor.
- Fix the wooden sleeve to the motor axle with a grub screw.
- Wire the motor into a circuit containing the battery holder with batteries, a basic switch and the clock with brush connectors attached to it's minute and second hands.
- Mount the clock onto the side of the box, keeping all other components and wiring concealed.
- Mount white box on the wall approx. 600mm above floor level.

Paper surface:
- Affix paper sheet to the wall behind the box and allow to fall along the floor in front of the box.

Light bulb circuits:
- Place the spare piece of white painted MDF at the bottom end of the paper lying on the floor.
- Along the top and the bottom long edges of this piece of MDF,

drill ten pairs of small holes and line up the 0.8m steel wires with these holes so that they run across the paper.

- To make one circuit, partially screw two 6mm dia washers into each of the first two holes nearest the paper. Sandwich a piece of steel wire and a piece of electrical wire (exposed at its end) between the washers and screw tight. One of the electrical wires should be 2m long and should be left to be wired into the power source; the other should first be wired through a light bulb connector block then to the power source.
- Repeat the above ten times to produce a line of ten light bulb connectors wired twenty pieces of steel wire lying across the paper. Screw ten mini light bulbs into the connectors.
- Wire the circuits back to an ac adapter.

Set up:

- Fill balloons with salt water solutions and place them into the wall mounted box. Arrange them so that they sit on the spiked axle but so that they are not actually pierced.
- Turn on the power to the electrodes lying across the paper.
- Turn on the power to motor within box and wait.

Additional notes:

- Make sure that none of the pairs of steel wire electrodes are touching at any time.

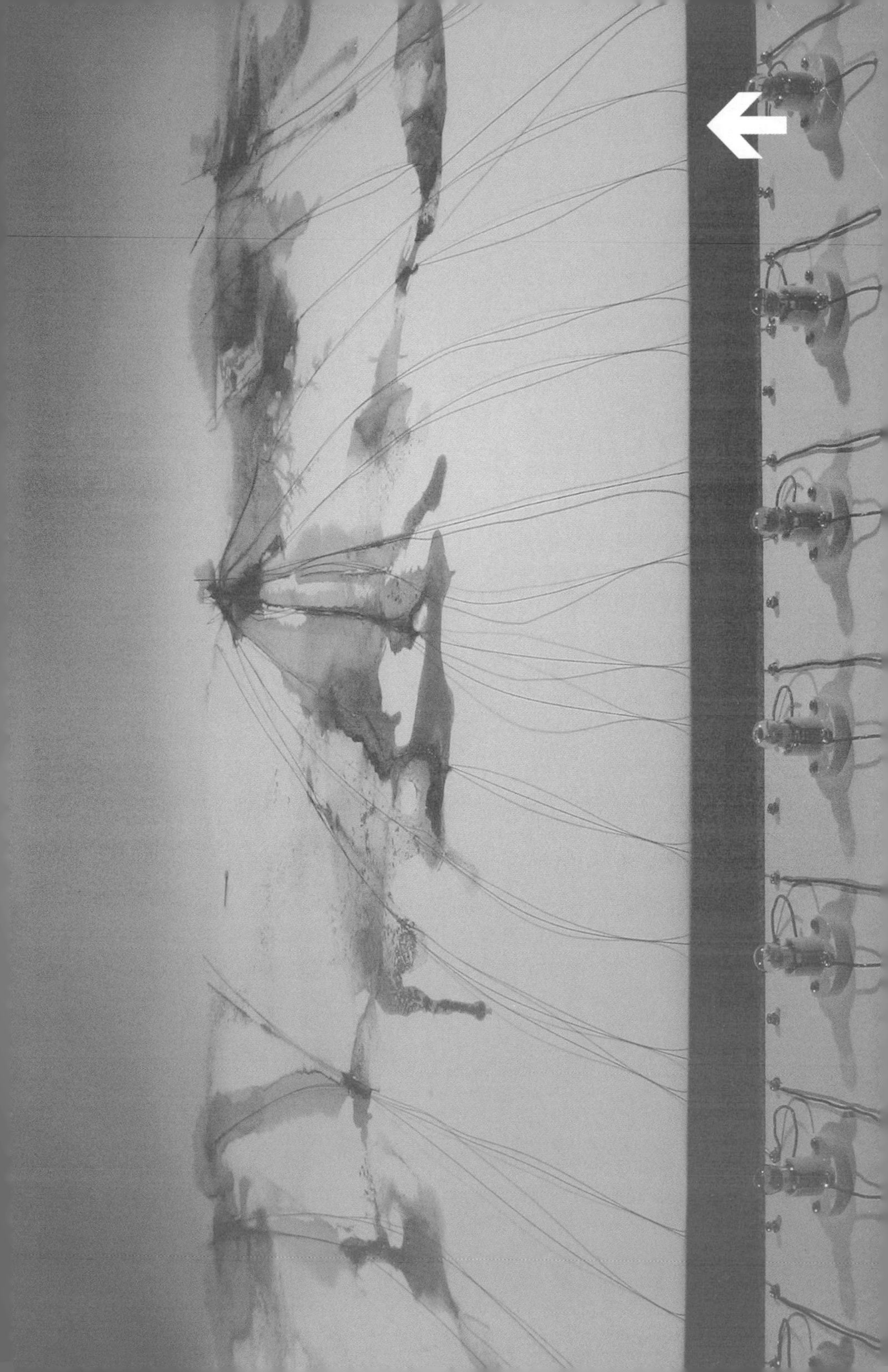

Designer: Bernd Felsinger

Device: Anticipation Navigator

Function: Instrument to record and navigate

Concept:
Central to the work is the inquiry into the nature of our spatial perception and the subjective understanding of spaces on the basis of one's memory and anticipation. The aim is to offer a method to communicate such ephemeral qualities.

The observer collects empiric data of a journey through the city. The device translates parts of the journey into a notation of lines embossed onto the surface of a plaster cast. These 'informed surfaces' are created via a mechanism consisting of 3 printing heads protruding through a latex screen, onto which soft plaster is poured and allowed to set. The device is essentially a 'drawing instrument' operating as an interface between the user and the city.

With the production of each new plaster cast, the previous one is fed back into the making process, affecting the surface condition of the successive cast. The previous plaster plate, representing a moment and position in the person's past takes on the role of a recent memory, subject to re-evaluation. As the user navigates through the city, 'recordings' in the form of notations are produced along the journey.

This journey through the city is finally represented through a series of interrelated casts, unique to and prescriptive of the personal experience and the decisions made along the way.

Dimensions: 1 x 1 x 1.2m

Fabrication time: 8 weeks

Assembly time: 15-20 minutes

Materials:
MDF: various thicknesses, machined and varnished
Perspex: various thicknesses, machined, heat treated, clear and frosted
Aluminium: plates and profiles in various thicknesses, machined
Latex: 0.2mm thick, white
Nylon: white, machined

Stainless steel: wires and hoses, bowden cables, nuts and bolts
Brass: fine tubes and rods, various diameters
Plaster + water
Circular spirit level
Compass
Ball bearings

Fabrication:
After several mock-ups and test props a series of 1:1 construction drawings were produced. During manufacture of the components, adjustments to the drawn production information became necessary, which shifted the design process from the drawing board into the workshop environment.

Manufacture of main structure, i.e. MDF support plate, MDF printing head support and memory cast tray, along with telescopic aluminium legs. All parts where subsequently reworked or completely replaced by refined versions.

Design and construction of printing heads. Starting with simple versions, tests were carried out to develop more complex assemblies. The final version of the printing head allowed for four degrees of freedom: rotation, incline, depth and alignment of the line. A series of three printing heads were produced in total composing the notation.
Formwork and cast release mechanism were designed, manufactured and added to device.

Production of carrier case, providing room for all components, tools for assembling, compartment for produced plaster casts, containers for water and plaster.

Additional notes:
As the device is a portable instrument intended for use in different locations, the emphasis was on providing a quick assembly procedure, lightweight but robust construction and space-efficient carrier case.

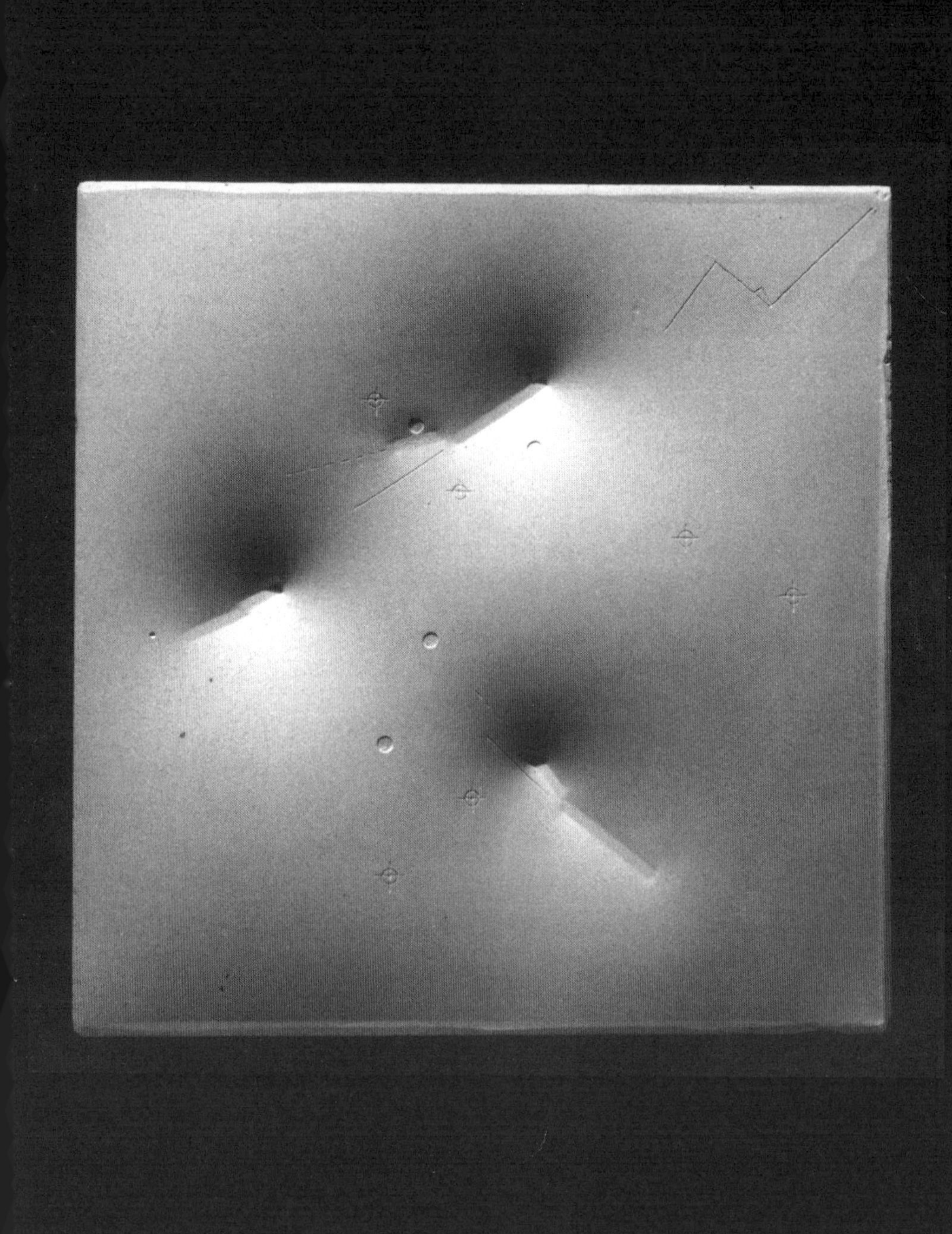

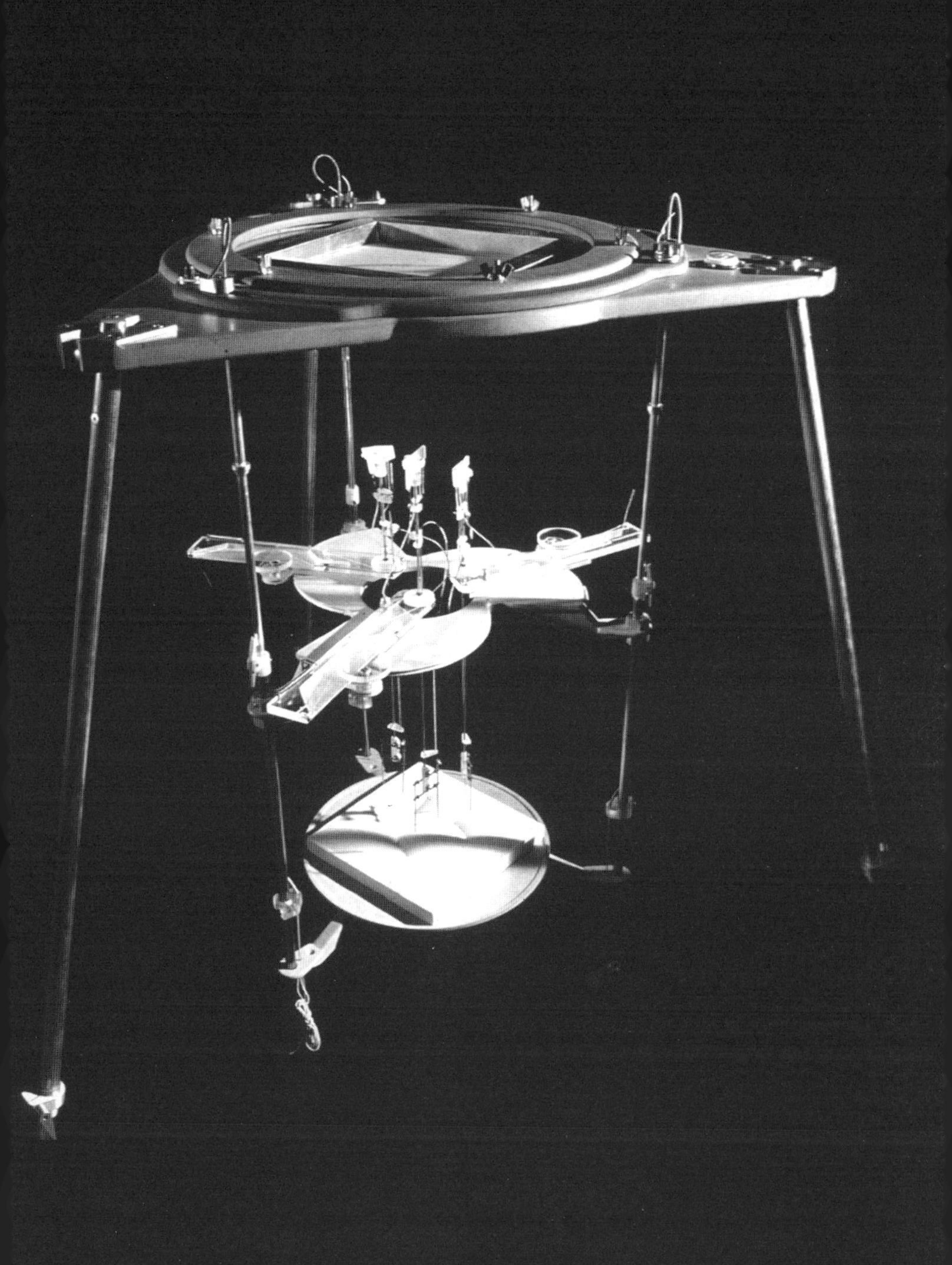

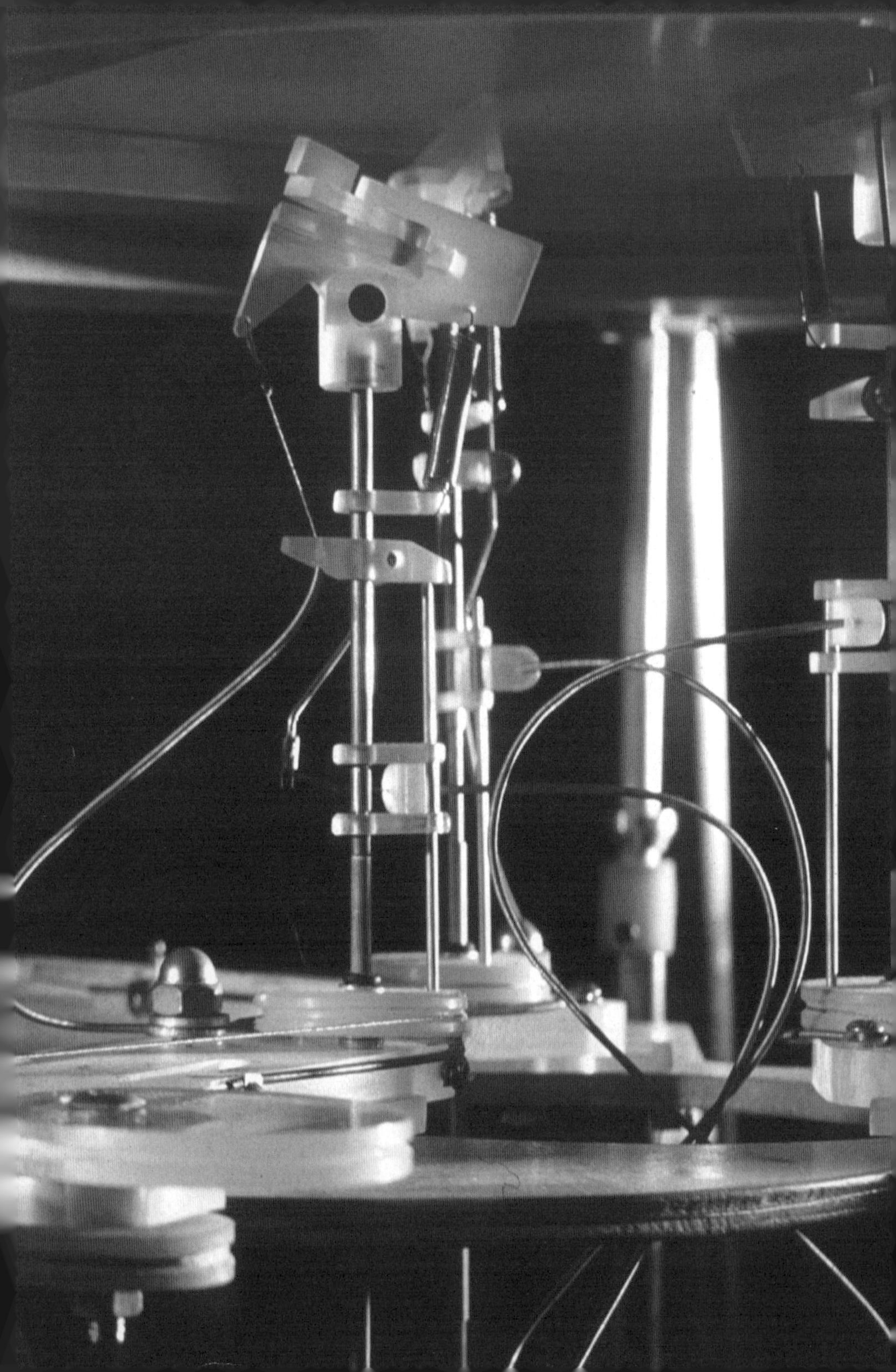

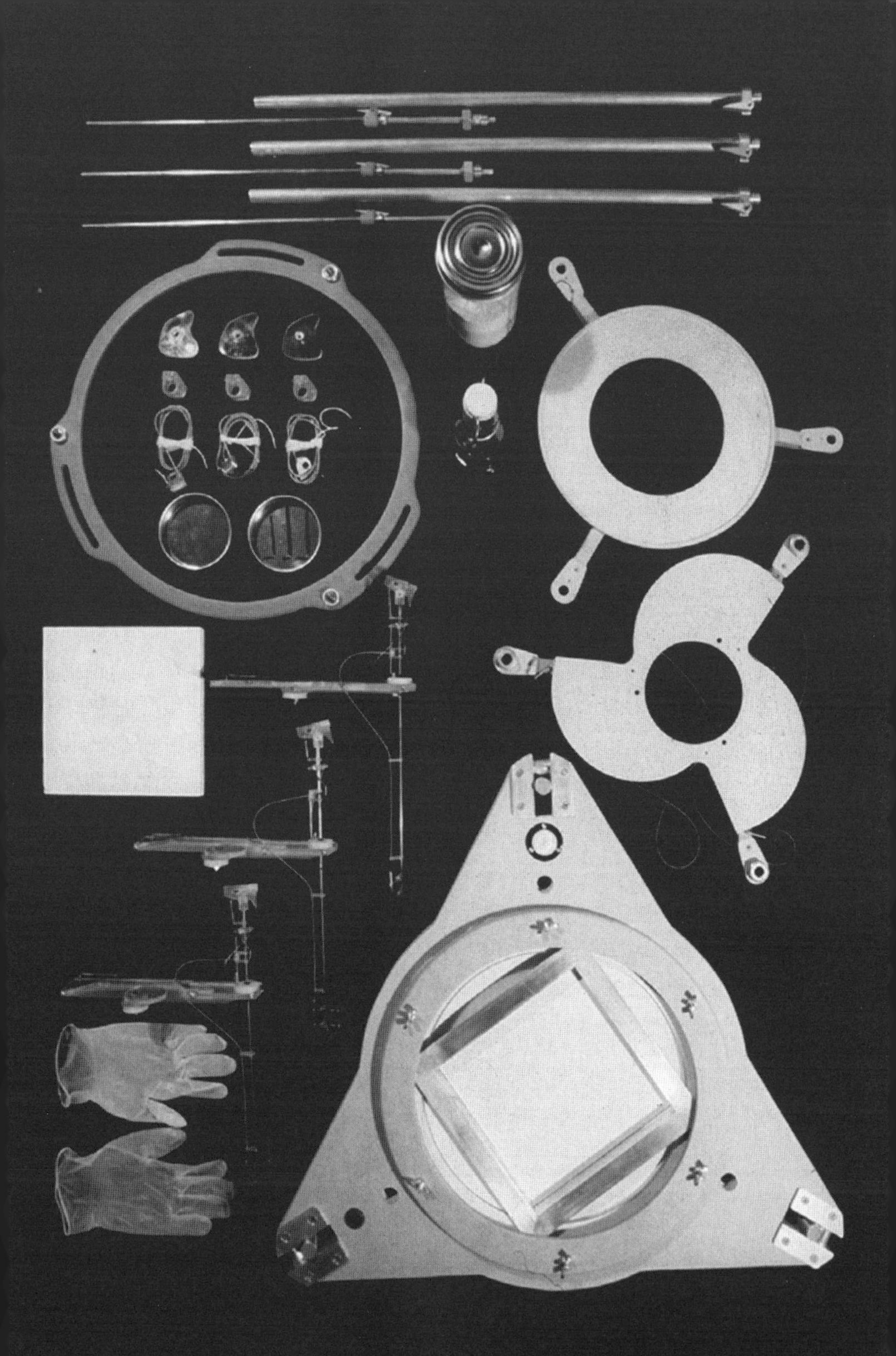

Designers: Lewis.Tsurumaki.Lewis (LTL Architects)

Device: Bellow

Function: Re-deployment of a Florida Voting Booth used in the contested US 2000 Presidential Election

Concept:
In a state of animated exhaustion, the case bellows open and closed.

Dimensions: 3 x 3 x 3ft

Fabrication time: 2 days

Assembly time: 1 hour

Materials:
Votomatic Booth
Steel Armature
Leather Bellows
Answering Machine (with heavy breathing)
Worm-gear Motor

Fabrication:
- Reconfigure Votomatic Booth legs and case.
- Using hinge as joint, connect steel armatures between legs and case.
- Attach Worm-gear motor and crank arms to inside of case.
- Wire answering machine's message to the rotating crank arm for repeated play.
- Attach bellows to inside of case.

Assembly:
- Screw steel armatures to legs.
- Plug it in.

Additional notes:
Photography by Michael Moran.
Project commission for group exhibition by Chee Pearlman and Paul Goldberger.
Votomatic Booth donated by exhibit coordinators.

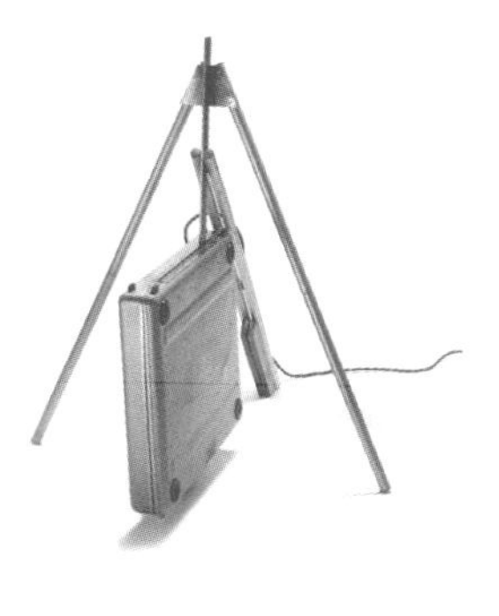

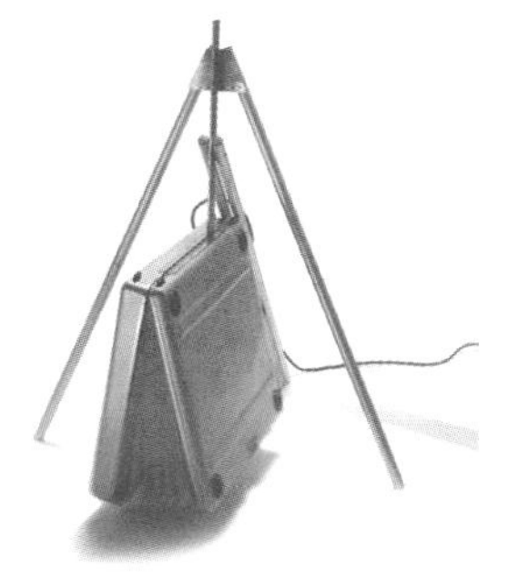

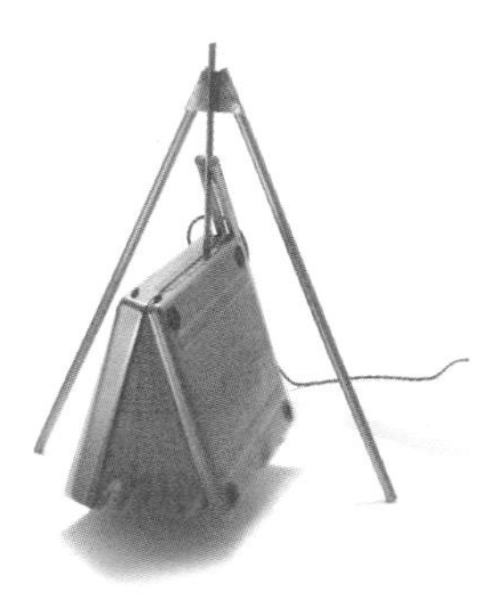

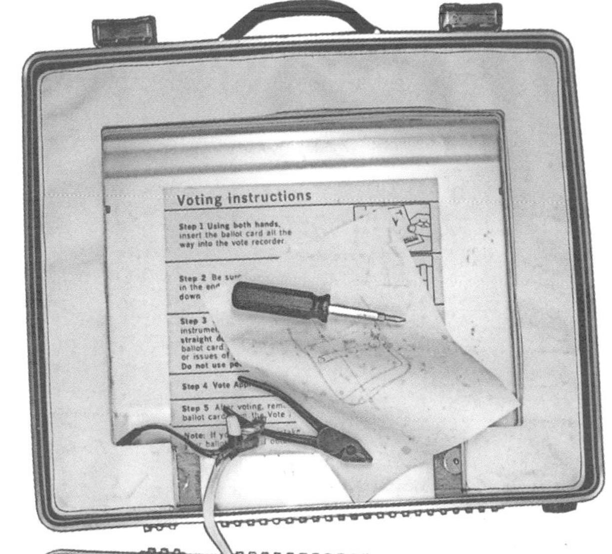
Voting instructions
Step 1 Using both hands, insert the ballot card all the way into the vote recorder.
Step 2
in the
down
Step 3
ballot card
or issues of
Do not use
Step 4 Vote
Step 5 After voting,
ballot card
Note:

Designer: Tsuyoshi To

Device: Blurred Spaces

Function: Creating an illusion of distorted spaces

Concept:
The idea for the device was to explore the boundary between reality and a virtual experience. The virtual experience was taken as a light space sited within a fixed room. By inserting an interactive element into the project the boundary between virtual and real is distorted through movement.

When the space is not occupied the only constant is the light reflection from the series of mirrored sheets. This creates a virtual space within the fixed room. When the occupants move around the space the reflection is distorted by breaching a series of virtual boundaries. This creates a moving form within the volume of light and the fixed volume of the room, thus creating a third 'blurred' space.

Dimensions: 720 x 930 x 1150mm

Fabrication time: 2 weeks

Assembly time: 4-5 hours

Materials:
Steel tubes
Steel rods
Steel sheets
Plywood
Mirror sheets
Piano wire
16no LEDs
4no motors
4no IR light barrier (emitter and receiver)
24no 9V batteries
M10, M3, M4 nuts and bolts

Fabrication:
Supporting arms for mirror table:
- Cut three tubes with diameter of 32mm at the length of 140mm.
- Cut four rods with diameter of 8mm at the length of 800mm and bend them so that the dimensions of the sides are 400mm, 100mm and 300mm at right angles at each corner.

- Weld steel sheets of 100 x 100mm, on both ends of the arm.
- Drill an 8mm hole through the middle of both sheets.
- Weld the bent rod to the tube; one each on two tubes and two on the other tube at angle of 130 degrees apart.
- Drill two holes at the back of the tube with 10mm at 95mm apart and weld M10 nuts on top of these holes.
- Insert these tubes onto the supporting structure and screw M10 bolts into the nuts to secure it at the appropriate height.

Motor and 'pinching' arm holder:
- Cut steel sheet into the shape for holding the motor.
- Bend appropriate parts of the holder at right angles at appropriate direction. Place mirror sheets on the table before attaching the holder on one of the sides of the mirror table with screws with washers. Secure motors to the holder.

Supporting arm for IR emitter:
- Cut four rods with 8mm diameter at the length of 250mm.
- Bend these rods at right angle from 100mm from the end.
- Weld 50 x 100mm steel plates with two holes to the shorter side of the arm.

IR receiver/emitter holder:
- Cut steel sheet at the dimension of 60 x 280mm.
- Cut out 40 x 120mm off one of the ends of the plate so that it leaves 10mm on both sides.
- Drill holes at appropriate places to hold the electronic board. Secure the board to the holder with nuts and bolts.
- Bend the holder towards the board so that it covers the top of the board. Attach the holder to the arm.

Assembly: (The room should not be bigger than 4 x 4m.)
- Attach mirror tables with components to the supporting arms.
- Attach IR receiver to the arms of supporting structure.
- Connect each IR receiver to each motor with electrical cable.
- Connect batteries on IR receiver/emitter, motors and LED.
- Drill four holes on the wall at appropriate places for the supporting structure. Using M6 masonry bolts, secure the device on the wall firmly.
- Attach IR transmitter to the wall using wall plug and M3 screws. Make sure that the line between the receiver and transmitter overlaps.
- The transmitter should be a few metres apart.
- Switch the IR receiver and emitter and LED on.

The device is ready to interact with occupants.

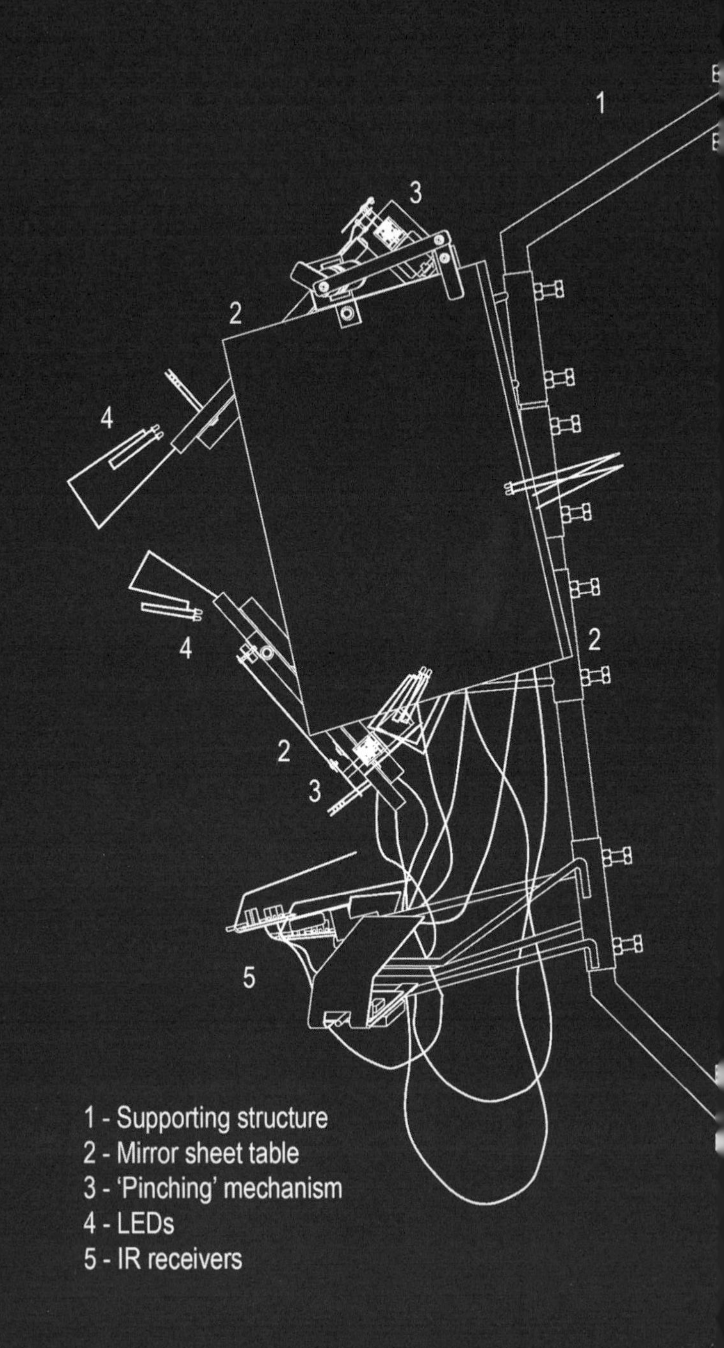
1
3
2
4
4
2
2
3
5
1 - Supporting structure
2 - Mirror sheet table
3 - 'Pinching' mechanism
4 - LEDs
5 - IR receivers

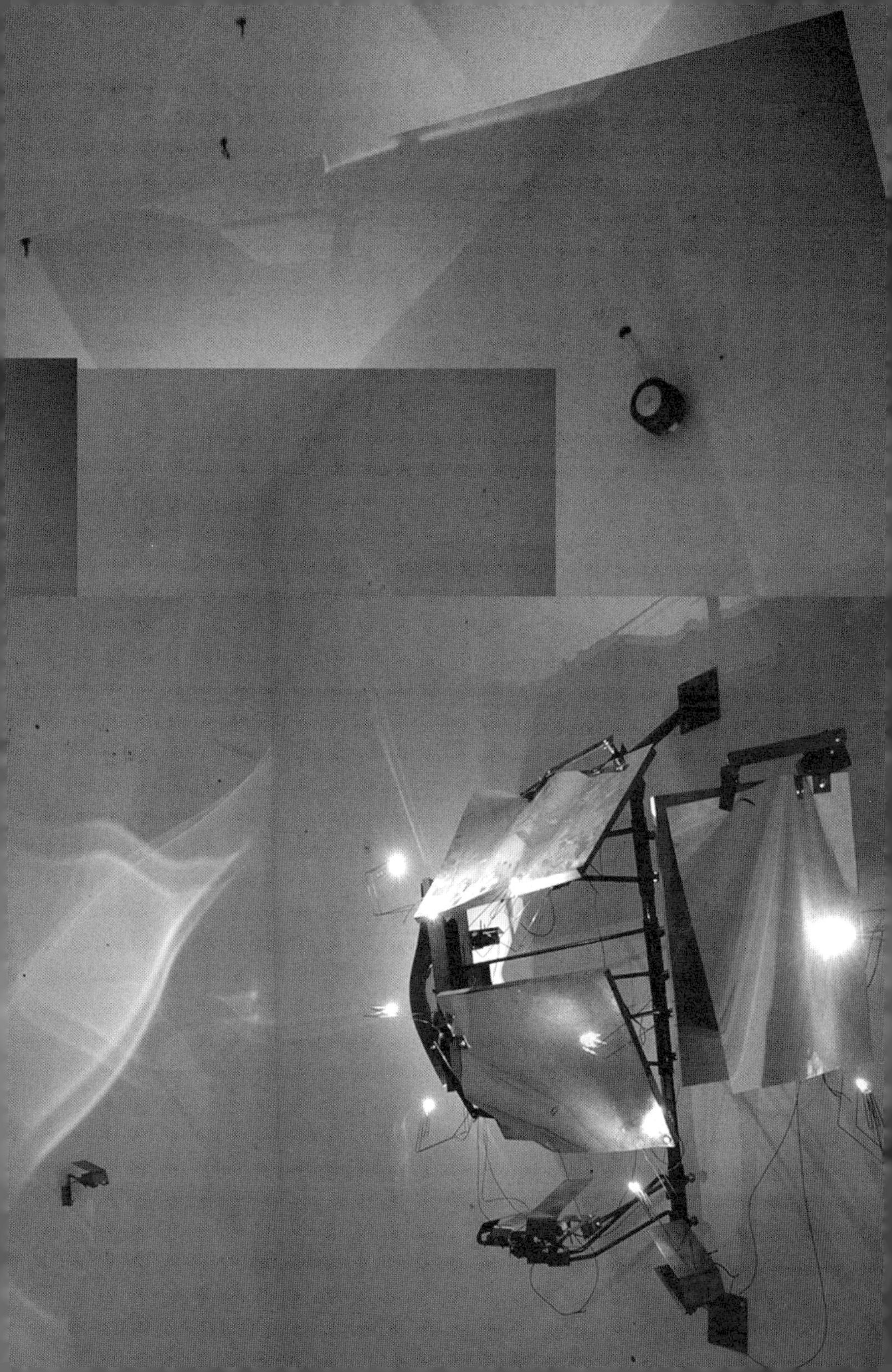

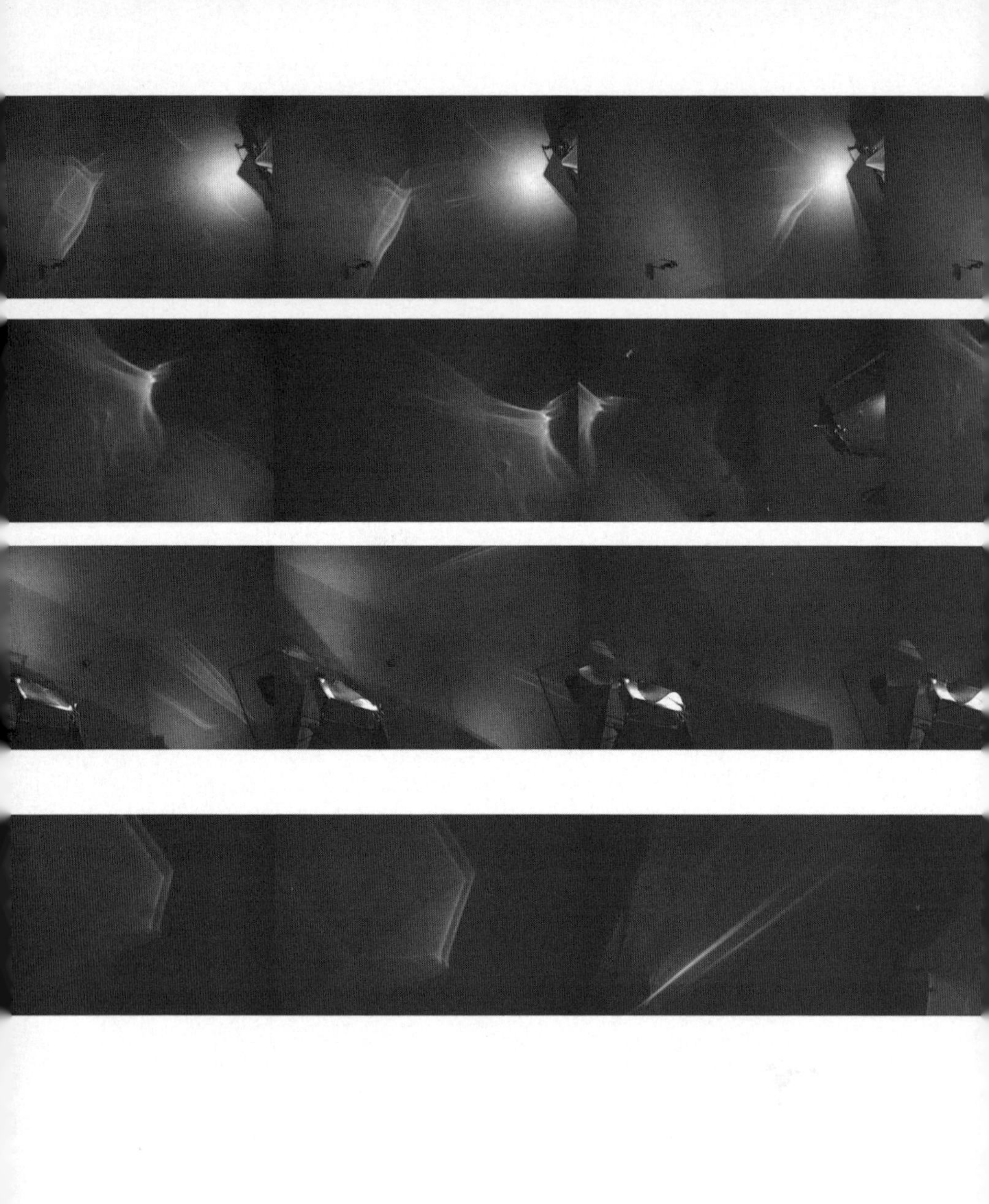

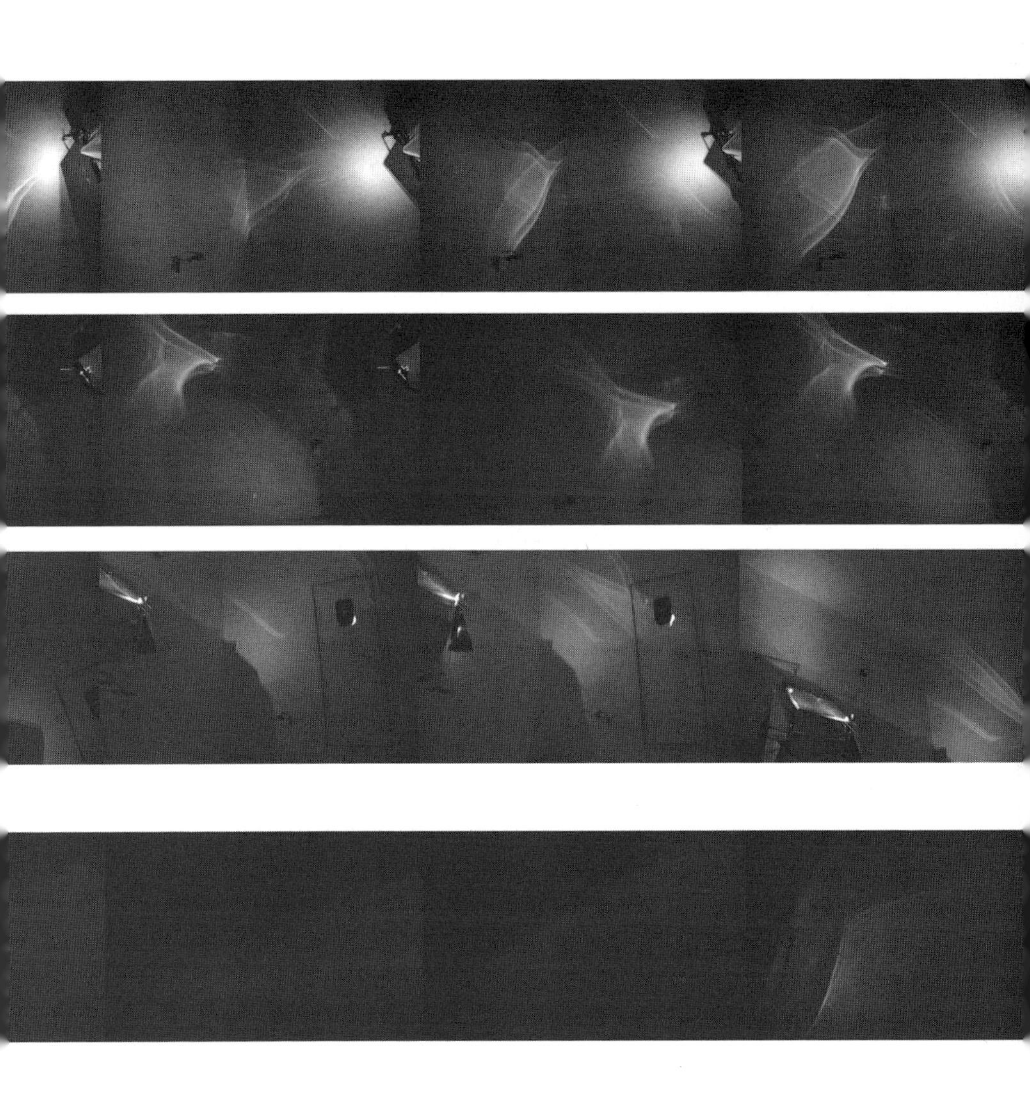

Designers: Lucy Evans, Kostas Grigoriadis + Adam Wood

Device: Climatic Threat Assembly

Function: Interactive response to the effects of climate in a subtropical environment

Concept:
The installation manipulates your movement through a notional landscape. Rotating horizontal arms define the space around them by projecting jets of steam and creating varying degrees of imminent threat.

Steel arms, suspended at assorted heights within a darkened set, support five glass vessels. Gas torches are positioned beneath these containers, heating the water held within. Air canisters act as counter-balances and pump cold air through the boiling water. The resulting vapour is forced through nozzles, blown into the glass, creating jets of steam, which are lit by small directional electric bulbs.

The rotating jets of steam were the main elements of the installation, symbolic of the cyclical threat of the monsoon floods. The Acrylic ribbon was a metaphorical representation of the landscape and the discolouration of the thermo-chromatic pixels mimicked the short-term physical effects of floods and landslides upon the island terrain. The pixels change from blue to clear before slowly returning to their former state.

Climatic pressure patterns passing over a plan view of Southeast Asia are projected onto the ceiling of the set, creating a swirling set of lines, which dictate the direction and speed of the moving arms and create nodal points about which they rotate. The installation created an exciting and dynamic spectacle for participants and observers, reproducing the ephemeral qualities of vapour and climate as well as highlighting the geophysical consequences of flooding.

Dimensions: 3.3 x 3.9m (Installation)
3.6 x 3.7m (Viewing area)
0.6–1.0m long (Individual device)

Fabrication time: 4 weeks development, 2 weeks fabrication

Assembly time: 4 days

Materials:
32no lengths of 5.0m 2x1 softwood
12no lengths of 5.0m 2x2 softwood
12no sheets of 1.3m x 3.5m MDF
4no boxes of 1.5″ wood screws
30no stainless steel angle joints
3no 5 litre tubs of black paint
12no 2.0m lengths of 6mm steel tube
3no 1.0m lengths of 4mm steel rod
5no black plastic kite joints
40no 2mm threaded bolts + screw nuts
5no stainless steel bearings
5no glass vessels
10no rubber bungs
5no gas torches
10no air canisters
5no small electric bulbs
10no 9V batteries
2no 1.0m lengths of 5mm steel flat
5no 12V motors
100m plastic coated electric wiring
5no multi-input timers
5no adaptors
3no extension leads
50m fishing line
60no stainless steel threaded hooks
9no 1.0m x 0.3m lengths of 5mm Acrylic
1no 2.0m x 0.3m length of 5mm Acrylic
250g Blue Thermo-chromatic Dye
1 litre of PVA Glue
20m fluorescent tape
Data Projector
Mirror
Steam

Fabrication:
- Cut steel tube to size for axles, armatures, and t-strut.
- Cut steel flat to 0.5m lengths for motor plates.
- Cut steel rod to 0.3m lengths for bulb holders.
- Cut steel sheet into strips for clasps.
- Cut steel rod to 5mm lengths and shaped for connective pins.
- Hammer pins in to top end of axles.
- Drill bottom end of axles with two 2mm holes.
- Drill kite joints and armatures in centre with two 2mm holes.
- Cut slots into one end of armatures, and drill two 2mm holes.
- Cut slots into both ends of t-struts, drill two 2mm holes

through each end.
- Bend T-struts into C shape.
- Bend bulb holders into shape.
- Weld T-struts onto opposite ends of armatures.
- Weld bulb holders onto t-struts.
- Slide kite joints to centre of armatures.
- Hammer 2mm threaded bolts through.
- Bend steel strips into clasp and turn ends 90 degrees.
- Drill ends with two 2mm holes.
- Drill motor plates with four 6mm holes at both ends.
- Bend motor plates into right angle.
- Place clasps into slots at ends of t-struts and armatures.
- Tighten joints with screws.
- Vessels blown in Chemistry department glass blowing lab.
- Saw softwood head and foot plates to 3.9m and 3.3m lengths.
- Saw softwood studs to 3.5 m lengths.
- Saw softwood batons to 3.9m and 3.3m lengths.
- Cut acrylic strips to size.
- Drill acrylic strips with 1.5mm holes top and bottom.
- Heat acrylic strips over strip heater and bend into shape.
- Attach fluorescent tape to acrylic strips.
- Mix blue thermo-chromatic dye with PVA and paint pixels onto acrylic surface.

Assembly:
- Bolt softwood head and foot plates into floor and ceiling.
- Drill and screw softwood studs into plates using stainless steel angle joints.
- Drill stainless steel hooks into floor and ceiling.
- Screw MDF sheets and staple into studs.
- Fill joints with polyfiller.
- Paint walls of set black (two coats).
- Paint MDF ceiling panels black (two coats).
- Screw softwood batons through MDF and into studs 2.75m above floor.
- Screw softwood joists into MDF ceiling panels.
- Lift and screw ceiling panels and joists into batons.
- Place softwood supports beneath ceiling panels.
- Drill holes through false ceiling.
- Attach fishing line to stainless steel ceiling hooks and thread through holes.
- Attach motors to metal plates and screw into upper side of ceiling panels.
- Solder wiring to motors, run across false ceiling and down wall.
- Thread other end of wiring into adaptors.

- Plug adaptors into multi-input timers.
- Attach steel axles to motor.
- Remove softwood supports.
- Attach steel armature to axle using kite joints.
- Screw MDF facing onto set to hide false ceiling, motors and wiring.
- Thread fishing line through holes in acrylic strips.
- Tie acrylic strips at correct heights and fishing line secured to floor hooks.
- Attach glass vessels and air canisters to armature with clasps.
- Position gas torches beneath vessels.
- Attach directional bulbs to bulb holder at end of armature.
- Attach batteries to kite joint.
- Position projector and mirror within set.
- Fill vessels with water.
- Light gas torches.
- Attach batteries to bulb.
- Switch on projector.
- Set timers.

Rods in place

Positioning arms

Arms in place

Ribbon in place

Installation in motion

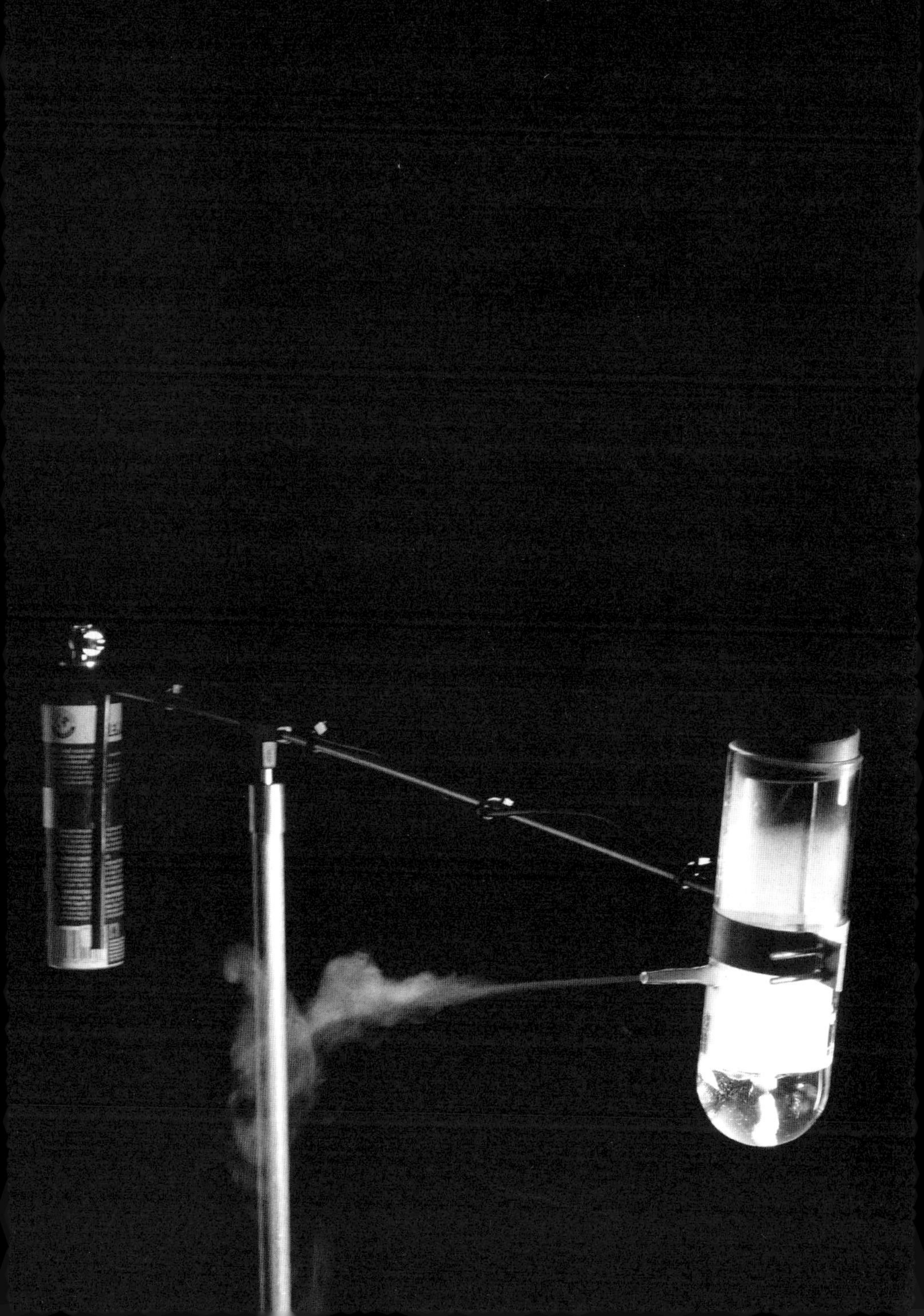

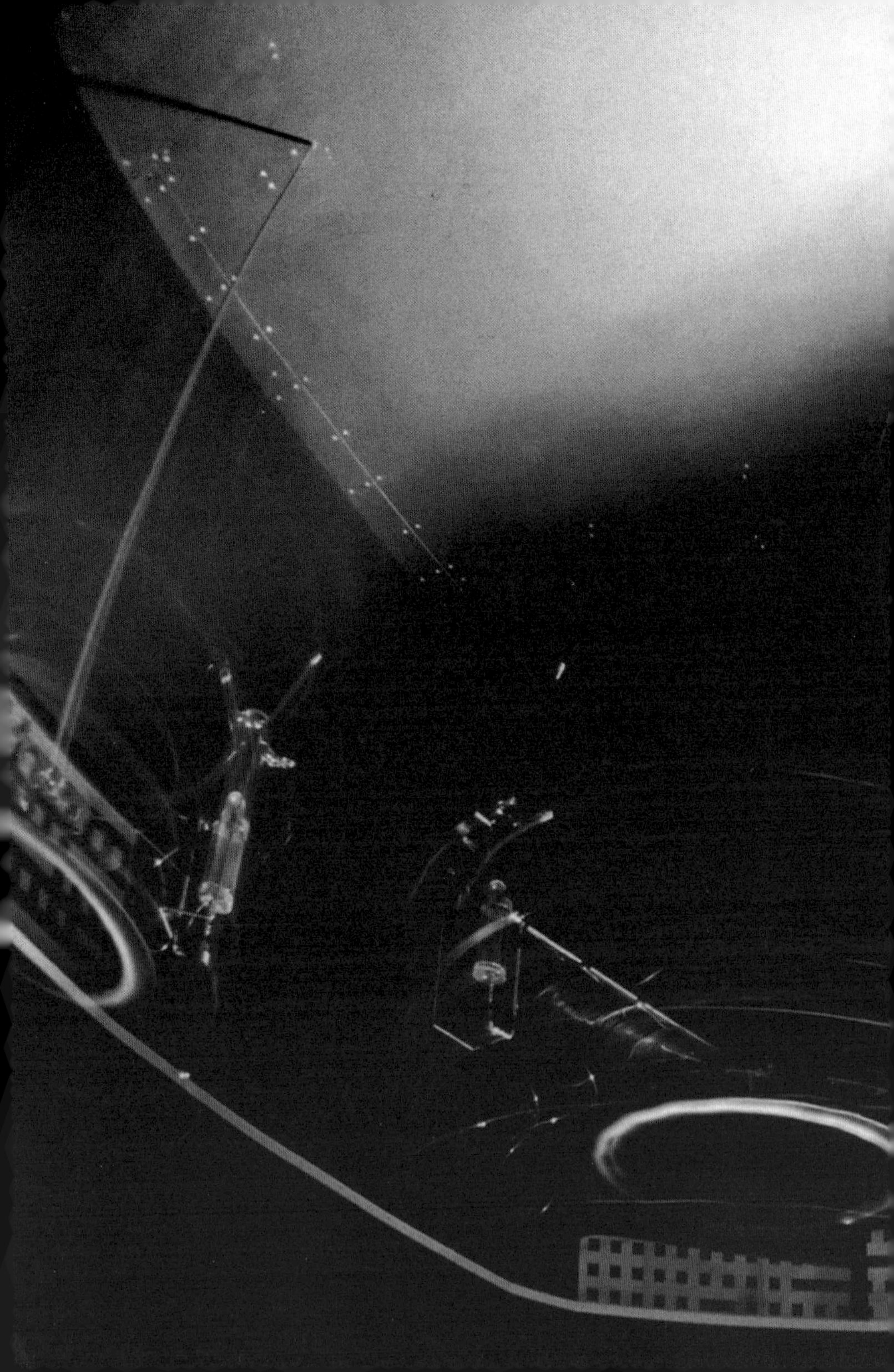

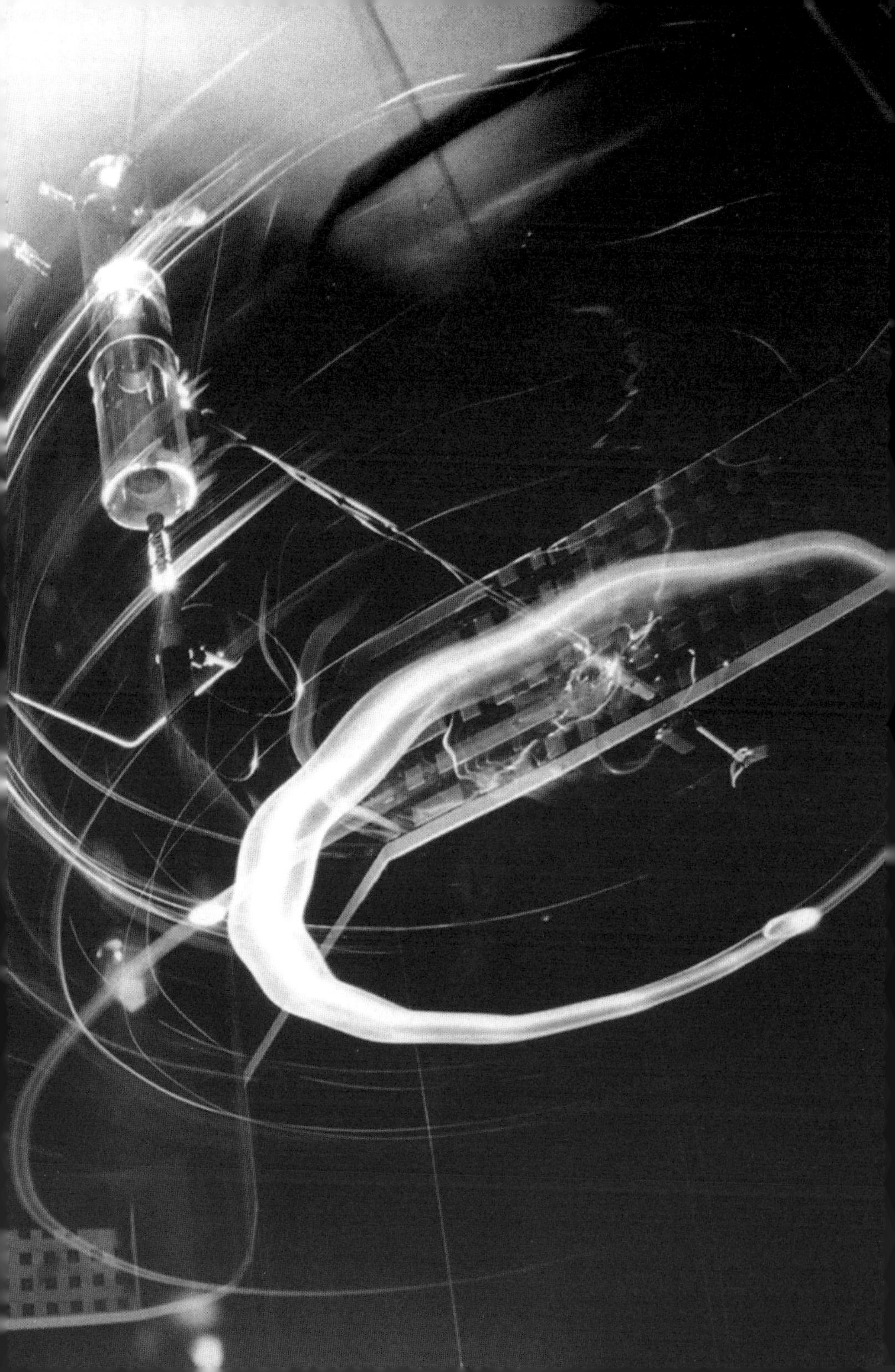

Designers: Charlie Sutherland + Charlie Hussey

Device: Daycaster

Function: Marking the location

Concept:
The Daycaster acts as a new gateway into the city of Exeter on the radial Honiton road. It celebrates and draws attention to the Met Office HQ's relocation to Exeter. It occupies a site between this new HQ and the old historical records office to the south.

The structure is expressed in 24 segments, such that each chronologically represents hours in the preceding 24 hours. It makes play of meteorological data using a changing lighting display. This light is reflected from stainless steel baffles to its transient audience. The Met Office constantly receives climatic data and the Daycaster acts as a visual manifestation of this ongoing measurement, analogous to a barometer.

A live feed of data from the Met Office is processed and continuously affects the hue and intensity 24 banks of LEDs underneath the length of the structure. The hue and intensity of the 1st LED will migrate along the device, hour by hour, until 23 hours later it drops off the other end.

The hues vary from blue to magenta via white. Average conditions are described with white light. When conditions are more inclement the lighting tends towards the blue spectrum; in contrast when warmer than average, it tends towards the magenta spectrum. Variables of temperature and humidity both shape the Daycaster's hues, intensity and display.

The information is supplied through a wi-fi web-link using the dynamic data-feed supplied by the Met Office. The radio receiver located at one end of the Daycaster receives data via wi-fi from a nearby building. The Daycaster's circuits process this data according to its own algorithms and control the LED colours and intensity accordingly.

The Daycaster mediates the ground between the ephemeral world of meteorology and the tangible reality of our weather in a responsive structure, slow but dynamic, reflective of climate both day and night.

Dimensions: 40 x 2.6m

Fabrication time: 2-3 months

Assembly time: 3 weeks

Materials:
Concrete strip foundation with galvanised grillage over lighting trench
Inset LED lighting arrays, with associated cabling and control system
Stainless steel reinforcement bars
Galvanised grille safety barrier
Stainless steel flats for bracing
Expamet stainless steel mesh

Fabrication:
- Bend stainless structural hoops in pairs, add flats and stretch and rivet the expamet mesh tight over form.
- Mount hoop structures to steel fixing plate for bedding into foundation.

Assembly:
- Strip foundation layed.
- Assemble segments on site and cleat together.
- Secure galvanised grille within structure to form structural barrier to car park side.
- Pack and secure foundation fixing plates into strip foundation.
- Complete concrete foundation around fixing plates.
- Install lighting in trench.

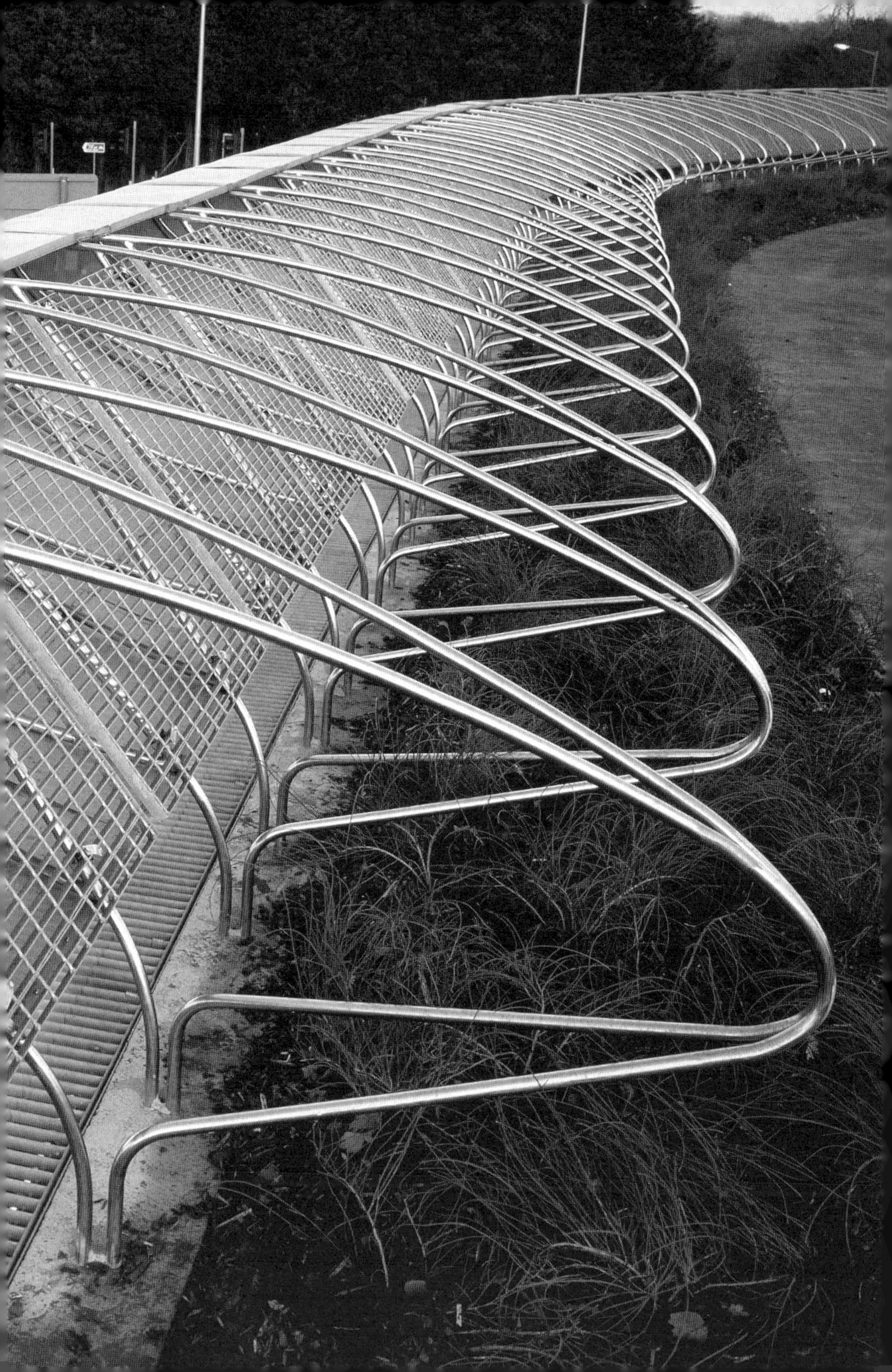

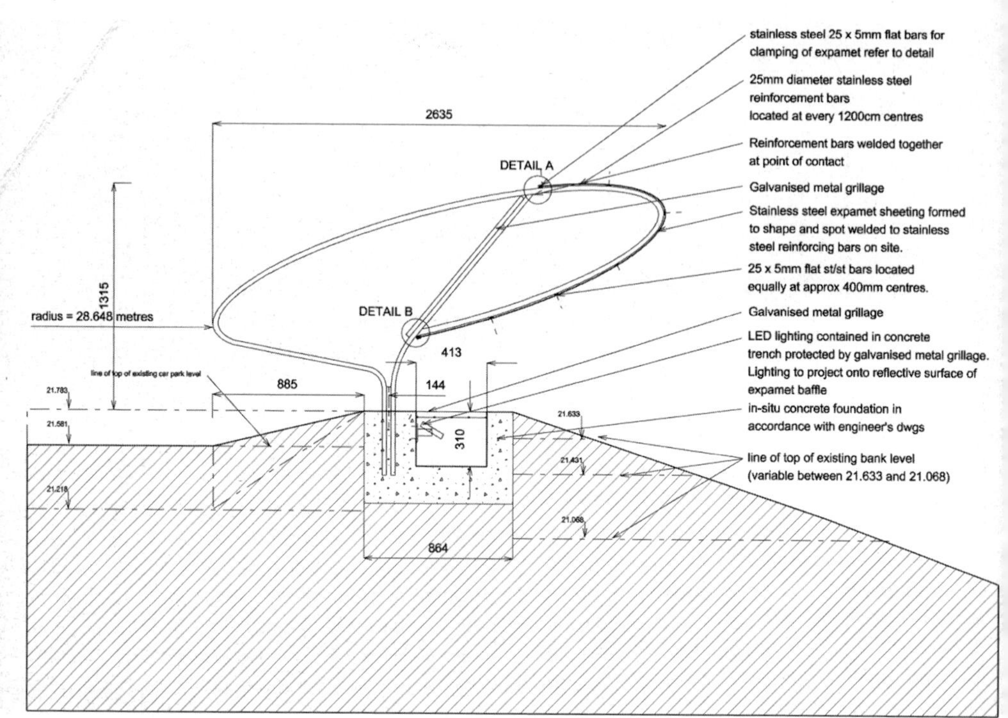
stainless steel 25 x 5mm flat bars for clamping of expamet refer to detail
25mm diameter stainless steel reinforcement bars located at every 1200cm centres
Reinforcement bars welded together at point of contact
Galvanised metal grillage
Stainless steel expamet sheeting formed to shape and spot welded to stainless steel reinforcing bars on site.
25 x 5mm flat st/st bars located equally at approx 400mm centres.
Galvanised metal grillage
LED lighting contained in concrete trench protected by galvanised metal grillage. Lighting to project onto reflective surface of expamet baffle
in-situ concrete foundation in accordance with engineer's dwgs
line of top of existing bank level (variable between 21.633 and 21.068)
2635
DETAIL A
DETAIL B
1315
radius = 28.648 metres
413
885
144
310
864
line of top of existing car park level
21.783
21.581
21.218
21.633
21.431
21.068
CROSS-SECTION

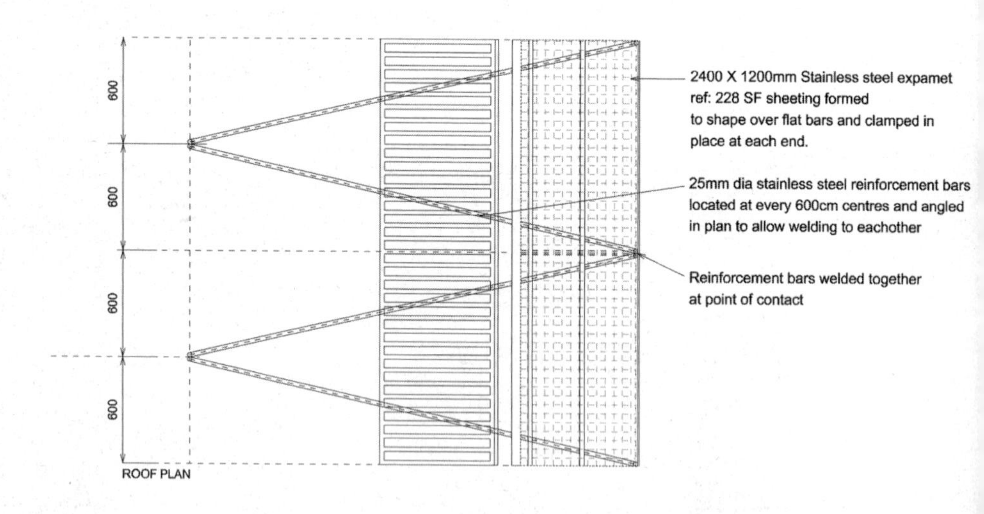
2400 X 1200mm Stainless steel expamet ref: 228 SF sheeting formed to shape over flat bars and clamped in place at each end.
25mm dia stainless steel reinforcement bars located at every 600cm centres and angled in plan to allow welding to eachother
Reinforcement bars welded together at point of contact
600
600
600
600
ROOF PLAN

Designer: Jerry Tate

Device: Drawing Fiction

Function: Drawing the imagined space to generate fictional relationships.

Concept:
The drawing machine interprets the interaction of three characters and critical site elements, demonstrating the spaces they establish between themselves. The product is the creation of fiction through the tension between all the elements on the site. The process was recorded at critical moments by taking castings of the surface of interaction in the drawing machine.

The drawing machine has three essential elements.

The first element is a group of components which represented the characters and the site. These are on the 'underside' of the instrument and are either fixed site elements, or mechanical 'characters' which could be adjusted to produce different individual representations and could be moved through the site using armatures.

The second element produced the plain of interaction, which in this case is a latex sheet stretched across the entire machine by a steel frame. It is through their input into this sheet that the characters and site elements produced an interaction.

The third element is the method of recording this process, by taking a plaster cast of the latex sheet at interaction points.

Dimensions: 800 x 900 x 1500mm

Fabrication time: 3 months

Assembly time: 2 weeks

Materials:
Drawing machine frame:
Mild steel welded channel section (base frame)
Mild steel angles (clamping mechanism)
Timber fillets
Steel plate (bracket connections)
Solid circular sections (legs)
White latex sheet

Armatures: Bright steel solid circular and rectangular sections and springs, nylon washers for hinged elements, lacquered.

Characters and site elements: MDF sheeting cut and planed to suit. Mild steel threaded bar for adjustments.

Castings: Mild steel angle welded frame lacquered and spray painted with silver enamel paint. Fine plaster. Bandages (as reinforcement).

Fabrication:
- Cut mild steel angle and weld to suit frame dimensions.
- Drill and tap holes for clamping bolts.
- Cut clamping angles with mitred joints to suit inside channel.
- Plane down timber fillets to suit.
- Ensure latex sheet stretching mechanism works prior to shot blasting.
- Lacquer immediately after shot blasting to avoid rust spots.
- Fabricate bright steel wall brackets and legs, generally TIG welded connections.
- Fabricate armatures from bright steel, as before.
- Test nylon hinges and springs to ensure successful operation relative to the latex sheet.
- Fabricate characters and site elements from profiled and shaped MDF. Test the characters during manufacture to ensure compatibility with latex sheet.
- Fabricate casting frames from mild steel angles, lacquer and paint.

Assembly:
- Drill holes for connections in both wall and floor. Fix mild steel frame.
- Bolt armatures together and clamp onto side of the main frame.
- Pull latex sheet across the main frame and pull taught. Ask a friend to bolt down the clamping mechanism.
- Arrange characters as desired for casting. Place the casting frame on latex sheet. Mix plaster and pour (ensure no air bubbles). Before plaster goes off reinforce rear of casting by laying bandages in a cross pattern on rear.
- Remove casting after twelve hours and store in a safe place (casting will be only eggshell thin!)

Additional notes:
The exact method of mixing, reinforcing and removing the plaster casts took some time to perfect and adequate time should be allowed for experimentation.

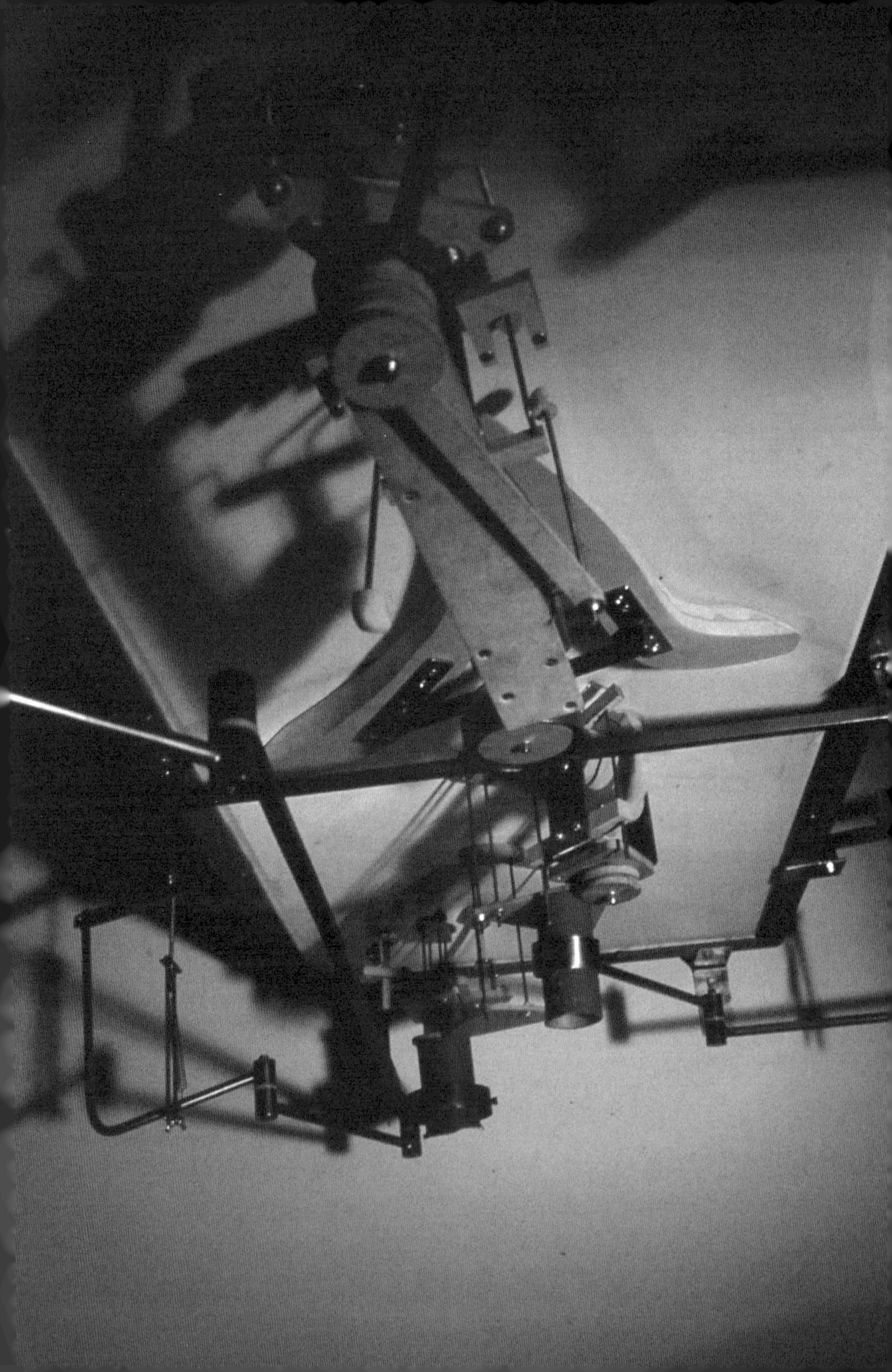

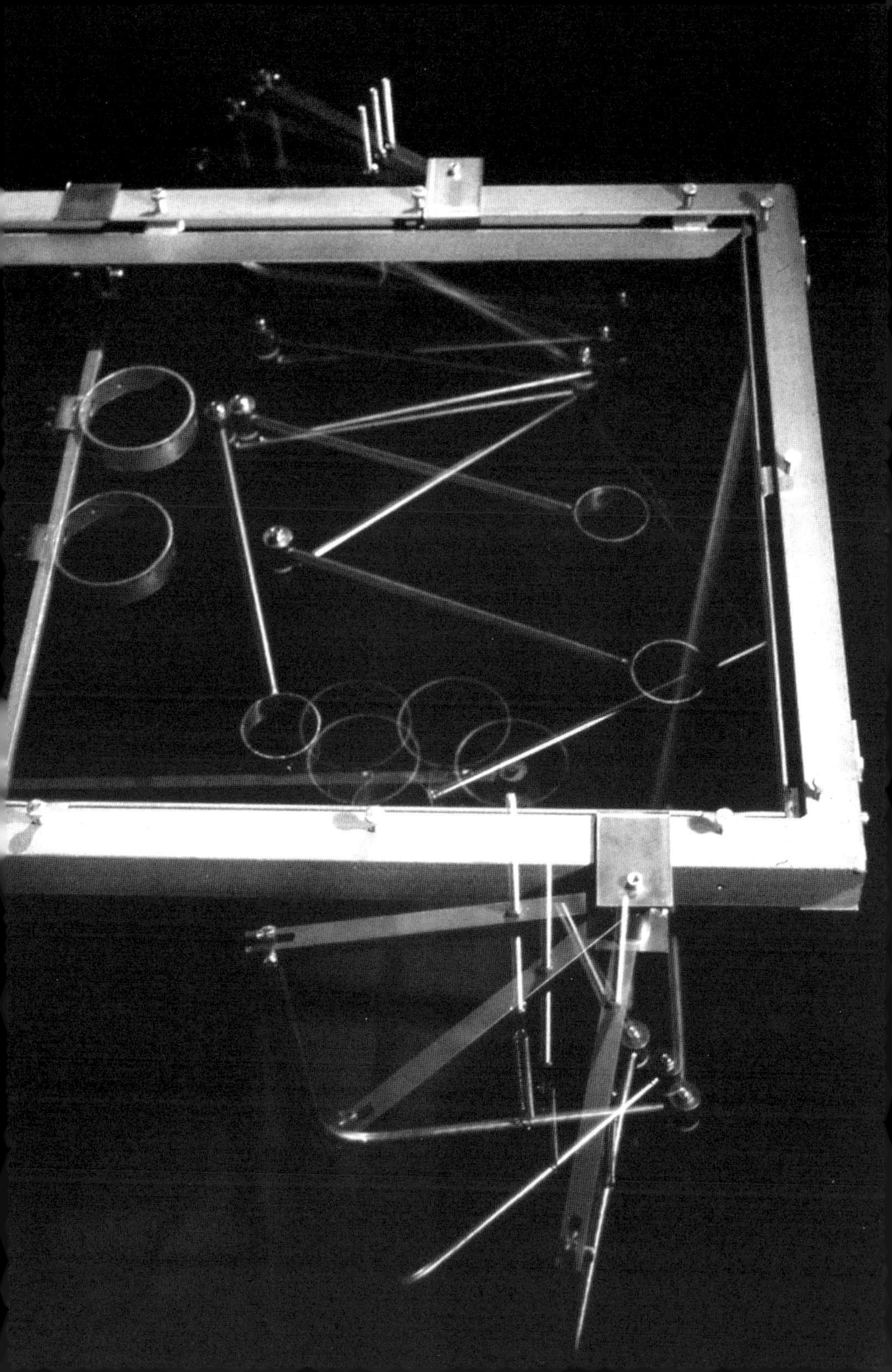

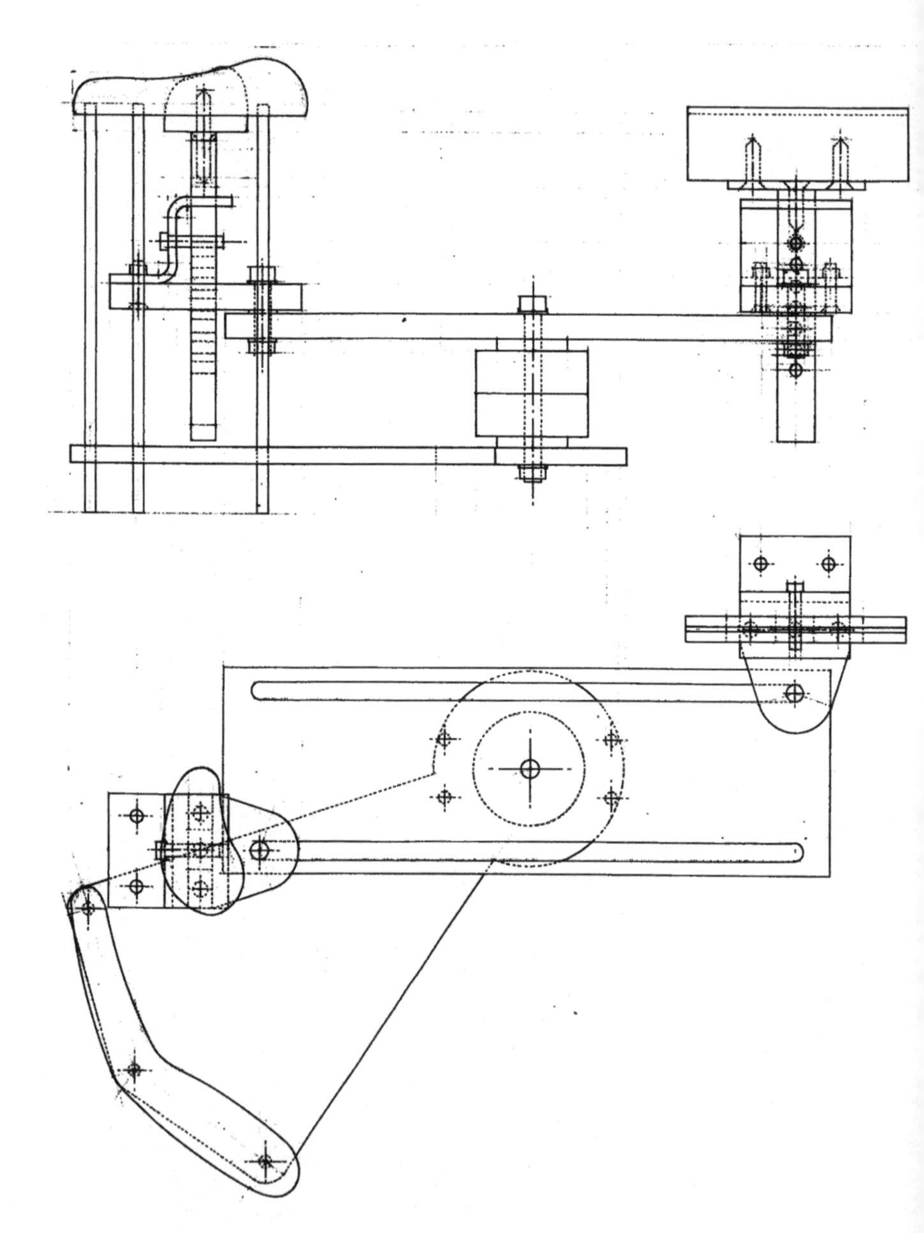

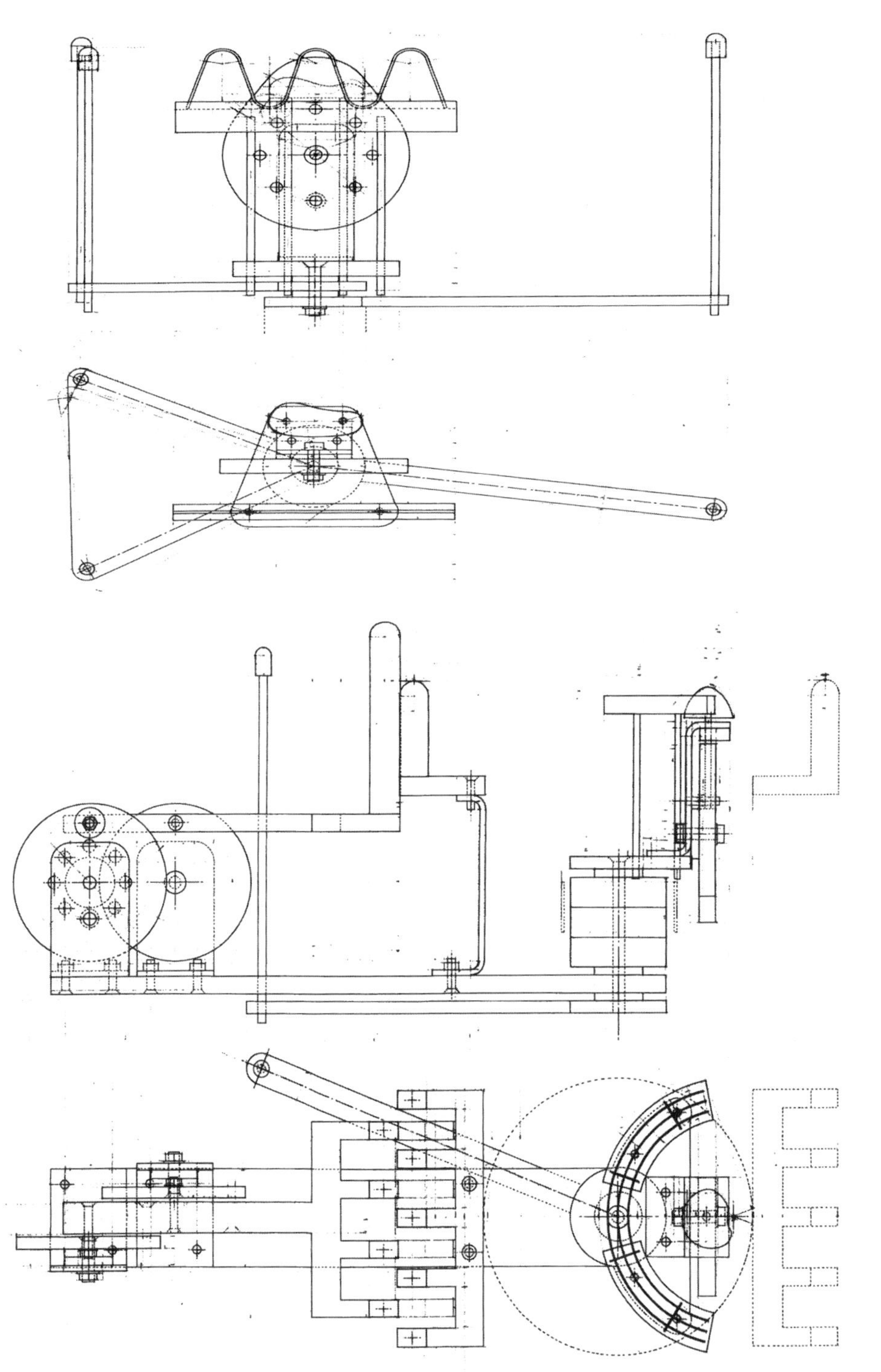

Designer: Nat Chard

Device: Drawing Instrument

Function: Exploring the possibility of the folded picture plane

Concept:
Architectural drawings need to be read by many agencies in the same way and have become laden with conventions to allow this. This ability to mean the same thing to everybody limits the possibility of the drawing to open up to more indeterminate possibilities. The instrument is one of several devices exploring the spatial possibility of the picture plane in making the drawing more active in the development of an indeterminate architecture. The two principle methods that are used to achieve this are through anamorphism - where your position with respect to the image implicates you in how it is constructed - and folding the picture plane, which can change the nature of how the elements of the drawing are assembled, again depending on your position.

A folded picture plane is supported by a series of mechanisms that are driven by information taken from a specially made camera. Each mechanism has two actions, one that is intended and one that is out of your control. The figure on the picture plane is constant, although elements of the figure can be obscured. Lights of different colour and intensity illuminate the figures. The final figure depends on the nature of the folds and the position of the viewer or the camera. The sequential photographs of the plane are assembled as colour negatives to make the final drawing of the whole experience.

Dimensions: 650 x 700 x 300mm

Fabrication time: Long story

Assembly time: 20 minutes

Materials:
Almost all the parts are CNC machined into patterns in Cibatool from which silicone rubber moulds are cast. The prototype is cast in plastic but the more developed version will be in bronze. Other elements are machined in Perspex or vacuum formed over MDF patterns. There is a range of roller bearings and electrical components that are off the shelf. The hinges in the

picture plane are made by machining the plastic surface to weaken it - too much in one instance. The figure blanking plates are steel and slide in pockets machined into the back of the picture plane.

Assembly:
There is a principle chassis to which all the main components are bolted (M4). The mechanisms sit in roller bearings that are a push fit. Once the picture plane is attached the electronic components are soldered together.

Additional notes:
This is a prototype. The components are sized to work in bronze. The current plastic legs are not strong enough to support the Bowden cables that link the instrument's mechanisms to the photograph reader. At the moment these actions have to be made manually.

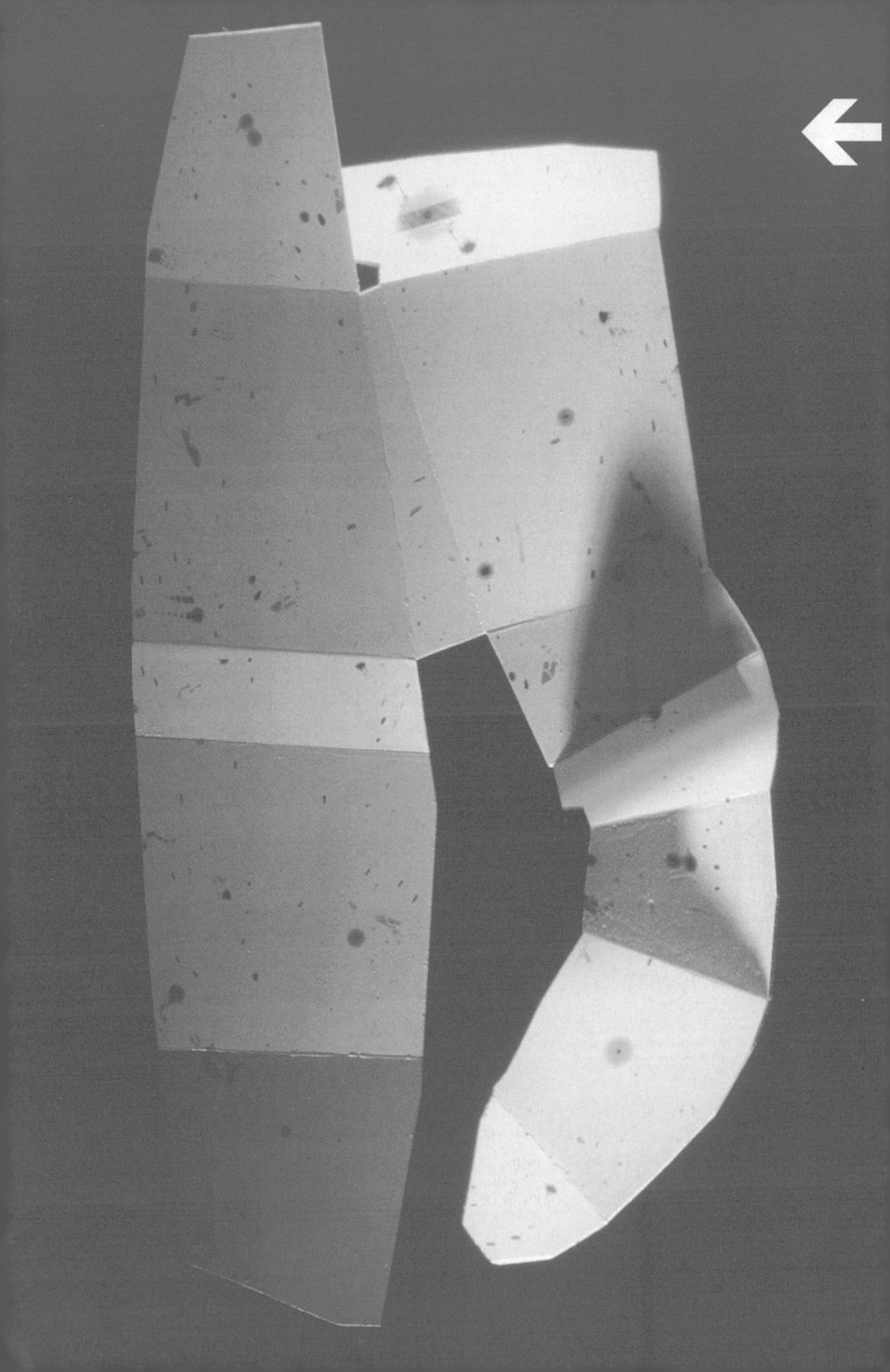

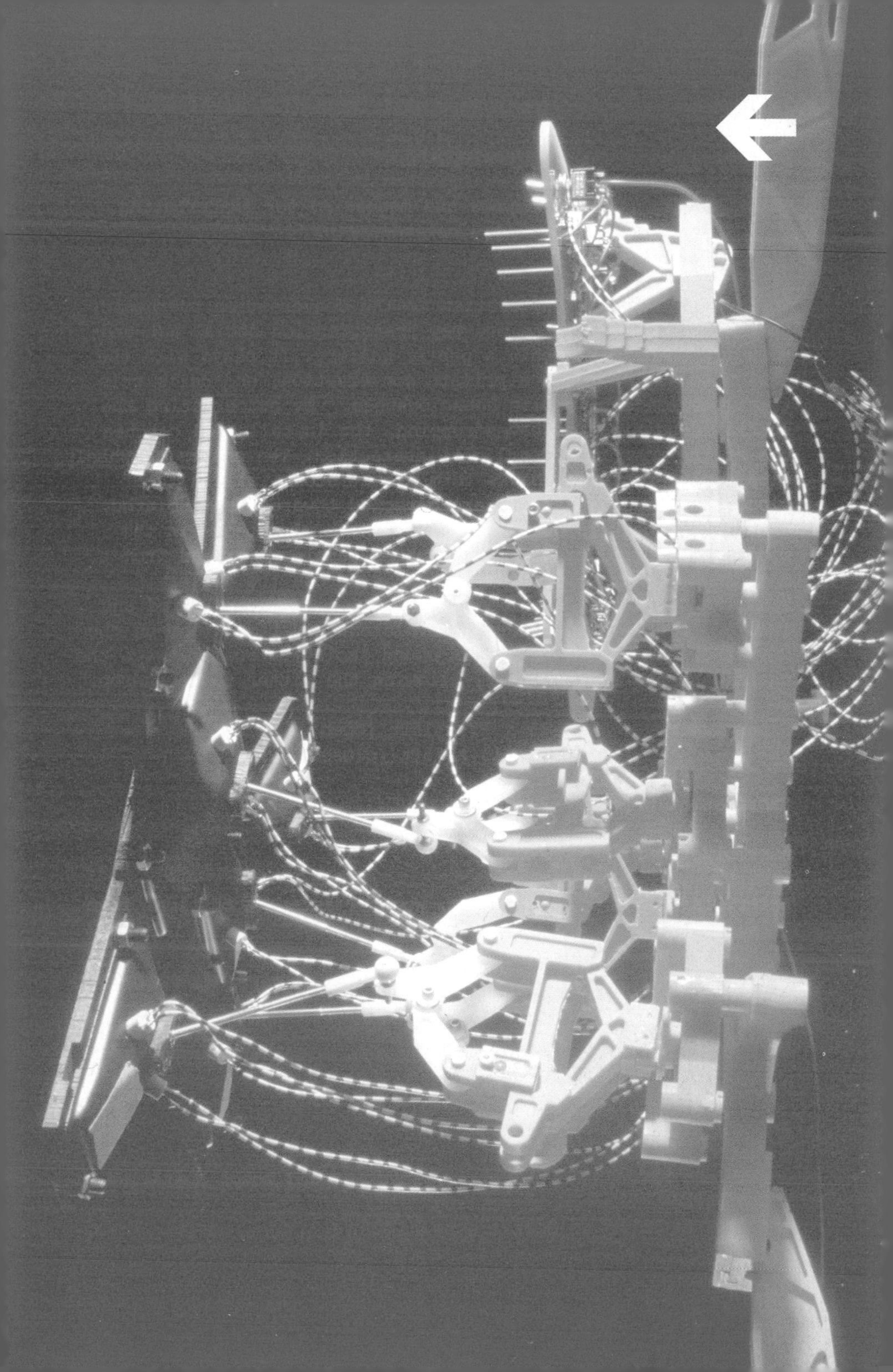

Designers: Lewis.Tsurumaki.Lewis (LTL Architects)

Device: Eavesdropping

Function: A space and mechanism for exacerbating gallery eavesdropping

Concept:
The most seductive conversation is the conversation overheard. Eavesdropping, takes the one-way transgression social act and ritually enacts it within a public gallery. It plays with the desire to listen-in to a private conversation, and calls this transgression into public consciousness. By exacerbating the spatial conditions of eavesdropping, the installation catches one at the moment of complicit interaction. Ten chairs on wheels with twelve-foot-high backs form a continuous wall in their closed position. The seats are directed towards ten isolated, low volume speakers connected to a remote microphone in the middle of the gallery. The microphone dangles overhead from a motorised pulley that slowly moves it across the gallery, scanning conversations. These private words are amplified and relayed to the ten speakers. Convoluted acoustical foam on the inside of the chairs creates a sound isolation room between the chairs and the speaker wall, allowing the sitter to eavesdrop.

Dimensions: 15 x 15 x 15ft (open)
3 x 15 x 15ft (closed)

Fabrication time: 2 months

Assembly time: 2 days

Materials: Aluminium, Wood, Plaster, Acoustical foam

Fabrication:
- Build chairs from aluminium and wood, with plywood surface.
- Skim coat outer surface in plaster.
- Cover inner surface in acoustical foam.
- Attach door track hardware to the top, steel wheels at the base.

Assembly method:
- Chairs fabricated in shop.
- Wireless microphone, receiver, speakers and motor installed.
- Door track attached to ceiling.
- Chairs attached to door tracks.

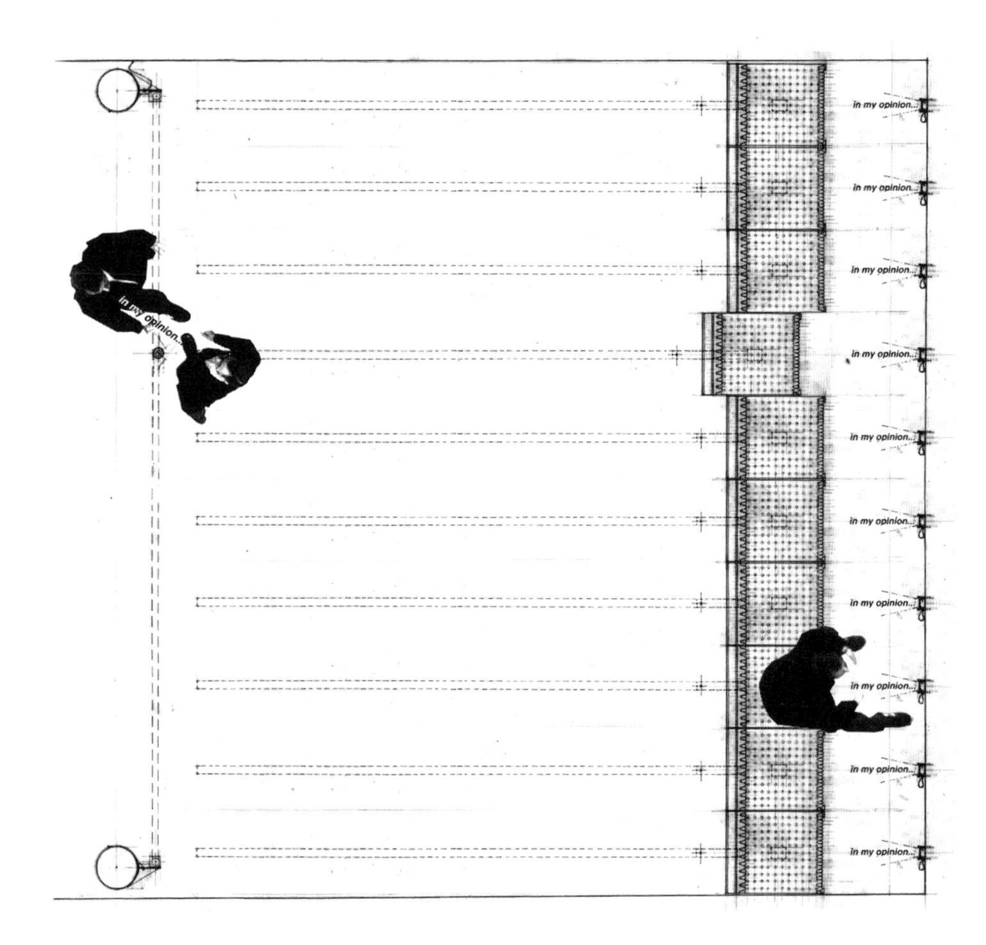
in my opinion...
in my opinion...
in my opinion...
in my opinion...
in my opinion...
in my opinion...
in my opinion...
in my opinion...
in my opinion...
in my opinion...
in my opinion...

Designer: William Thorne

Device: Edge Monkey

Function: Prototyping a climbing robot

Concept:
Edge monkeys trade off their local technical complexity against the possibility of very simple multiple façade actuators. The same monkey can activate shading devices, ventilation devices, movable insulation and security screens. These could all be standard products with a mechanical monkey interface. Monkeys could also clean the windows. Monkey actions could be 'read' anthropomorphically in terms of mood and culturally in terms of contemporary theatre and dance. Edge monkeys have potential individual and collective behaviours. It is this possibility that leads us to consider that building envelopes which contain edge monkeys could enter the realm of 'time based art'.

Dimensions: still evolving

Fabrication time: 4 months
The whole device was modeled in 3D in Micro-station before fabrication.

Assembly time: 8 hours

Materials:
Aluminium
8 pic microprocessors with support circuitry
Stepper motors
Electromagnets
Brass gears

Fabrication:
Mask and etch circuit boards
Water-jet cut aluminium parts
CNC machine on vertical milling machine excess material

Assembly:
Slot and bolt parts together.

Additional notes:
The device was designed to be flexible, to allow parts of the mechanism and the software to be switched for more evolved designs. In some ways, I designed it never to be completed!

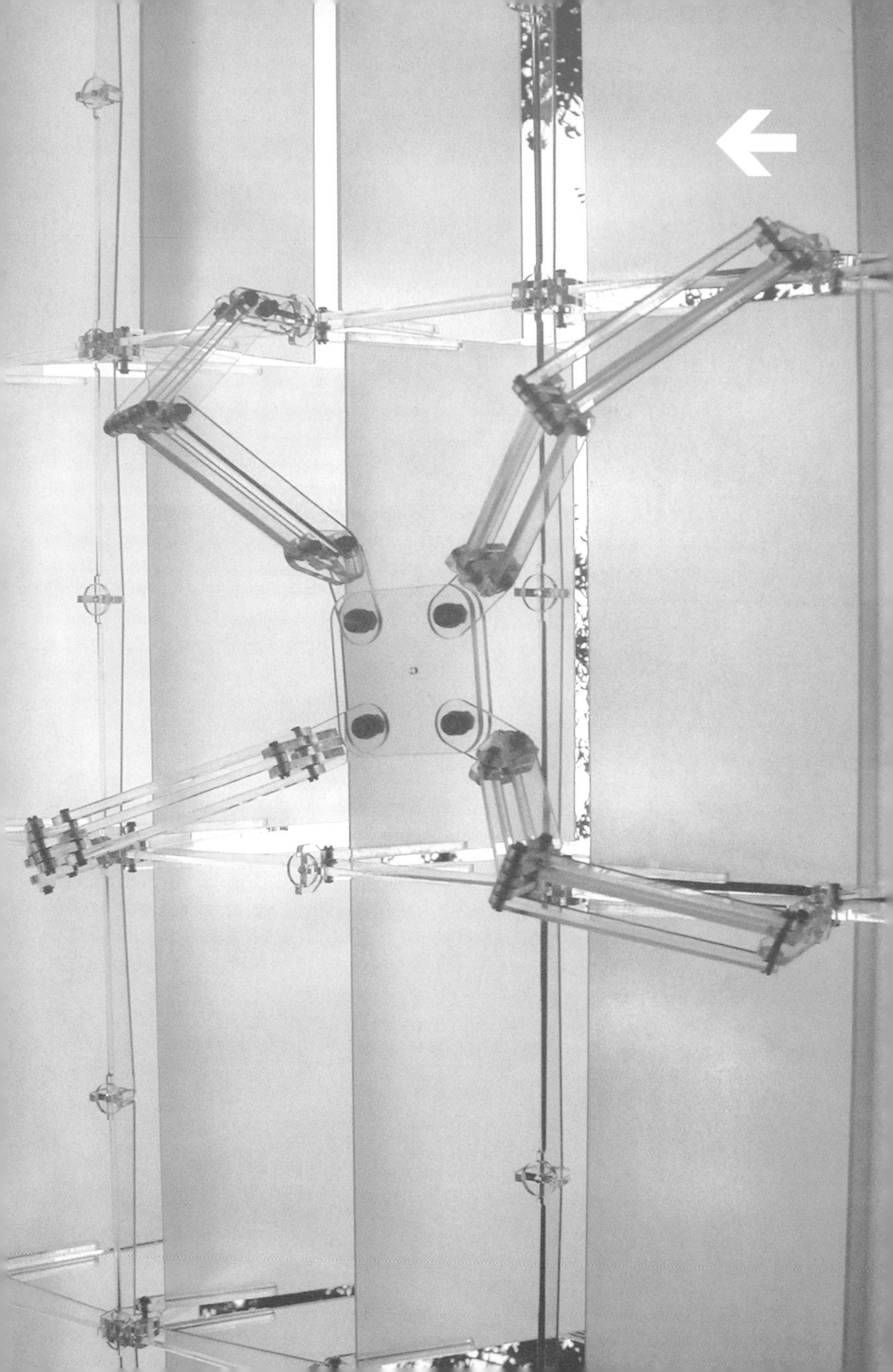

Designers: Louise Yeung, Anthony Lau + Denis Tsang

Device: Floating Lanterns

Function: Flood warnings

Concept:
Flying paper lanterns have been used as warning signals in ancient times as flood warnings.

The flame heats the air inside the lantern causing it to rise into the sky and the lighted lantern can be seen from a distance. The paper lantern has been designed with a fuse that will cause it to self-destruct and burn after a period of time. Sparkler fragments have been fixed to the tissue paper skin so that when it burns, it will release a shower of sparks.

This device lay dormant around the city awaiting the rising sea-level. The arm of the device measures the surrounding level of water, and upon reaching a certain threshold, triggers the device. An electric motor turns a sparking wheel which ignites the lantern wick. The lantern slowly unfurls and rises into the sky as a warning of the imminent flood. As the city floods, the whole sky will fill with floating lanterns.

Dimensions: 420 x 350 x 500mm

Fabrication time: 3 days

Assembly time: 1 hour

Materials:
Electric motors
Acrylic body
Battery pack
Sheet steel legs
LED
Crocodile clips
Electrical wiring
Piano wire
Pop rivets
Steel screws
Tissue paper
Aluminium foil
Cotton rolls
Tin candle trays

Paraffin lantern oil
Lighter sparking wheel
2-way switches
Ground up sparklers

Fabrication:
Paper lantern:
- Fold and glue the sheets to form the shape.
- Use steel wire to hold the lantern wick tray. Coat the paper with ground up sparklers.

Wick:
- Roll cotton rolls up in an aluminium sleeve.
- Cut and bend the acrylic body to shape.
- Bend steel legs to shape and insert into position.
- Attach motors and sparking wheel.
- Solder 2-way switches and wiring into position.
- Connect floating arm and LED to main body.
- Install battery pack.
- Mount lantern guides.

Assembly:
The paper lantern is folded and held by the lantern guides above the base device. The device is placed into position in the city and it lies dormant awaiting the rising sea levels.

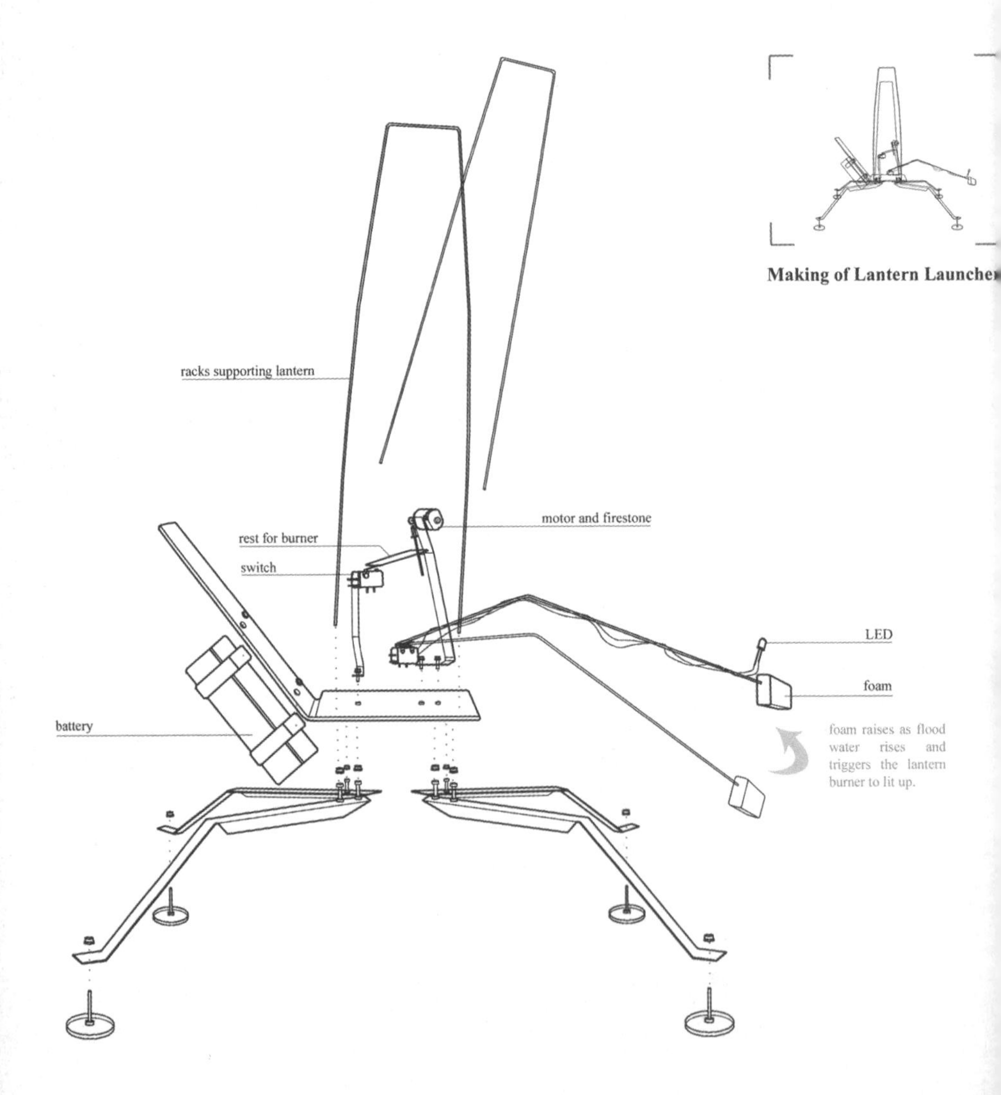

Making of Lantern Launche

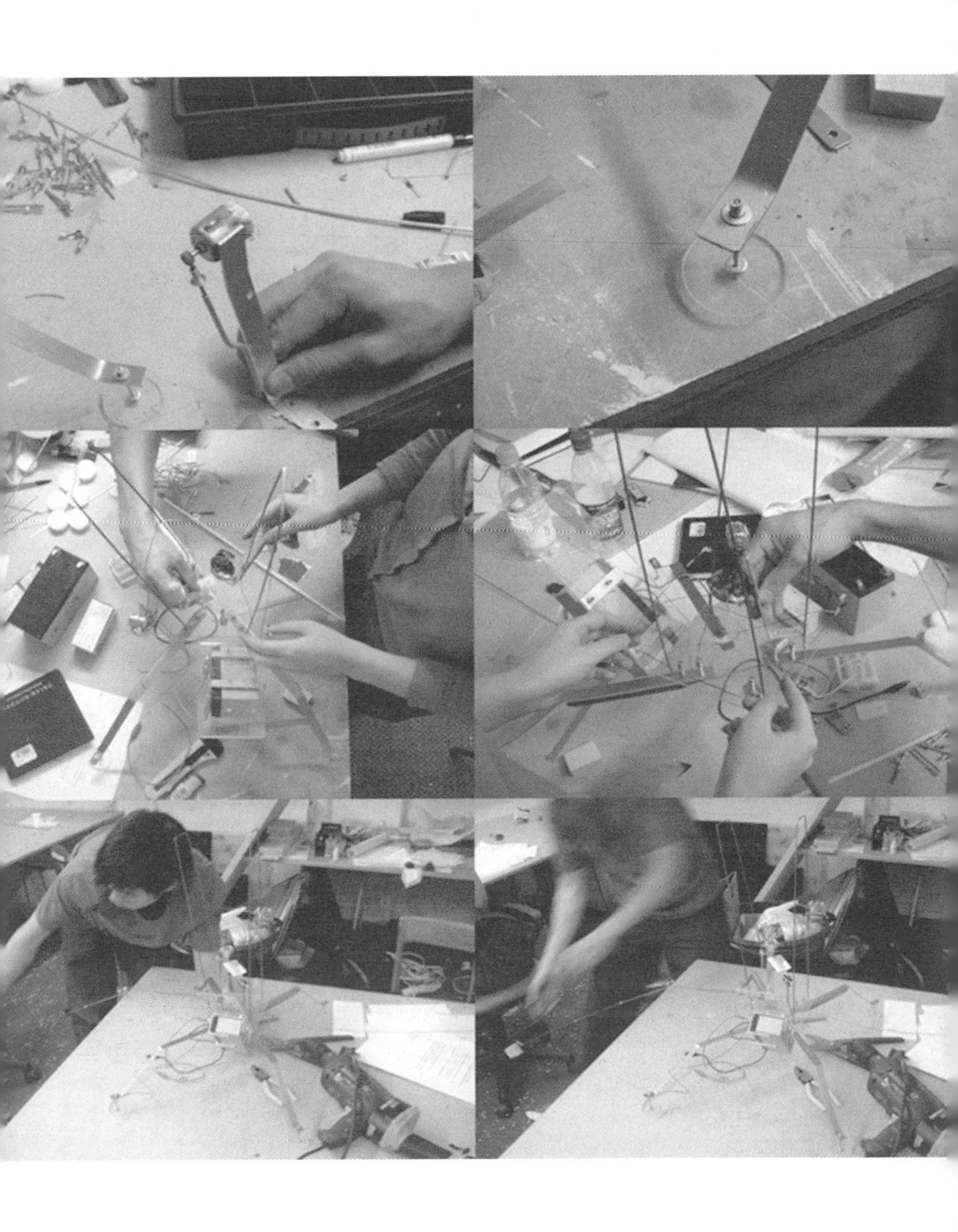

Designers: Denis Tsang, Louise Yeung + Anthony Lau

Device: Floodscape

Function: Investigating rising sea levels

Concept:
An artificial world that simulates a city and its relationship with the water is created with our landscape and its various electronic and mechanical components.

An artificial flood is created, which creates both a gradual and cataclysmic flooding. The balance between the rate of water draining and flooding is controlled by a valve and this represents the balance between human activity and the global warming.

A series of mechanical devices are positioned along this landscape and they are activated by the rising flood waters. The water acts as a conducting medium for the electricity, which flows from aerial mesh down into the devices, and through the water and into the electrodes.

The objects are arranged orthogonally as a notional city. The city comes to life with the water, and the cityscape begins to shift and change as the devices vibrate and move. LEDs begin to flash and emit light, some of which is projected upwards and captured by the mesh and the ceiling of the room. This play of light represents the poetic beauty of the flooded city.

The devices are designed with individual characteristics; some are on stilts, some can float, whilst others are static or become submerged. This suggests the notion of how the city responds in a flood where some structures will survive, some will reposition, and some will die. At the end of the flood cycle, the machine is switched off and we can observe a landscape of floating and sunken objects and the new arrangement of the city after the flood.

Dimensions: 1000 x 2100 x 3000mm

Fabrication time: 1 week

Assembly time: 2 weeks

Materials:
Much of our installation was made from materials sourced from scrap yards. In total, we took apart four washing machines for pumps and mixing tanks. The main water tank was adapted from a plastic street divider found on the street. The steel frame was made from scrap metal.
Steel structural frame
Main tank
Upper tank
Water distribution system
Drainage system
Electrode landscape
Electronic control junction
Conducting mesh
Lighting

Fabrication:
- The wooden frame for the landscape was first constructed. The MDF is then bent onto the framework and finally a wood veneer glued on. Perspex sides bolted and sealed with silicone sealant, surface of wood painted with varnish.
- Steel frame welded in workshop and mounted under wooden frame. Main tank made from plastic street divider. Pump installed and pipes connected.
- Upper tank made from steel sheet and washing machine tanks.
- Magnetic trapdoor made with floating trigger. Sprinkler system connected to upper tank.
- Drainage holes made in landscape surface and connected back to main tank. Overflow gutter made from steel sheet and bolted to edge.
- Electrodes made from pop-rivets and arranged in a grid on the landscape. Wiring connected to DC packs.
- Multi-extension lead taped to steel frame to form electric junction. All DC packs plugged into this point.
- Steel rods bent and welded to form mesh frame. Mesh tied to frame with chicken wire. Framework is suspended from ceiling with steel wire and expanding bolts. Crocodile clips connect the DC packs to the mesh.
- Lighting system created using LEDs connected to a DC pack.
- Individual Floodscape devices made.

Assembly:
The device had to be installed in a 3 x 4m room. The main components were constructed in the workshop and it was assembled inside the room. Once the wood frame was installed, the remaining components were built onto it.

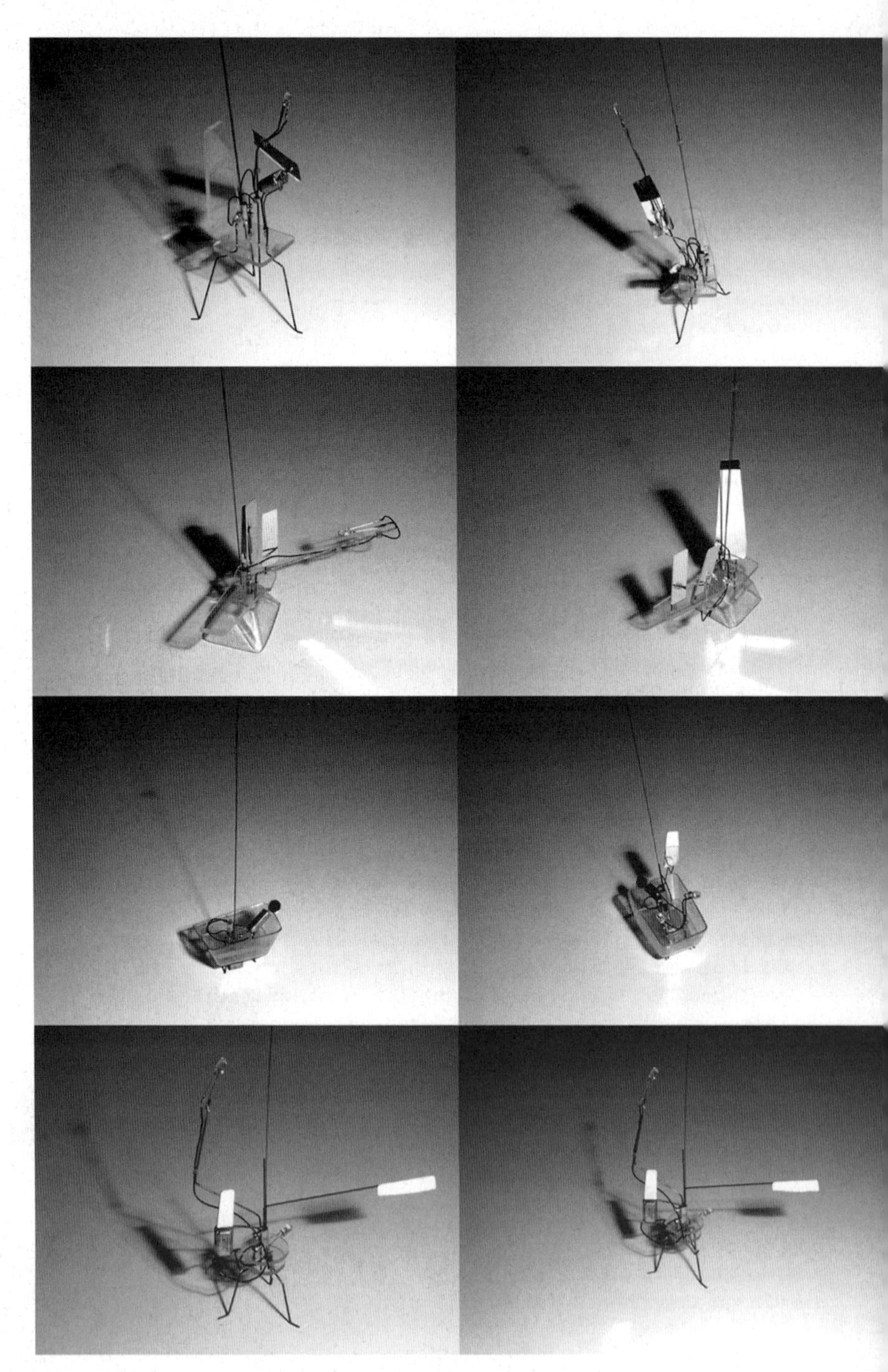

Designer: Shuheng Huang

Device: Haircutting Machine

Function: Transforming human desire

Concept:
This is an apparatus made of organised interacting parts used for the transformation of human desire: a haircut! The scissors glide and rotate on tracks demonstrating the analogy between three dimensional spatial choreography and tectonic form.

Dimensions: 1.5 x 0.25 x 0.2m

Fabrication time: 12 days

Assembly time: 3 hours

Materials:
1no scissors
3mm plywood
6mm MS rods
MDF wheels
Stainless steel wheels
Nuts + bolts
MS rotating hinges

Fabrication:
- Laminate and bend three sheets of 3mmm plywood to make frame.
- Adapt scissors for fixing.
- Using hinge as joint, connect scissors to steel armatures.
- Attach MDF wheels to MDF track using bolts.
- Bend MS rods to right radius to suit main frame.
- Attach stainless steel wheels to steel frame.

Assembly:
- Bolt MDF track with wheels to main frame.
- Attach steel frame and scissors.

Additional notes:
Used under supervision of an adult and preferably a barber!

Designers: James Ward + Juliet Aston

Device: Haptic Gloves

Function: Communicating tactile stimulations

Concept:
Operating as a partnership, two users (sight sensitive and touch sensitive) use remote devices to investigate a boundary using their own bodies as tools for collecting and receiving data.

Although the sight sensitive user has his visual information restricted by a visor, he leads and his touch-sensitive partner follows directly behind him. One eye on his feet for orientation, the other sees straight ahead or at the whim of his partner is redirected to the boundary beyond.

The pace of the journey is varied to the touch sensitive user's desire. The sight sensitive user determines the temporal space of investigation, by searching for a subjective reading of the boundary's edginess. Investigations by the touch sensitive user's haptic glove are translated to sensations. Through a prosthetic device, the palm of the sight sensitive user receives tiny abstracted tactile stimulations. The gloves limit the users' senses, and make them interdependent.

Dimensions: Touch glove: 71 x 122 x 31mm
Sight glove: 89 x 117 x 38mm
Visor: 135 x 146 x 52mm

Fabrication time: 2 weeks

Assembly time: 3 hours

Materials:
Polycarbonate
Nylon tubing
Thin-wall polycarbonate tube
Magnetised iron
Mirror plastic
Neoprene
Cotton thread
Uncoated single core copper wire
PVC-coated wire
Epoxy resin
Aluminium sheet

Stainless steel rod
Brass rod
Solder
Push/Pull solenoid 12 DC
2x Miniature tilt switches
3x Double pole switches
5x Variable resistors

Fabrication:
- Sight sensitive user's haptic glove:
- Solder wiring loom together to produce in series circuits connected to a battery pack.
- Produce plaster mould of users hand.
- Coat plaster mould with release agent and cast.
- Vacuum form inner polycarbonate sheet over plaster cast.
- Bond wiring loom and nylon tubes to outside face of polycarbonate.
- Vacuum form outer polycarbonate sheet the inserts.
- Drill out the nylon tubes, trim and finish polycarbonate to fit user's hand.
- Coil uncoated copper wire around the top of polycarbonate rods and insert magnetised iron to produce a solenoid.
- Connect solenoids to the wiring loom and insert them into the nylon tubes.

Touch sensitive user's haptic glove:
- Solder sensors to wiring loom.
- Cut neoprene sheeting to pattern.
- Sew neoprene patterns together.
- Sew on sensor elements and wiring loom to the rear of glove.
- Cut aluminium sheet to patterns.
- Bend pattern over jig to shape.
- Bond mirror plastic to the rear face of aluminium pattern.
- Bend armatures linkages to shape.
- Connect the fan mechanism to the circuit board.
- Solder a light dependent resistor to the piano wire.
- Feed the arm into the tin through the small holes and connect to the circuit board.

Assembly:
- Assemble armature linkages.
- Connect solenoid and neoprene glove into the wiring loom.
- Solder battery pack and variable resistors into series circuits.
- Connect separate looms together.

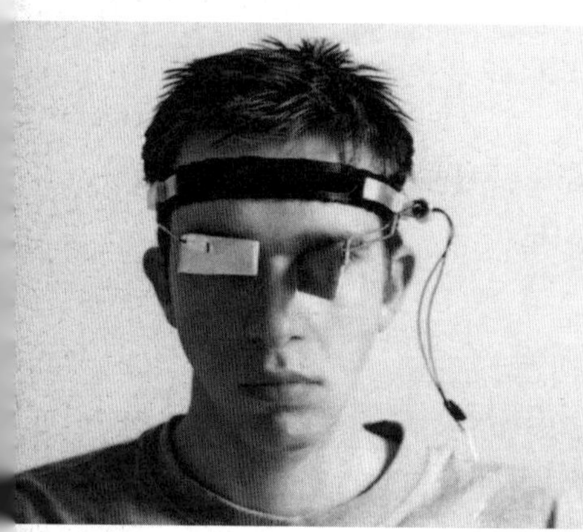

I AM

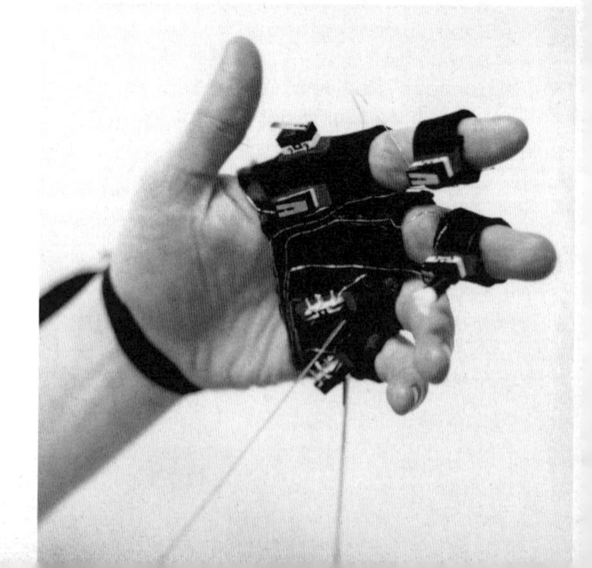

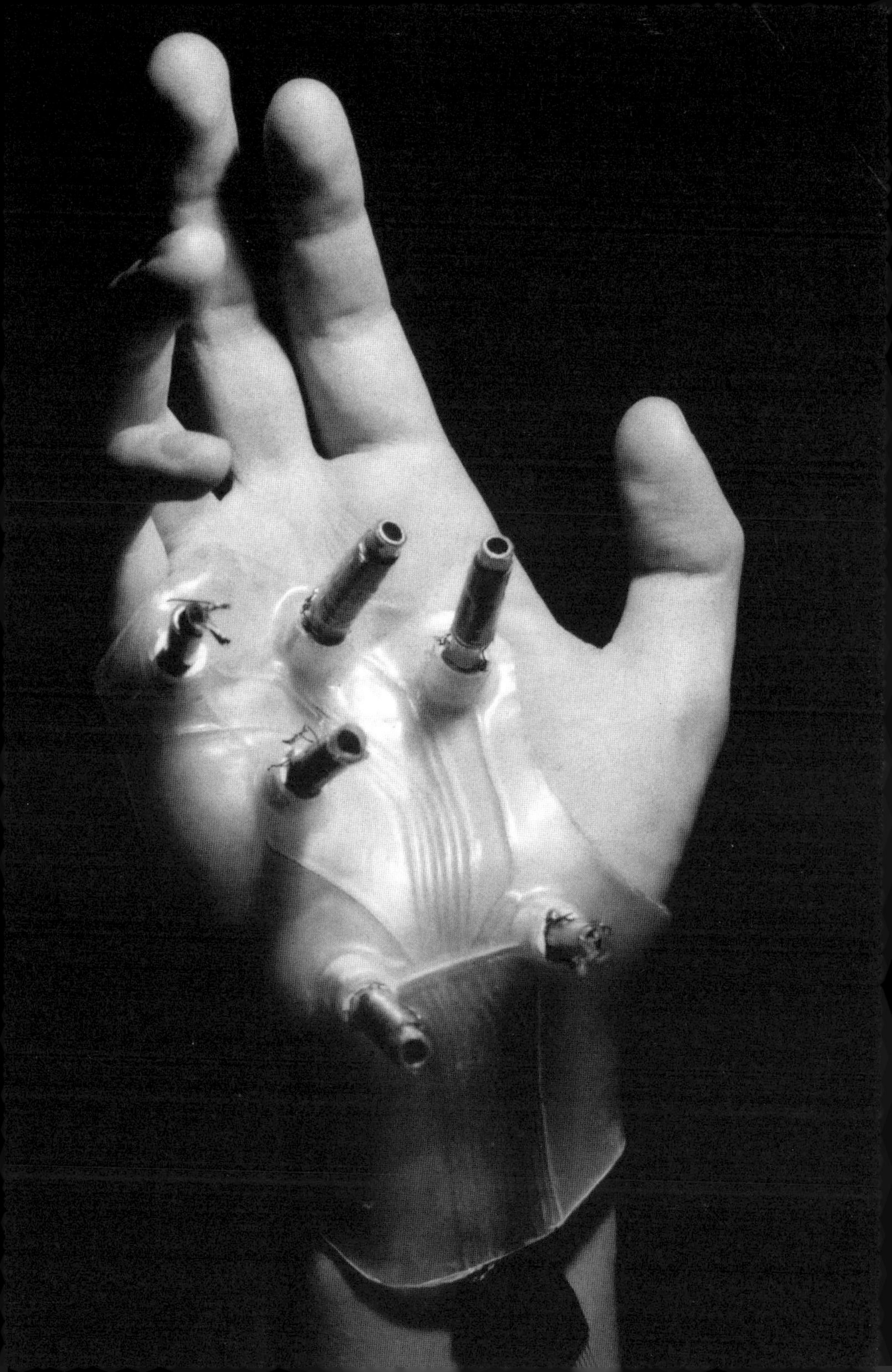

Designer: Matthew Springett

Device: Hydro-kinetic Hinge Assemblage

Function: Screening in response to occupancy

Concept:
In London's Smithfield meat market, hanging animal carcasses create a mobile and fluctuating spatial landscape. They screen the hall when they are hung up, and animate it when they are being moved around or dissected. Inspired by this process, the assemblage uses a two-way hydraulic system, enabling an attached surface to alter its location and shape in an orientation.

Dimensions: 2500 x 600 x 1000mm (Assemblage)
300 x 45 x 60mm (Component)

Fabrication time: 4 weeks

Assembly time: 24hrs

Materials:
Module: Syanate resin body, perspex + silicone mechanism, vacuum formed UPVC, Polythene tubing, latex balloon, clinical syringe, stainless steel grub screws, car body filler + spray paint.

Counter weights: Vacuum formed UPVC, lead, perspex, thread.

Frame: Lacquered steel, perspex, threaded rod, nuts + bearings.

Fabrication:
Module:
- Make plaster moulds for casting; cast, sand fill, spray units.
- Make mould for 2nd leaf, vacuum form 2nd leaf.
- Fabricate perspex hinges.

Counter weights:
- Make mould for vacuum former, vacuum form containers.
- Fill with lead, glue seal and paint.

Assembly:
- Sub assembly of modules, counter weights and frame.
- Assemble table in position.
- Fix pulley frame to ceiling, hang modules and counterweights.
- Fill balloon bladders and syringes with water.
- Test and adjust.

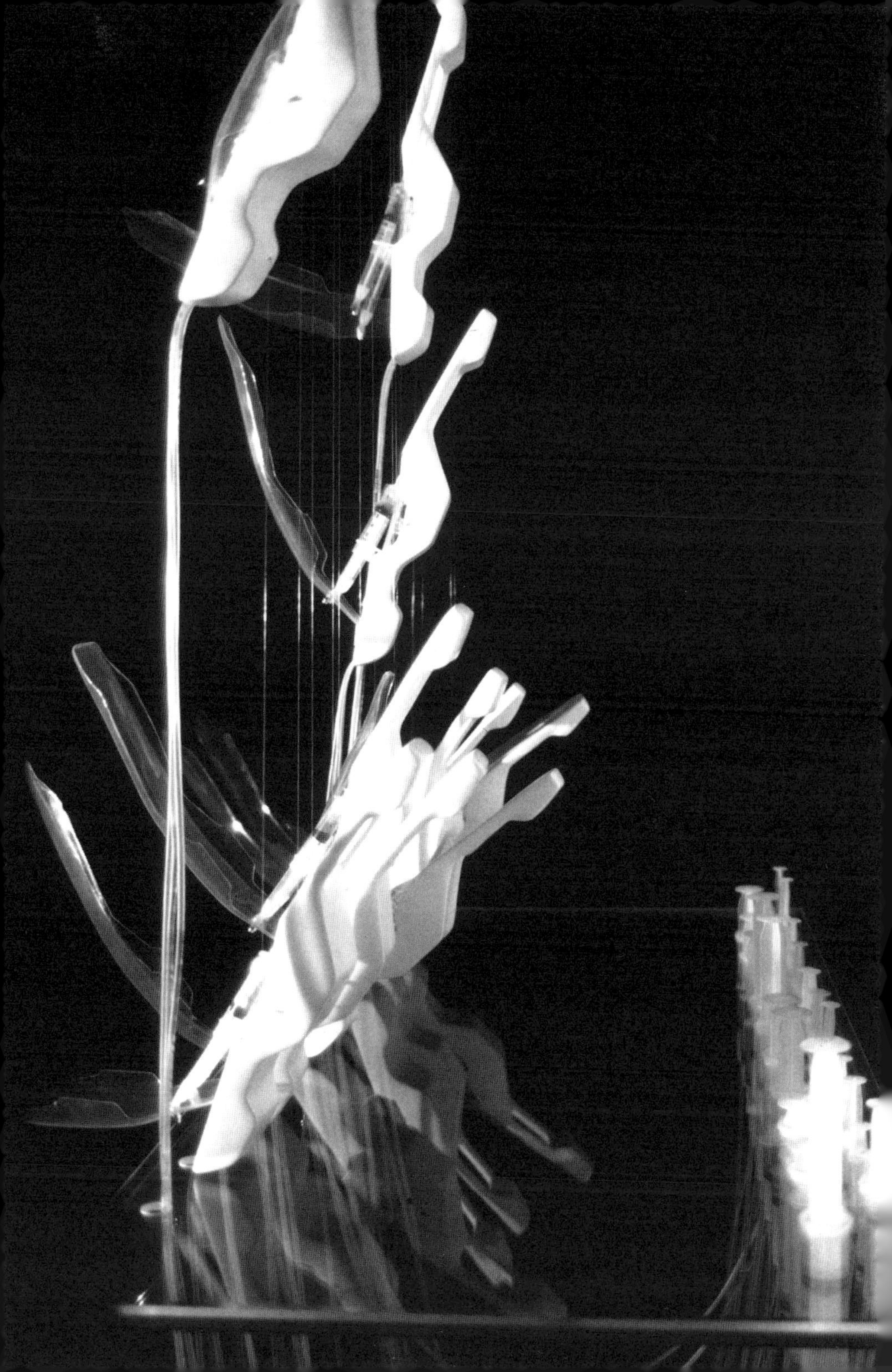

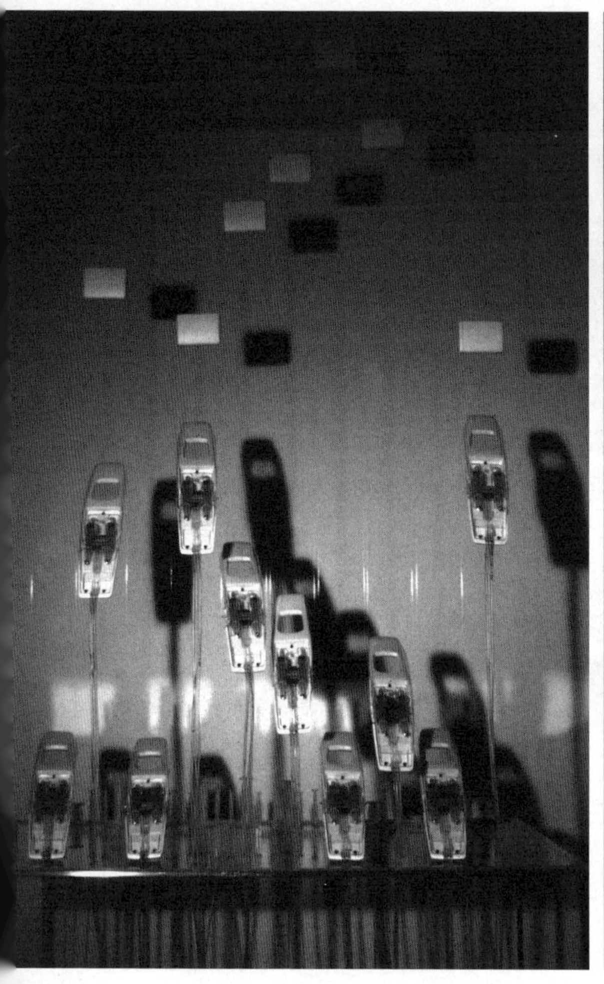

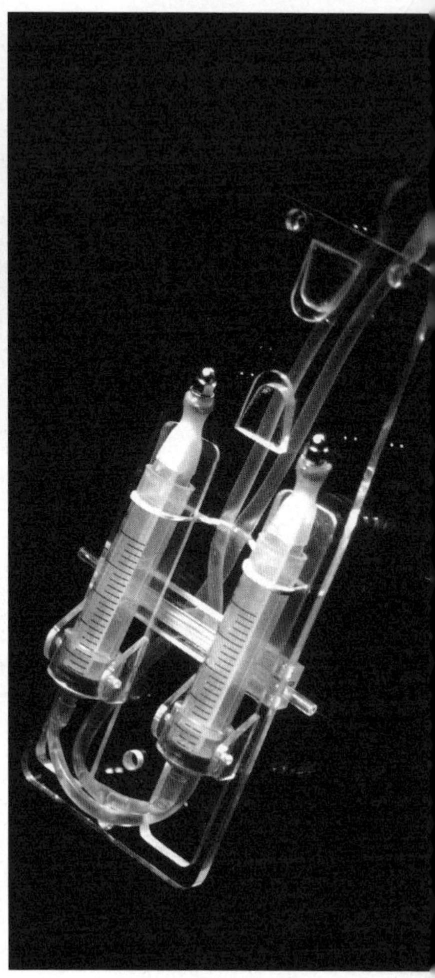

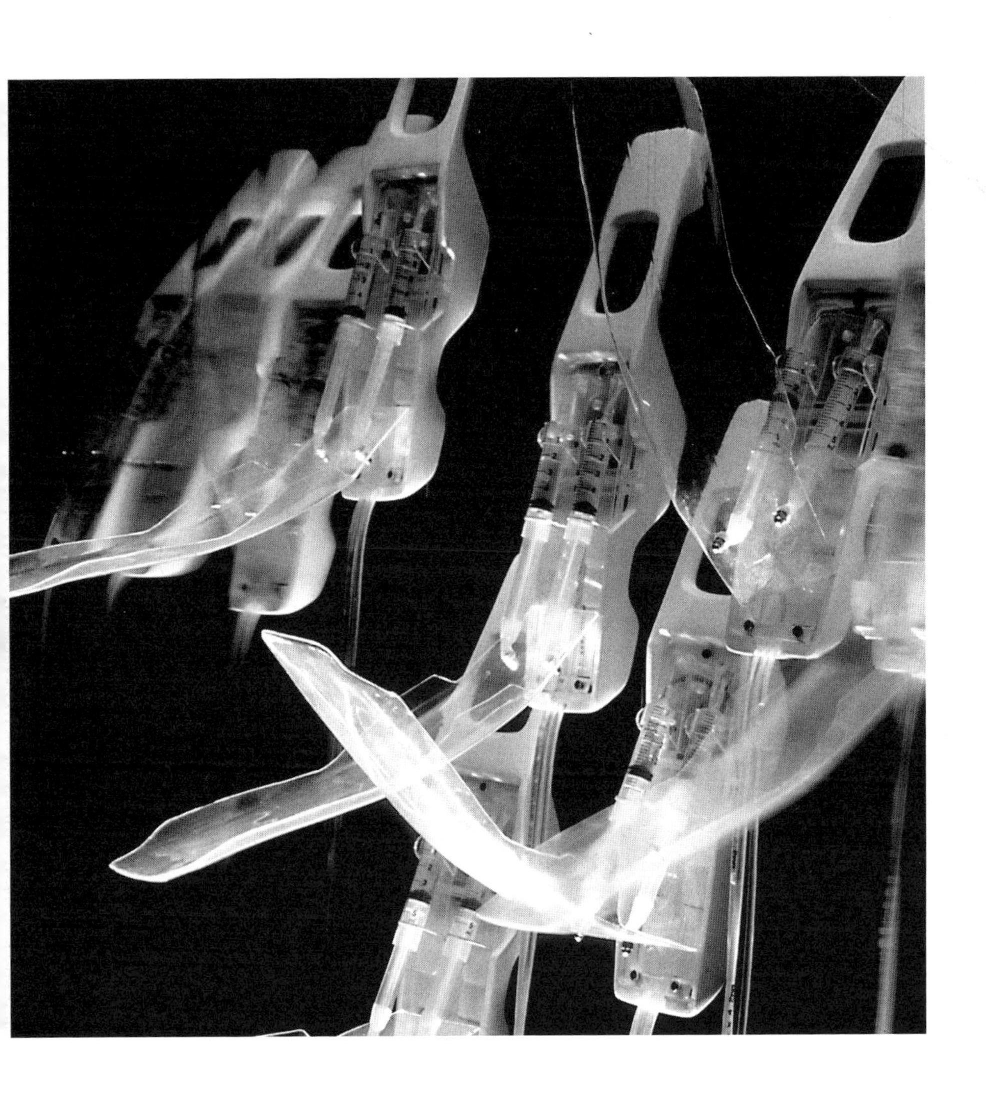

Designers: Mette Ramsgard Thomsen
with Jesper Mortensen + Chris Parker

Device: I See What You Hear

Function: Interactive sound installation

Concept:
'I see what you hear' is an interactive installation where users interact through sound and movement. Talking, singing, making noises, the users generate swarms of leaves, insects and numbers, creating a fluid space around the presence and action of the user. Like a snowstorm, the space is a condition rather than a limitation, generated through the moment of interaction and sited fleetingly around the presence of the users.

The installation is the making of an embodied interface mapping the users' sound output to the dynamic production of a graphical three dimensional space. The environment is generated as clouds of matter that the user 'blows' into being. The sound interface determines the parameters of pitch and volume along with a notion of silence, that are mapped onto a particle system. As the users sing, talk, whistle or clap they change the spread, speed and density of the stream. Silence becomes a means of dissolving the stream, of cleaning the space out and starting again.

The environment draws a fantastical world akin to a childhood dream. Butterflies mix with leaves, numbers and circles as the users scale the environment through their voice. As two-dimensional objects occupying a three-dimensional space, the objects spin and twirl, drawing the depth of the stereoscopic environment. A second camera based interface tracks the user's movement in the installation space. The users wear polarised glasses so as to see the stereoscopic space. One of the glasses is mounted with an infrared LED which is tracked by an infrared camera. The user movement is mapped onto the virtual viewpoint allowing the user to 'look around' the objects as they are generated.

'I see what you hear' is an intuitive and auto-didactic environment, where the continual filling and dissolving of space creates fuzzy boundaries, mirroring the open parameters of the interface. Here, new sounds (clicking, clapping or blousing) create unexpected results. As users engage with the environment they learn to explore a new sense of agency within the interactive dimensions. The digital becomes an enacted reality, instantiated in the present and taking place through the moment of interaction.

Dimensions:	3 x 5m (installation space) 2.6 x 2m (projection screen)
Fabrication time:	3 months
Assembly time:	2 days

Materials:
Interactive environment:
1no dual processor PC (visualiser and camera tracking system)
1no laptop (running sound interface)
1no Ethernet hub
2no 1500 Lumen data projectors
2no polarised filters to mount on the projectors
1no high-end graphics card with dual DVI-I monitor output
1no perforated stereoscopic projection screen (retro-reflective)
1no shotgun microphone
1no infrared camera
10no pairs of polarised glasses (with a mounted infrared LED)

Fabrication:
Interface and display:
'I see what you hear' is made of three independent programs communicating through TCP/IP. The sound interface analyses for pitch and volume, the camera interface determines the x and y position of the primary user and the visualiser maps the incoming data to the parameters of the particle stream.

Sound interface:
The sound interface computes the pitch level (through a Fast Fourrier Transform) and amplitude (volume) of the sound signal deriving the two core parameters of interaction. The sound analysis takes place in real time and is dynamically mapped on to the particle stream. Pitch determines the y axis of the particle stream while volume determines the width of the stream (local x and y axis of the spray), along with the density (number of particles) and velocity (speed of the particles).

Camera interface:
The camera interface tracks the position of an infrared LED mounted on one of the stereoscopic glasses. The two-dimensional tracking data is mapped onto a semi-spherical plane allowing the

user to 'look around' the particles. If users choose not to wear the LED mounted glasses the system reverts to a basic centralised viewpoint.

Visualiser:
The visualiser maps the interactive parameters to the particle stream. Designed as a graphical user interface, the visualiser is also a design tool through which multiple visualisations can be explored. The visualiser allows setting of the particles' size, texture, spin axees as well as the overall environment's gravity level and colour.

Projection:
The digital environment is projected using a passive stereoscopic projection system. The visualiser outputs two coupled viewpoints into the digital space corresponding respectively to the left and right eye. This dual output is projected onto a retro-reflective projection screen which directs the light straight back, thereby limiting the diffusion of the image. Using polarised filters and glasses the two projected images are separated allowing for stereoscopic vision. The stereoscopic display is presented before the picture plane of the projection screen, meaning that the users see the swarms of objects in three dimensions as sited around them rather than beyond the picture plane.

Assembly:
The installation takes place in a sound dampend space allowing users a sense of privacy as well as reducing noise from the surroundings. The installation space is lined with a soft dark fabric that cushions both sound reverberation and light refraction. In contrast, the projection screen is perforated resulting in a subtle visual connection to the outside.

'I see what you hear' is both a single and multi-user system. A wall mounted shotgun microphone produces a defined sound cone, again limiting the noise from the outside while simultaneously enabling multiple users to interact with the system.

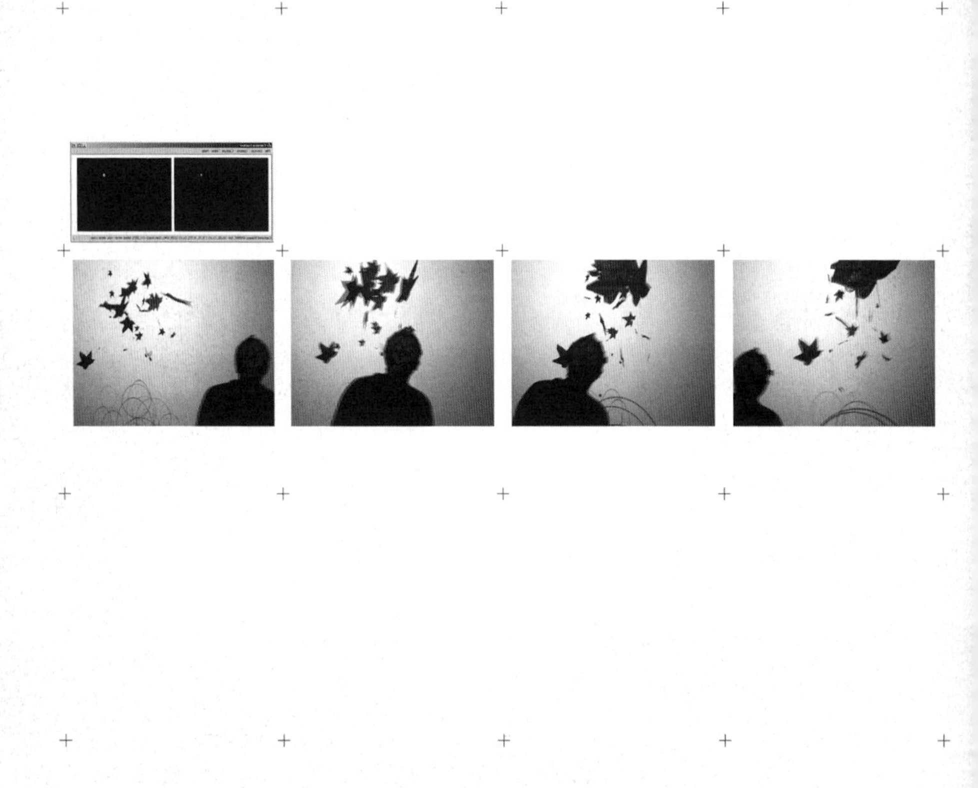

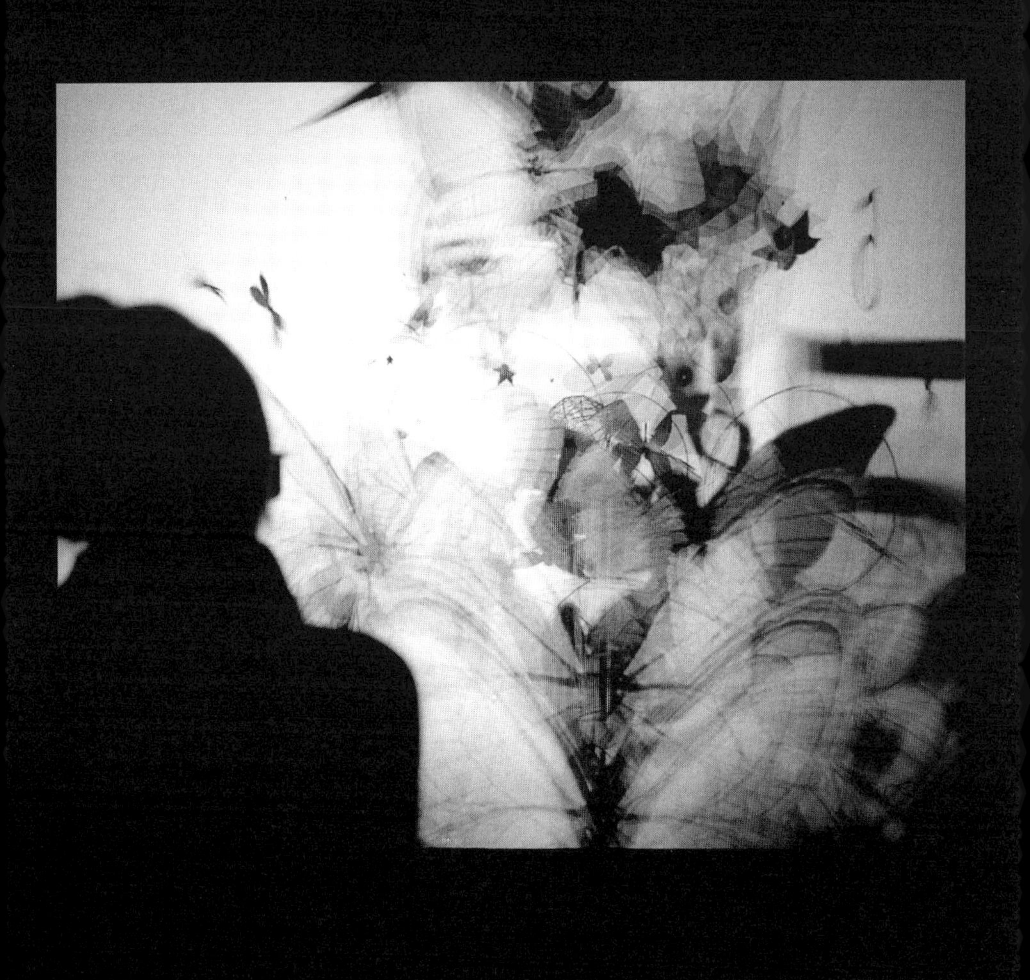

Designer: Chris Leung

Device: Light Fibre Field

Function: Four-dimensional space-time and occupant movement mapping devices

Concept:
The objective was to build a system that would explore its environment and build a time-based map of its surroundings.

The project started by developing one 'lighting emitting mast' that contained a switching lighting source and a computer controlled mirror to direct a narrow light-beam, together with eight directional light sensors. The system demonstrated self-learning properties in identifying the location of each respective neighbour by horizontal direction, and estimating their distance by altitude and light intensity. The system also demonstrated adaptive properties in coping with changing ambient light levels, changes in the installation space as well as changes in object arrangement. The changes observed in the field's behaviour with the presence of people amongst the objects were the most intriguing, with evidence of emergent shadow and edge-following behaviours.

Dimensions: Each Light Emitting Mast 1550 x 200 x 200mm and weighs 14kg. The field with 15 objects is 7500 x 4500mm.

Fabrication time: 6 months; Software development 18 months+

Assembly time: 4 days to install and self-calibrate nine Light Emitting Masts

Materials: Required for one Light Emitting Mast (all quantities multiplied by 15)

Power

1no 0.1uF mains X-2 suppression caps	RS 115-196
1no PCB F/H with cover 6.3A @ 250V A/C	maplin KU29
1no 18VA triple-out transformer	RS 201-8794
2no In-line 400V 2A rectifier	RS 183-4090
1no T220 voltage Reg MC7812CT	maplin QL32K
1no TO2205 MIC29301 3A LDO/EN	RS 217-4973
1no T220 voltage reg 78S05 2 Amp	maplin UJ54J
3no Electrolytic 220uF cap general	RS 228-6997
2no Electrolytic 2200uF 25V/16V	RS 228-6701

1no Electrolytic 1000uF RS 228-6818
10no 0.1in 0.1uF ceramic cap 63V RS 264-4927
1no Heatsink TO220 17.9oC/W RS 263-251
2no Heatsink T220 35x27x16 9deC/W RS 234-2407
1no 12V cooling fan 500mA maplin RG03D
1no TO220 silicone pad and bush RS 298-443
6no Polyester cap 1uF 63V smoothing RS 823-998
3no Polyester cap 10uF 63V RS 179-4368
1no 5V internal resistor LED red RS 228-5562

Lighting Control
1no 10Kohm vertical potentiometer RS 160-095
1no 50W tungsten halogen lamp 12deg. 12V UV glass
1no Compact dimmable electronic lighting transformers 60W
1no Velleman K8003 Dimmer Kit maplin VF58N
1no LTC 1257 CN8 Digital-to-Analog chip RS 217-0397
1no 50W halogen ceramic lamp holders maplin VJ11M
2no Nom. 5V 3.5 Kg torque servo-motors various
1no Nom. 10mm dia. 1 metre cast acrylic rod various
1no Dentist non-magnifying/magnifying mirror various
1no 12V 500mA Cooling fan RS

Sensing
1no Erwin Sick retro-reflective beam sensors RS 263-8247
1no 50x50mm polarized retro-reflectors RS 265-2754
1no HEF4067BP 16-ch multiplexer RS 169-7920
8no 10K Ohm Light-Dependent-Resistors Maplin N53AY
1no 0-5V 1000W/m^2 Pyranometer Unit with amplifier SkyeSKL2650
1no P.I.R. sensors gaurdscan type RS 239-7182

PCB + CPU + Networking
1no PIC 16F877 20/P microprocessor crownhill-associates
2no PIC 16F84a 4/P microprocessor crownhill-associates
3no 4MHz ceramic resonators 3-terminal RS 179-3725
1no MicroChip 24LC16B 2K EEPROM crownhill-associates
1no BUZ10 N-channel MOSFET maplin UJ32K
1no 16-way D.I.L. 0.3inch pitch pin socket maplin FZ49D
1no Tripad Strip Circuit Board 3962 maplin JP52G
1no 40-way D.I.L. 0.6inch pitch pin socket maplin FZ67X
3no 8-way D.I.L. 0.3inch pitch sockets punched maplin BL17T
1no TO92 format DS1813 uP supervisor chip RS 262-9035
1no MAX202 RS-232 transceiver RS 299-913
1no SN75 176B RS-485 transceiver maplin AE09K
2no 18-way D.I.L. 0.3inch pitch sockets maplin HQ76
1no 3mm tricolour LED 5V RS 228-5685
4no 4k7 1% 0.6W metal-film resistor RS 164 9195

10no10k 1% 0.6W metal-film resistor	RS 164 9280
1no 8-way SIL resistor 10k Ohm	RS 140-978

Connectors + Fixings + Enclosure + Switches

1no e case c 220mm	maplin PL93a
2no end plate c	maplin PL94
1no IEC socket PCB chassis snap-fit	RS 311-8031
1no 9-way D-type socket chassis solder bucket	maplin RK61R
1no high-voltage warning plates	maplin WH48C
2no RS-485 bus DIN 4-way chassis	maplin HH33L
2no RS-485 bus DIN 4-way plug	maplin HH26D
1no 3mm LED chassis mount bezel	RS 262-2983
1no M3 eyelet earthing straps	RS 433-028
2no 2-way pluggable SKT 0.3″ pitch	maplin RH98G
2no pins for above 0.3″ pitch connector	maplin RJ27E
1no rubber grommets for cable strain relief	maplin JX71N
1no pin strip 1x36 St 0.1 in.	maplin JW59P
1no 3-pin IEC mains plugs	maplin NH65V

Fabrication:
Each object integrates several systems together to control light emission, direction control, light sensing and communications. There is fabrication of electronic, electrical, mechanical and optical components each connected together and orchestrated under software control. The electronic controller boards were custom-designed, hand-built and individually tested with matching hardware. The aluminium rod and sheets were hand-machined and lathe-turned to make the customised mechanical components. The next step was authoring the software both at the scale of software-drivers for low-level control, such as motor parametric control, as well as the high-level planning of search strategies and learning control functions.

Assembly:
Each object is made up of three assemblies: the base-section, the lighting-section and the controller/sensor assembly. The base-section is installed first and wiring for power and communications is connected through to all the objects. The lighting-section of each object is then installed and levelled up using the three-point screw mountings. At this point the controller/sensor assemblies are connected onto the body of each object and the system goes through a list of self-testing and self-calibration program routines. After a unique networking address has been assigned to each object and the central controller loaded with an initial search strategy, the objects are left to their own means to explore the given installation space.

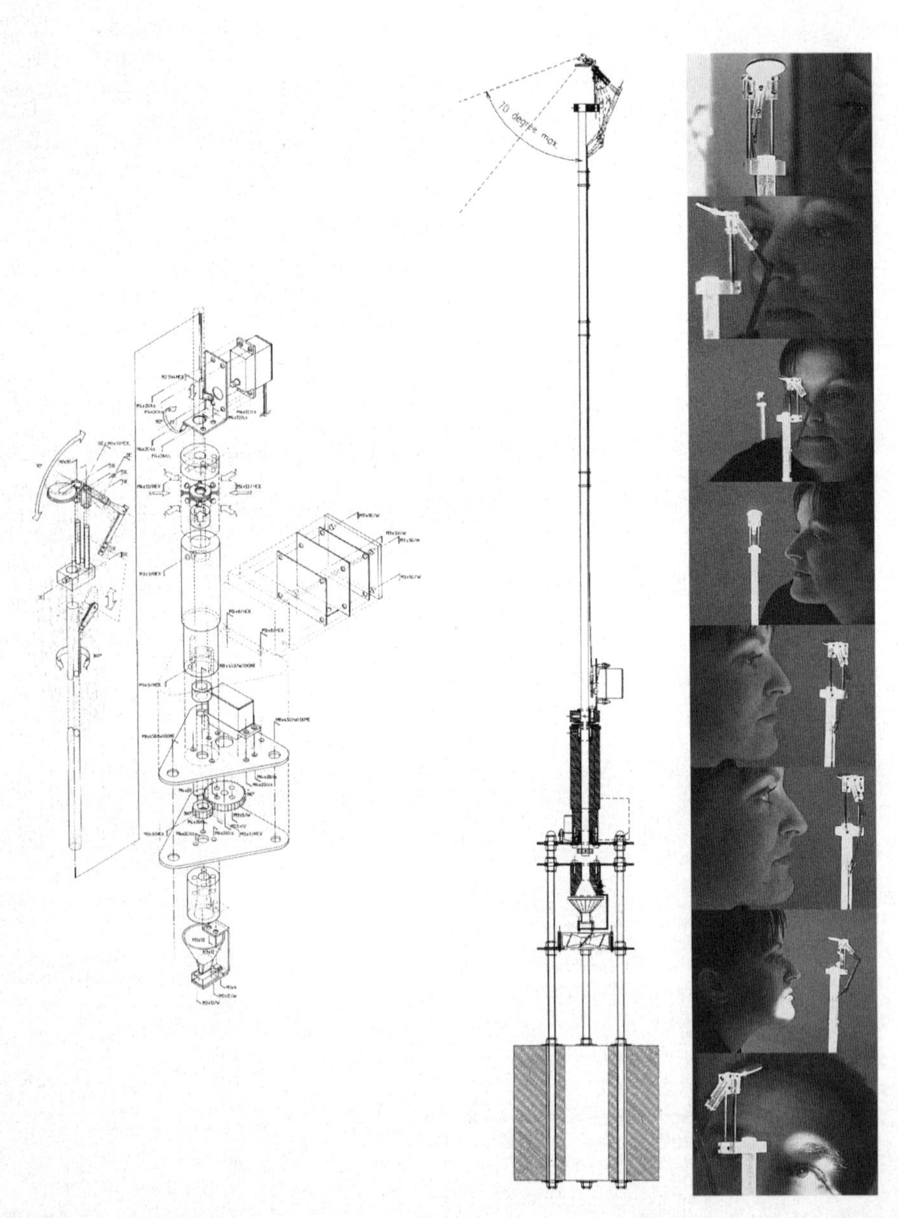
70 degree max.

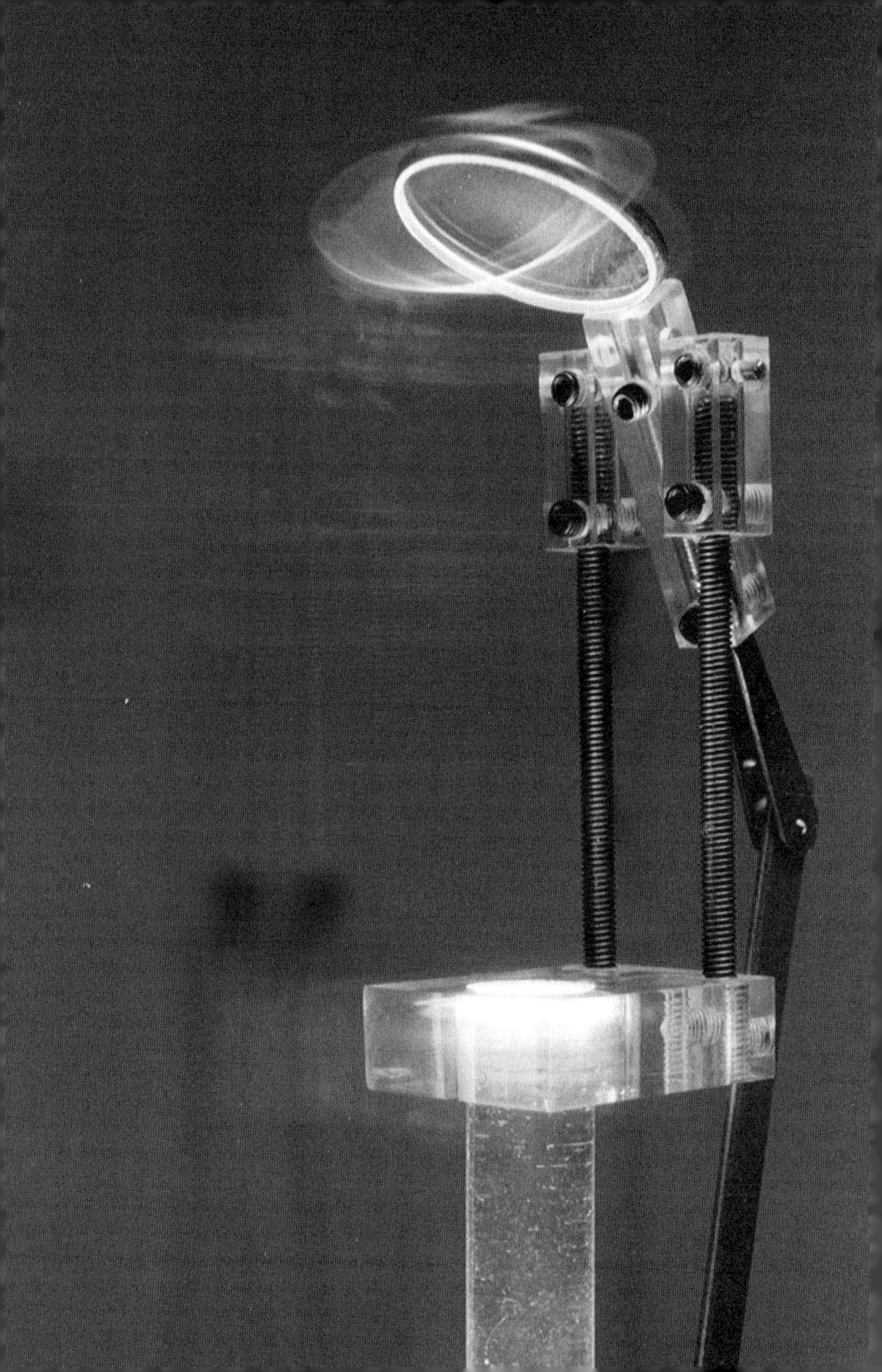

Designer: Dimitris Argyros

Device: Light Rings

Function: Examination of diffraction and halo formations via superimpositions of a natural and artificial light

Concept:
The device, together with photographic documentation, is used to inform of the ambiguous state of twilight. This assemblage comprises of four light rings placed next to each other on site.

A natural fire source and an artificial LED are simplified metaphors of the two adjacent elements, employed to, firstly, simulate the cyclical nature of diurnal light and secondly, to accentuate the particular moment of twilight, when the two elements blend within each other.

The two light sources are positioned perpendicular to each other and are set on a slow rotational path, creating natural and artificial 'light ring' formations. At a specific point, the two sources are hidden from each other's view behind a plastic sheet with a small aperture in the middle. Through diffraction and reflection, the two light sources are made to interfere and superimpose with each other through the formation of a light halo. The effects become apparent only through long exposure photography.

Dimensions: Each light ring has a diameter of 900mm. The rings are to be placed next to each other covering a total surface area of 1800 x 1800mm. Each device is 550mm in height.

Fabrication time: 7 days

Assembly time: 25 minutes

Materials:
Spine + base:
800mm oak wood 70mm diameter
400mm steel tube (10mm outer diameter, 8mm inner diameter)
1000mm steel rod (15mm outer diameter, 12mm inner diameter)

Waist:
3000mm squared steel plate 3mm thick
5000mm plastic-coated conductive wire

4no motors, 30rev per minute speed
8no AA batteries
4no 9V batteries
1no 60mm diameter steel gear (15mm inner diameter)
1no 16mm diameter steel gear (6mm inner diameter)
4no ball bearings (15mm inner diameter)
Nuts and bolts 3M + 4M

Arms:
4000m hollow steel tube (8mm outer diameter, 6mm inner diameter)
500mm hollow steel tube (6mm outer diameter, 4mm inner diameter)
4no candleholder
4no candles
4no bright white LEDs
1no 200 x 200mm acrylic sheet 0.5mm thick

Head:
4no 190 x 150mm plastic plates 0.5mm thick

Fabrication: (all quantities multiplied by 4)
Construct spine:
- Cut 15mm diameter rod to 350mm length. At one end make a slit using a hand-saw.
- Slide big gear up and using nuts connect at halfway.
- Slide ball bearings through 15mm rod but do not weld as yet.

Construct waist:
- Cut two 70 x 40mm plates and drill 8mm hole on each face.
- Drill appropriate 3mm holes for mounting motor and battery pack on same faces.
- Cut two 40 x 40mm with 15mm hole in centre.
- Weld plates to construct rectangular section.
- Attach small gear to motor and then using M3 nuts and bolts attach motor and battery pack to square section.

Join spine and waist:
- Slide square section with motor and gear attachments through 15mm rod over ball bearings, so that small gear of motor is level with fixed gear. Accurately, lightly weld ball bearings to 15mm rod in horizontal position.

Construct fire arm:
- Cut 8mm hollow steel rod at 900mm.
- Cut 6mm rod at 30mm.
- Drill 6mm hole at small candleholder.
- Weld 6mm rod to candleholder and then to 8mm arm.

Construct wind protector:
- Cut acrylic sheet to 10 x 80mm, curve and superglue to construct a hollow tube, 20mm diameter.
- Balance in-between candle using small steel rods to pierce through candle and sheet.

Construct LED arm:
- Cut 8mm hollow steel rod at 900mm.
- Cut 6mm rod at 30mm. Bend 90 degrees halfway.
- Weld lightly 6mm in 8mm steel rod.
- Drive conductive wires through both 6mm and 8mm rods.
- Attach white LED at top of 6mm rod and attach to wires.

Construct base:
The base depends on ground conditions. For soft soil, one should be able to drive 15mm rod through ground. For harder clay, a dagger has to be constructed out of wood in the shape as shown in drawing, with a 15mm hole in the centre.

Construct head:
- Cut plastic sheet at 190 x 150mm.
- Make a 0.5mm diameter hole at plastic sheet, 30mm from bottom.

Assembly: (all procedures repeated four times)
- Drive timber base in to ground using a hammer. Ensure it is at 90 degrees to ground.
- Place 15mm steel spine with attached waist through the base so that the device stands horizontal.
- Attach plastic sheet to 15mm steel spine, superglue if necessary.
- Squeeze fire and LED arms to waist through 8mm holes. Friction should ensure that the arms stay horizontal.
- Attach cables to AA battery pack to turn on LED.
- Light candle and place wind protector over the top.
- Attach motor to 9V battery pack to start rotation of light rings.
- Long exposure photography is recommended during operation of light rings.

Additional notes:
Things can go wrong, so one should have extra set of:
- Batteries
- Film
- White LEDs
- Candles and matches
- Warm clothes

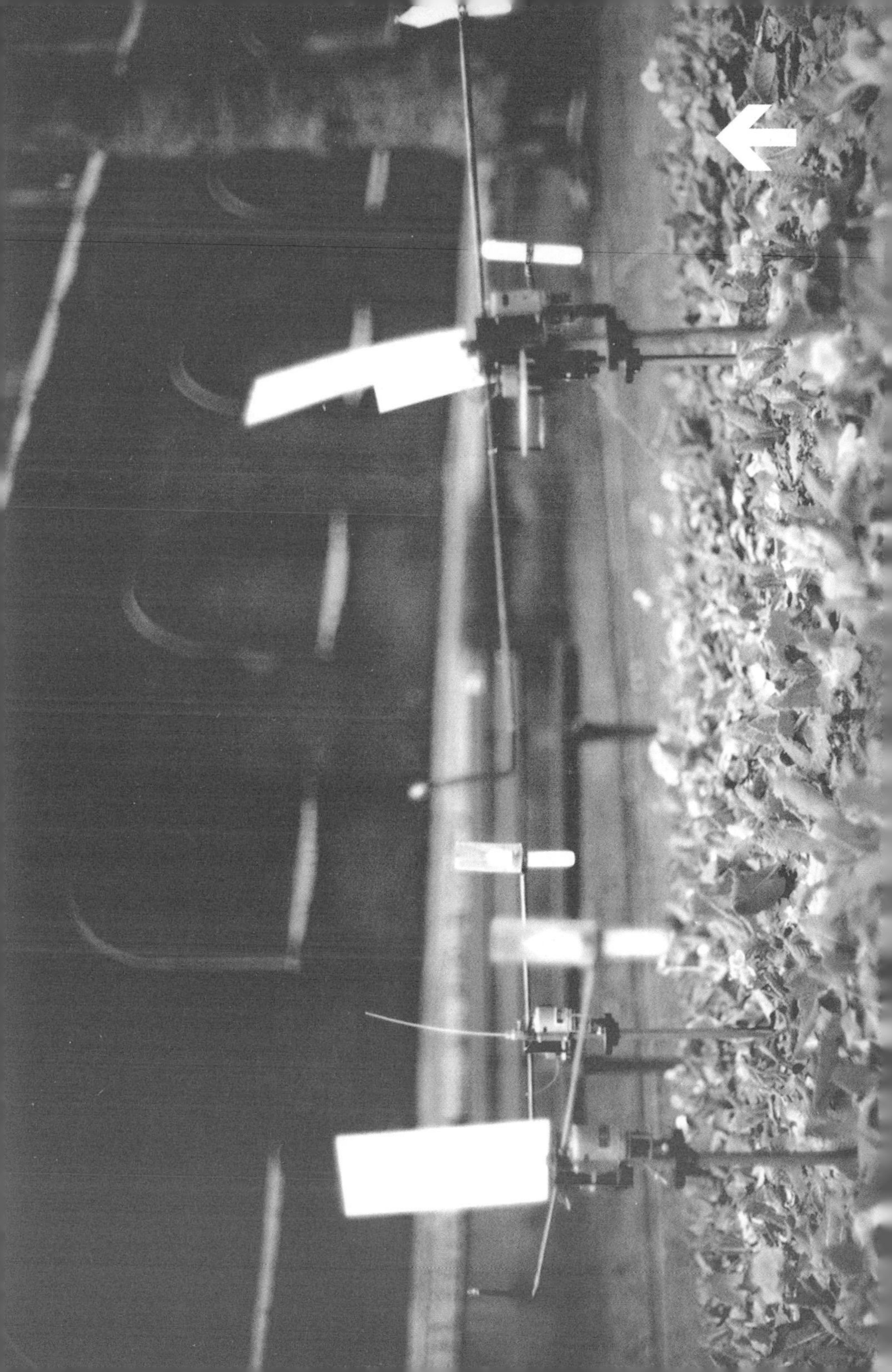

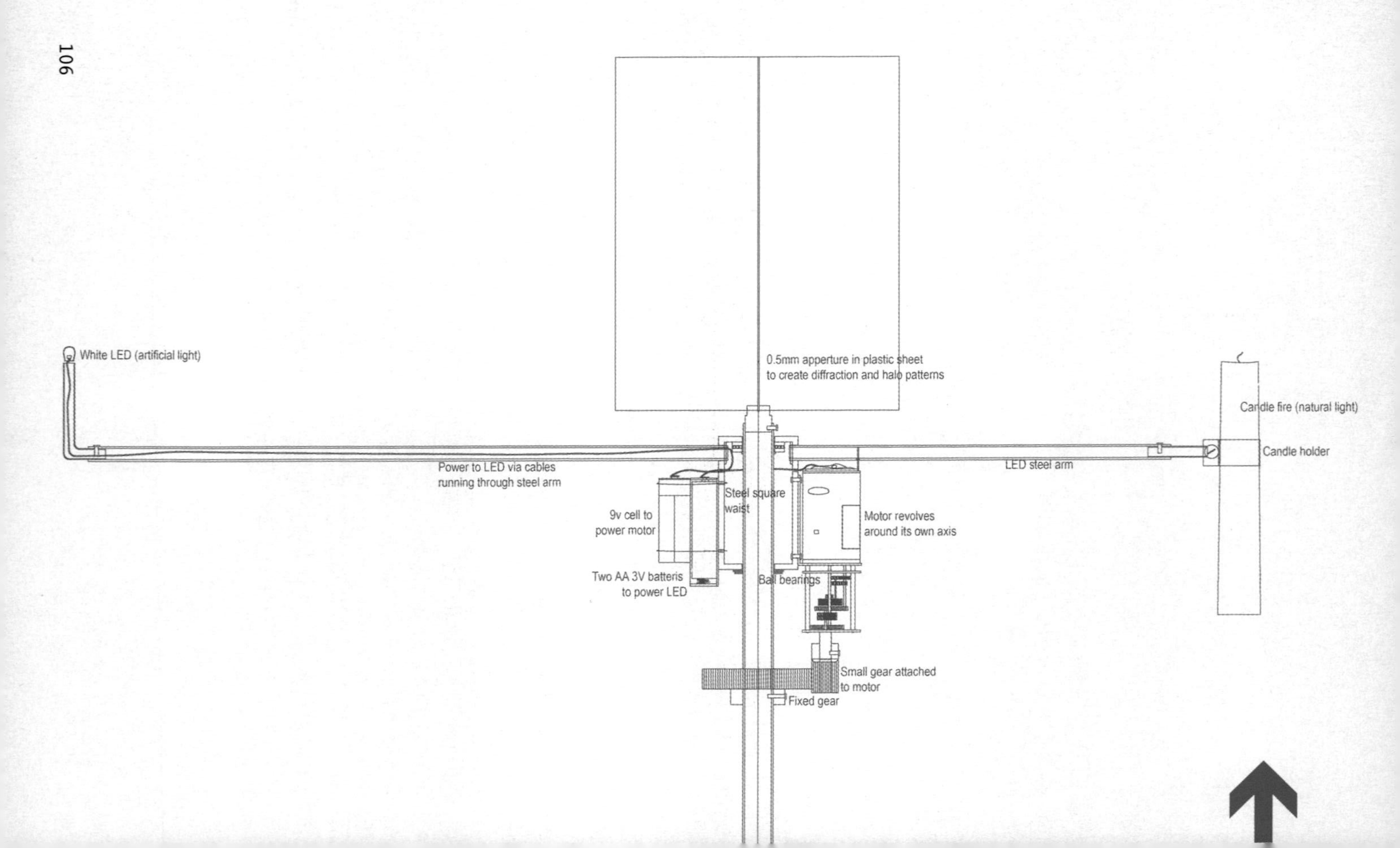

White LED (artificial light)
0.5mm apperture in plastic sheet
to create diffraction and halo patterns
Candle fire (natural light)
Candle holder
Power to LED via cables
running through steel arm
LED steel arm
Steel square
waist
9v cell to
power motor
Motor revolves
around its own axis
Two AA 3V batteris
to power LED
Ball bearings
Small gear attached
to motor
Fixed gear

Designer: Imogen Long

Device: Light Volumiser

Function: Revealing the fluctuating daylight conditions within a room

Concept:
Daylight becomes apparent to the eye when it hits a surface and is reflected. This project examines the way that unseen rays of light are travelling through space before they hit surfaces such as walls and floors. The imperceptible fluctuations in daylight entering a room and its shifting patterns over time are recorded, augmented and distorted by the interaction of simple devices.

The single suspended device responds to the presence of light, which activates the motor, spinning the limp fabric and transforming it into a solid, circular shadow-casting barrier. The light sensor, located at the end of an arm, reaches out from the body of the device, giving a reading of the light levels at an isolated point in space. This reading is visible in the motion of the fan. The resistance in the circuit can be modified to enable differing levels of sensitivity to light.

Arranging a number of devices in close proximity allows a complex interaction to begin. Those closest to the source of light are activated first, their augmented shadow obscuring light to those behind, which therefore remain inactive. As daylight moves through the space over time, its shifting angle catches the sensors of different devices in other locations, the ones in front falling inactive, and those behind coming alive, only to obscure yet further devices. A relay of activity and inactivity is set up.

The active devices animate the space, a colour change occurring as the hidden inner layer of the fan is revealed upon opening.

Dimensions: Tin: 60 x 105mm
Tin, fan and sensor arm:
60 x 350mm (shortest)
60 x 560mm (longest)

Fabrication time: 2 weeks

Assembly time: 2 hours

Materials:
Painted and sandblasted sardine tin
Piano wire arm
Double-layered silk fan (white inner and grey outer)
Thin metal chain
Brass sheet and rod for fan mechanism
Clear plastic tubing
Cogs
Electronic components
Light dependent resistor
Motor
Resistors
Diode
Circuit board
AA battery (x2)

Fabrication:
Paint the tins internally and sandblast externally.

Fan mechanism:
- Cut the brass sheet to form the base support for the motor, batteries and the fan mechanism holder.
- Attach the brass rods and cogs.
- Cut a circular double-layered fan from white and grey silk and rivet together at its centre.
- Stitch a thin metal chain into the circumference of fabric.
- Attach the fan to the brass rod through the rivet and secure using small pieces of plastic tubing.

Circuit board:
- Place the circuit board in a tin and secure the fan mechanism.
- Connect the fan mechanism to the circuit board.
- Solder a light dependent resistor to the piano wire arm.
- Feed the arm into the tin through the small holes and connect to the circuit board.

Assembly:
- Feed the two lengths of fishing wire running perpendicular to the arm through small holes in sides of devices.
- Arrange the devices around the room and suspend from the side walls by attaching fishing wire to hooks in the walls.
- Allow light to enter the room through small apertures in the otherwise covered window.

The devices will begin to register the presence of light and interact with each other.

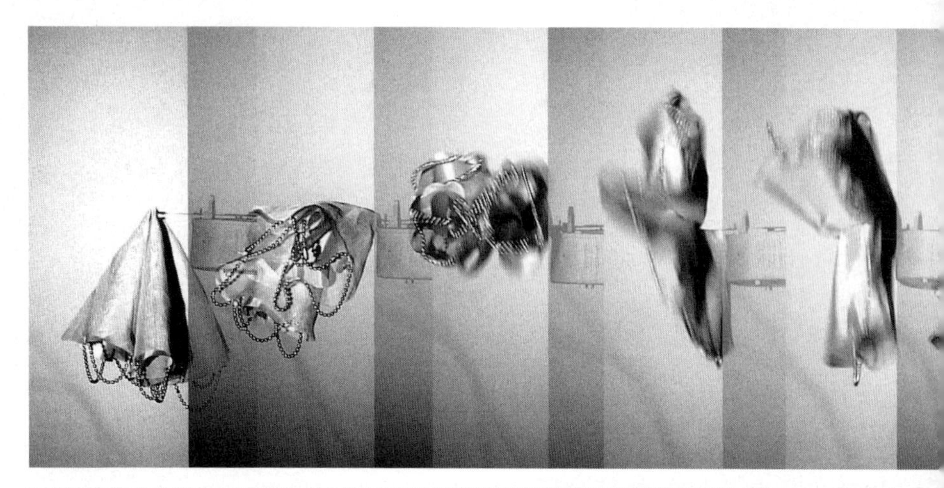

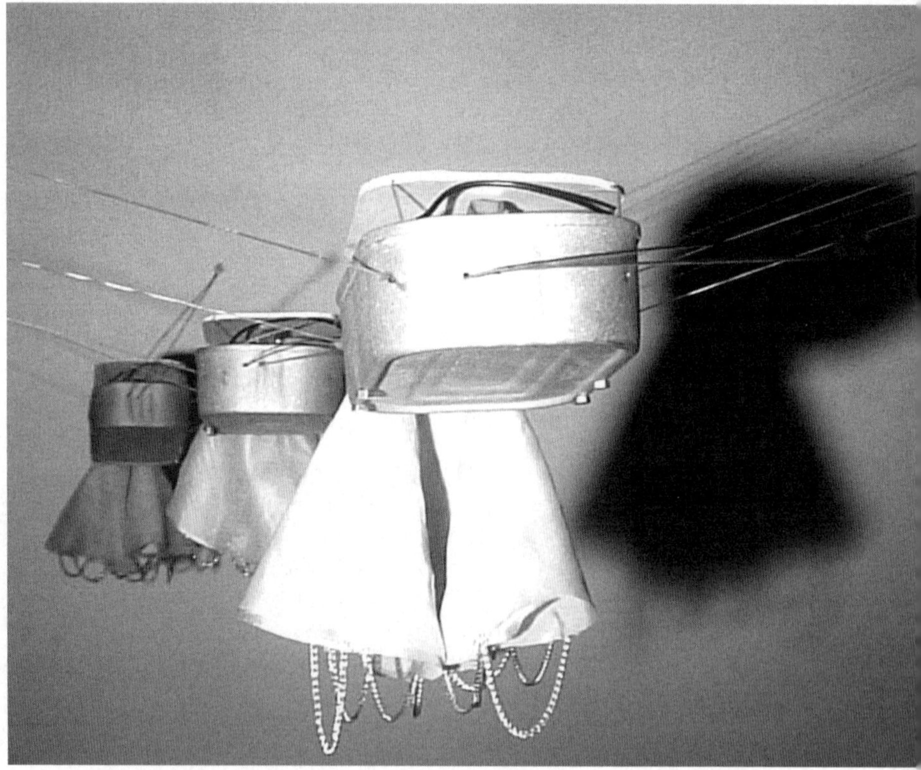

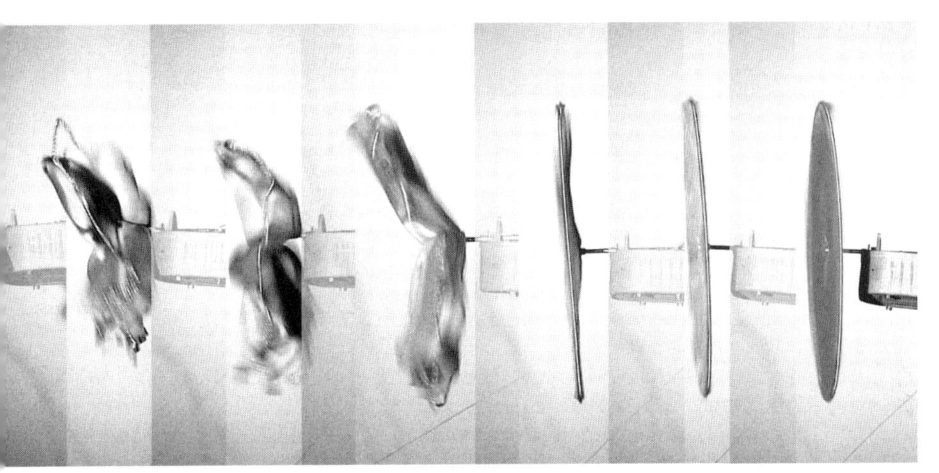

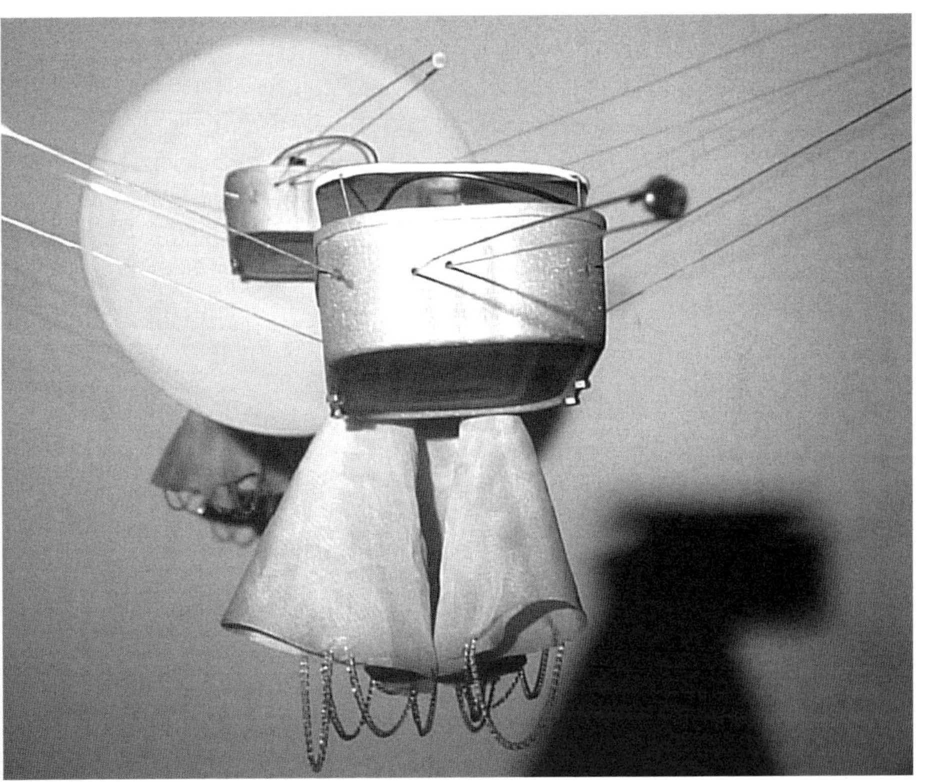

Designer: Jason Bruges Studio

Device: Litmus

Function: Interactive environmental art

Concept:
Four interactive sculptures are programmed to act as giant litmus papers, sensing and responding to a variety of environmental stimuli such as daylight, wind and tides in this riverside area. Placed on roundabouts near the A13, the tall, 12m high 'Litmus' sculptures are visible to motorists passing by. The sculptures have a steel framed acrylic structure, which supports an array of LED pixels. Each 'Litmus' tower reacts to its environment, gathering information and displaying it using differently coloured LEDs. Two of the towers are situated near Ferry Lane, marking the borders between an industrial zone and the Thames marshes, whilst measuring and displaying the light levels and tide levels at Tilbury.

Marsh Way is the site of a further two towers, located where the traffic turns off the A13 into the Rainham area. The southern 'Litmus' tower displays the power generated by the neighbouring wind turbine while the northern tower counts and displays the amount of traffic entering into the Rainham area.

Dimensions: 1000 x 1200 x 12000mm
2750kg (Individual artwork)

Fabrication time: 4 months

Assembly time: 4 days (Piling)
2 days (Installation)

Materials:
1no top angle framework
1no anti-bird mesh panel
4no main steel uprights
4no bottom horizontal steels
17no M16 x 60 LG B-N-SP'W-FW
34no M16 x 50 LG B-N-SP'W-FW
9no M12 x 40 C'SK B-N-SP'W-FW
3no M12 x 40 LG Bolt
4no lightning finial
4no metre cabinets
4no metre cabinet support brackets

17no M16 x 50 LG B-N-SP'W-FW
4no hasp and staple
4no padlock
4no power isolators
4no steel pile caps
16no screw piles various lengths
4no bird deterrent assemblies
4no base tie diagonals
16no steel connection plates
1no light level sensor
1no traffic count sensor
1no tide sensor
1no frictionless wind sensor
80no acrylic panels
20no polycarbonate panels
197no polycarbonate washers
500no thick black rubber washer
500no M10 LG Panhead
500no carbon/glass fibre stalks varying lengths
500no LED assemblies
7500no LEDs
85kg marine grade glue
4no LED control + power boards

Assembly:

- Cut and rivet the steel frames using CAD-CAM.
- Hot dip galvanise the frames then later assemble off site.
- Cut and drill the polycarbonate and acrylic panels on a CAD-CAM routing bed.
- Wind the composite stalks.
- Glue the stalks to the polycarbonate and acrylic assembly.
- Fabricate the LED assembly.
- Fix all the acrylic panels to the steel frames.
- Fit the power and data wiring looms to the steel frame.
- Attach and test the LED assembly.
- Print the LED control board circuits.
- Pile the site and fit the pile caps. Commission the power supplies.
- Bolt the artworks onto the pile caps.
- Attach sensors to the artworks.
- Commission the power and data connections.
- Test and commission.

Designer: Alvin Seng Chun Tan

Device: Mayflies

Function: Energy storage and release system

Concept:
'Mayflies' is an energy storage system that stores energy via a mechanical means. This mechanical energy can then be transformed into kinetic energy using the very same system, and the result is a self-propelling device that travels in any random direction; the rotation of the paddles encourages the generation of limited lift, much like a helicopter rotor.

As a single individual item a mayfly alone is as interesting as any wind-up toy available in toyshops. The construction of an entire swarm exponentially increases the resulting fun factor, but at the same time also increases the frustration factor in regard to resetting for the next firing sequence. The unpredictability of the entire system makes each activation sequence a unique experience, ranging from the entire swarm expanding all of its energy in one explosive second to a series of minor flares.

Dimensions: 80 x 25mm (Individual Mayfly)
Variable (Base)

Fabrication time: 10 minutes (Individual Mayfly)
3 hours (Base)

Assembly time: 5 minutes (Individual Mayfly)
2 minutes (Base)

Materials:
Individual Mayfly:
2no white plastic sheet, 1.5mm thick
1no spring steel, 5mm width, 0.2mm thick
1no piano wire, 1mm diameter
1no M3 machine screw 20mm
1no M3 machine screw 12mm
6no M3 nuts

Base:
MDF
Aluminium rod 10mm diameter
Black spray-paint

Fabrication:

Individual Mayfly:

- Cut plastic into the upper and lower paddles following the template using a scalpel.
- Drill holes for the screws using a 3.5mm drill bit.
- Drill holes for the piano wire and trigger using a 1.5mm drill bit.
- Cut piano wire into a 50mm length and bend into trigger shape.
- Cut the spring metal to a length of 250 mm.
- Coil spring metal; this is achieved by clamping with a vice and coiling the metal.
- Bend both inner and outer ends of the springs to form hooks.

Base:

- Cut base into platforms from the MDF. Each mayfly takes up approximately 200mm^2; ensure there will be enough space for the desired number of mayflies.
- Drill holes into the platforms to hold the mayflies in place using a 8mm drill bit.
- Drill holes into the platforms to dock aluminium rods using a 10 mm drill bit.
- Spray paint the platforms black. Allow several coatings for an even finish.

Assembly:

Individual Mayfly:

- Insert screws into the upper paddle. The core screw (20mm) is inserted at the pivot end and the other screw closer into the other hole.
- Lock in all the nuts. The core screw is left slightly loose to allow rotation. The other screw (12mm) is locked firmly into place with a nut.
- Inserted spring with the inner hook locked onto the core screw using two nuts.
- Lock outer hook onto the other screw with a nut.
- Lock lower paddle onto the core screw with a nut.
- Inserted trigger into the hole on the lower paddle.

Base:

- Inserted aluminium rods into the dock holes of primary base.
- Dock secondary platforms onto the rods.

Additional notes:

Winding up the mayflies takes time and patience. Also, as the triggers are very sensitive to pressure, care should be taken to avoid premature release.

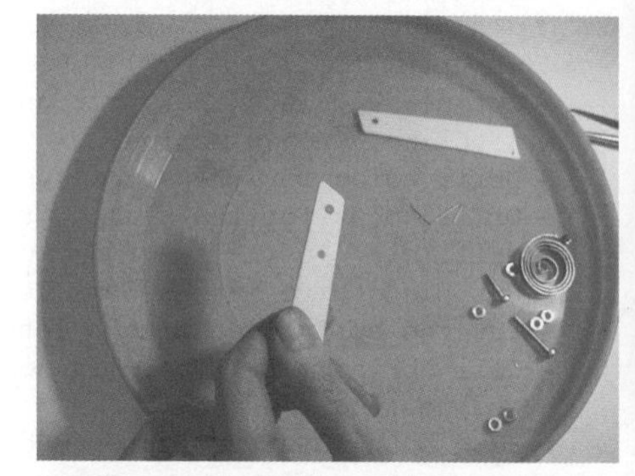

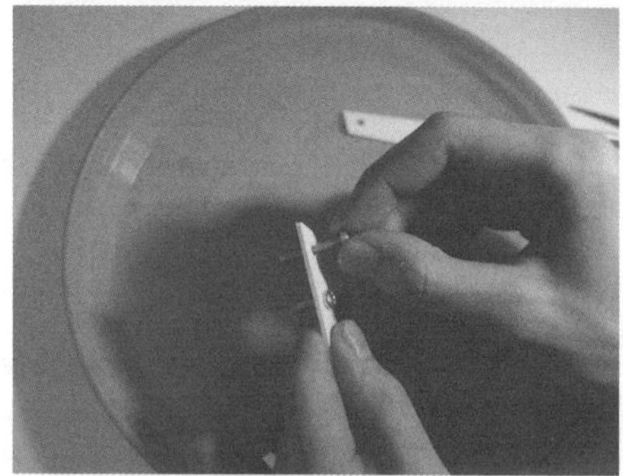

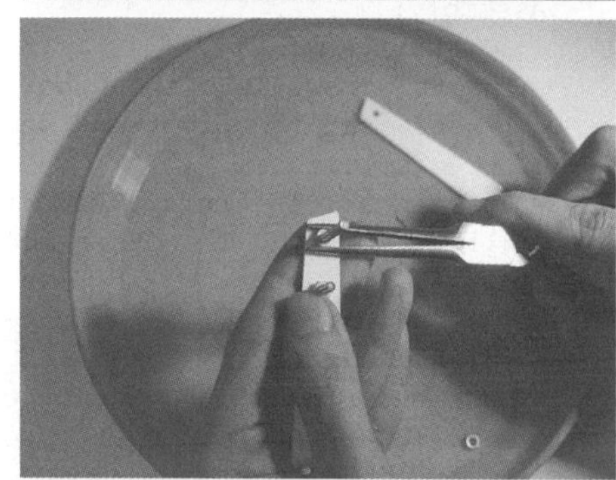

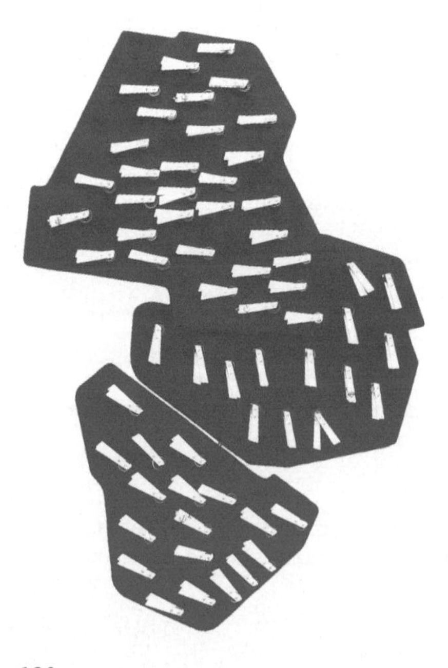

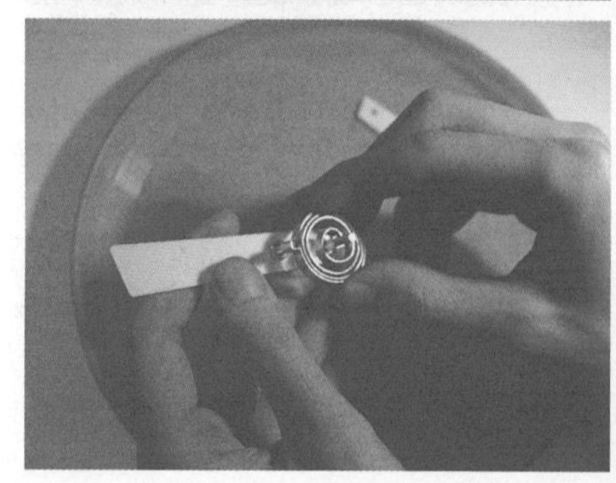

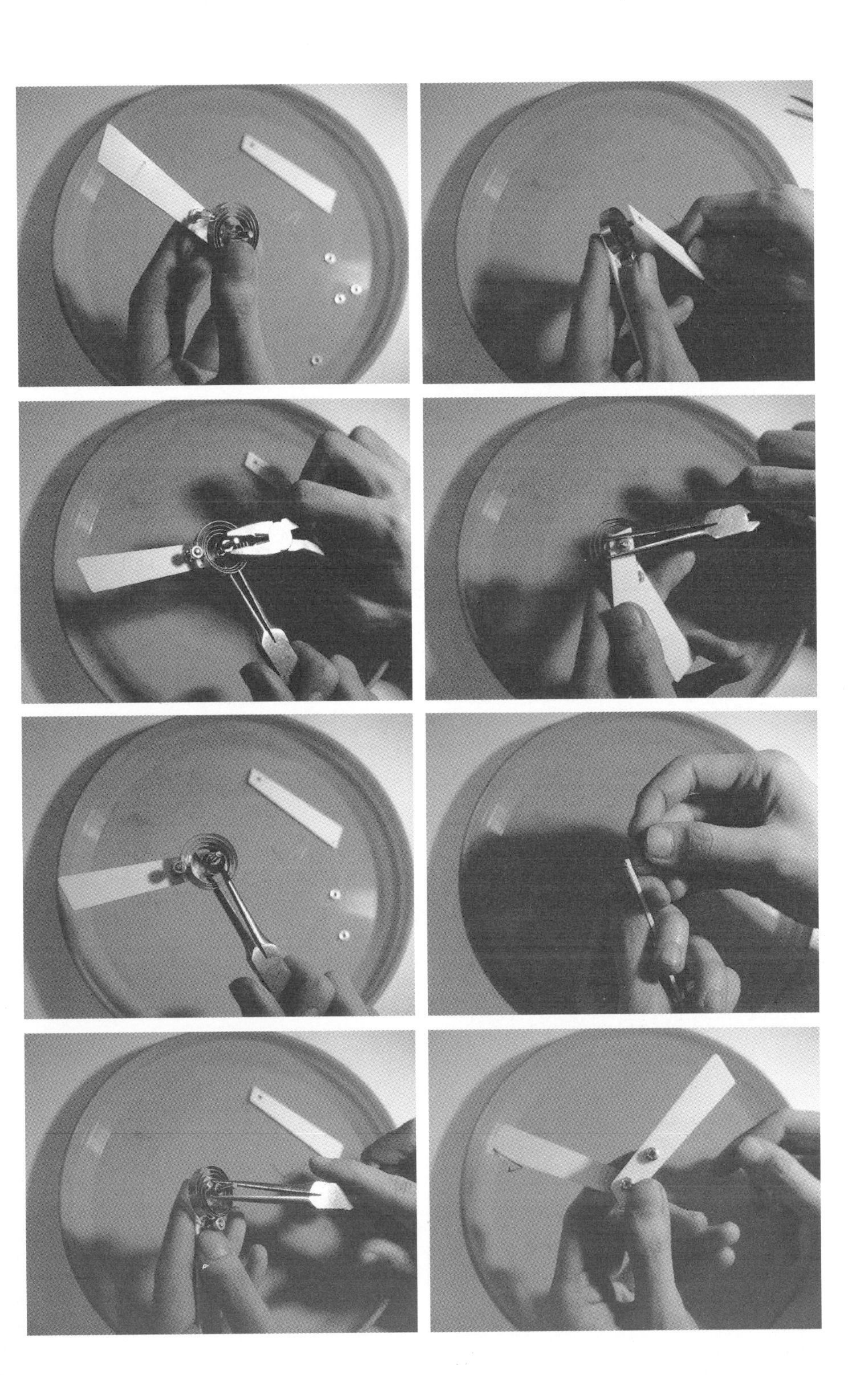

Designer: Jasmin Sohi

Device: Mealtimes

Function: Reminding my grandfather to eat

Concept:
My grandfather has an obsessive habit - always having his meals at the same time everyday. The device acts as his reminder. Everyday for 10 minutes at 8am, noon and 8pm, this clock-based circuit illuminates the rice threaded with fibre optics. Meanwhile, the clock stops for 1.5 minutes at sunset and sunrise everyday: hence mealtimes are continuously shifted, reflecting winter daylight patterns. Potatoes are electrolysed to produce a small current. Without the potatoes the device is useless; the owner must aeroponically mist the roots using the pump - a symbiotic relationship between a human and his food.

Dimensions: 1900 x 550 x 400mm

Fabrication time: 2.5 weeks

Assembly time: 1 hour

Materials:
6 x 6mm mild steel rod, bent + welded
3no fresh potatoes (Jersey Royals work particularly well)
Rice, cooked
Fibre optics from novelty lamp
Boiling tube
Victorian brass plant watering spray pump, nozzle removed
Maplin clock movement mechanism
Electronics (optical switches, LDR, transistors)
2no transformers
3no perspex scientific beakers
6V halogen bulbs
Colour acetate
Transparent silicon sealant
Sandblasted perspex tube + 3mm perspex sheet
Base from spring-form cake tin
3mm rubber tubing
0.1mm steel wire
Piano wire + solder
Insulated wire, various colours
Copper strips
3no Jaguar car windscreen spray nozzles

Clear plastic for use with heat sealer
Aluminium foil
25mm wide steel flat, holes drilled
Small springs (2mm diameter)

Fabrication:
- Bend 6 x 6mm steel rod into required shapes.
- Drill holes for object support in steel rod lengths.
- Weld together steel rod lengths.
- Take strip of sheet steel, form thin strip.
- Coat on one side for grip with silicon sealant.
- Wrap around top edge of beaker.
- Fasten to steel frame using M3 nuts + bolts.
- Thread each rice grain with fibre optic, leave rice to harden.
- Drill large hole in spring-form cake tin base.
- Take one bunch of fibre optic rice and thread through hole.
- Bend rice flat and secure to cake tin using loops of 0.1mm wire, soldered to cake tin base.
- Form open enclosure out of sandblasted perspex tube and 3mm perspex, glue together.
- Insert assembly of clock movement with coloured acetate on the axle and two halogen bulbs, one pointing towards the acetate and one remaining clear of it.
- Line perspex tube with aluminium foil to prevent light leaking.
- Construct lid out of sandblasted perspex, drill large hole.
- Insert fibre optic into lid, pointing towards halogens.
- Construct perspex box.
- Build electronic circuit and enclose in perspex box, leaving wire ends protruding and fitted with connection blocks for easy detachment and transport.
- Enclose light resistors in heat-sealed clear plastic.
- Make harness for potatoes out of loops of piano wire and springs; solder to steel loop around beakers.

Assembly:
- Fit electronics, rice plate and perspex tube onto frame.
- Wire up device and secure wires to frame with 0.1mm wire ties.
- Attach potatoes to beakers using potato harness.
- Attach nozzles to tubing and poke into beakers.
- Run tubing along steel frame, securing with 0.1mm wire ties.
- Screw in device.
- Connect electronic parts using connection blocks.
- Fill boiling tube with water, insert pump, attached to frame.
- Plug in transformers, hiding wire behind radiator.
- Move piece of paper between optical switch on the clock to reset device.

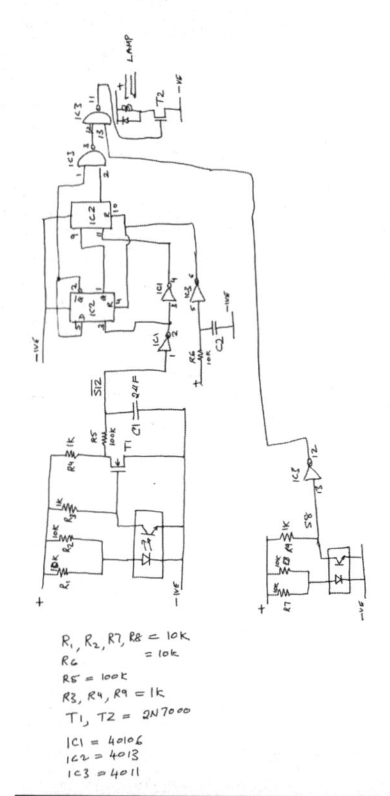
R1, R2, R7, R8 = 10K
R6 = 10k
R5 = 100k
R3, R4, R9 = 1k
T1, T2 = 2N7000
IC1 = 40106
IC2 = 4013
IC3 = 4011

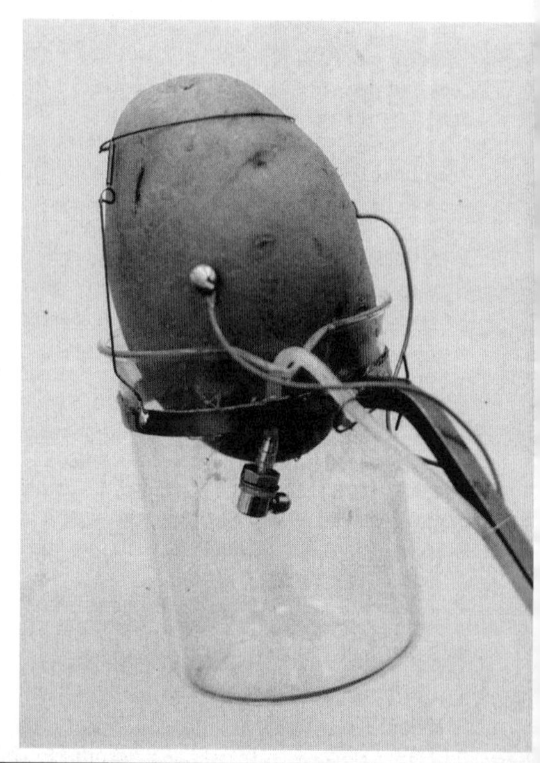

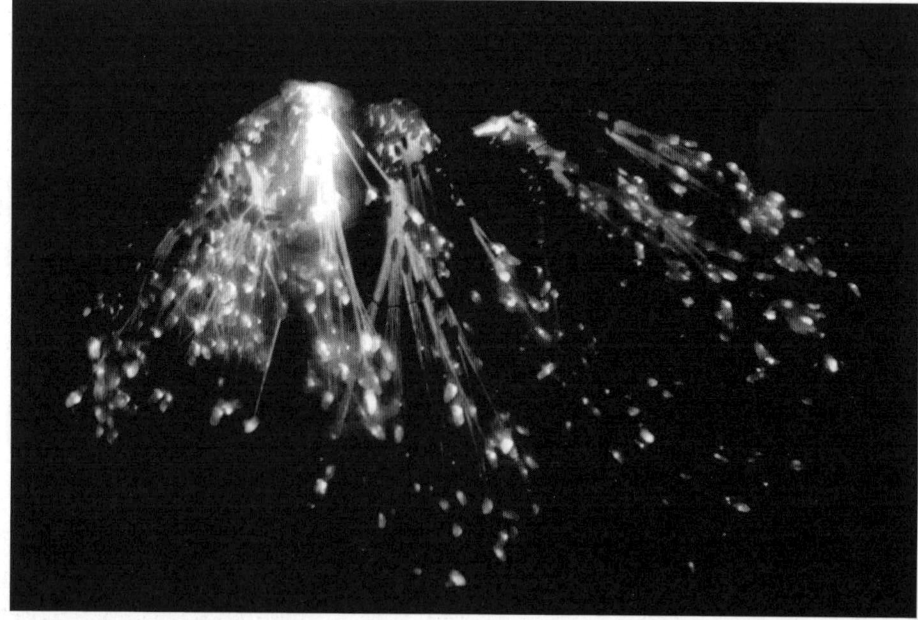

Designer: Marcus Brett

Device: Microclimate of a Bedroom

Function: Measuring moisture, pressure and wind speed within a bedroom

Concept:
The device is a homemade multifunctional tool, combining a barometer and anemometer and is hung from the ceiling of a bedroom. The device enables the measurement of microclimates at specific points in a room over time. Moisture levels, wind speeds and air pressures can and do vary considerably within small points in a room and can be read directly from the instrument. When several hundred are arranged within a space in a cloud-like formation, localised readings at all points in a room can be determined.

From the combination of the long-term observation of the device over a period of three months [or longer for seasonal variations] a general weather pattern of a room can be determined. Within the bedroom where the experiment took place, frequent storms occurred at the following: the head of the bed [when inhabited], above the drawing board [when drawing] and at the door [when opening]. The site of the most frequent violent diurnal storms took place in the vicinity closest to the exposed solitary light bulb [when switched on]. The tilted window generated few storms but caused a high velocity prevailing wind. The window vicinity indicated the highest moisture content and the radiator vicinity the lowest moisture content.

Dimensions: 150 x 150mm (individual device)
2.4 x 4.5m (the cloud)

Fabrication time: 10-15 minutes per device
2-3 days in total (100 devices)

Assembly time: 6 hours

Materials:
4 A1 sheets squared tracing paper 220gsm
20m piano wire 0.3mm
200 disposable glass pipettes
200 Blick Stikkers plain white 5mm x 8mm
100 Rizla cigarette filter tips
50m white cotton thread

2 litres Indian Tonic water (flattened) must contain Quinine
100 lead free fishing weights (pierced)
100 sellotape double-sided Velcro pads

Fabrication:
- Refer to pages 130–131 for instructions:
- Take a 70-80mm length of piano wire and bend at point shown.
- Bend piano wire again at the point shown to make U-shape.
- Bend piano wire at all points shown to make clip-shape.
- Heat the disposable glass pipette at points shown with a blowtorch.
- Bend the hot glass pipette into a U-shape.
- Fill with 20ml Indian Tonic, stopper with cigarette filter tip and insert clip.
- Cut a 200mm x 60mm piece of squared tracing paper and fold in half.
- Unfold and flatten the piece of paper and cut two triangular pieces from the tips.
- Re-flatten the folded paper.
- Cut two oblong pieces from paper as shown.
- Score along lines shown and fold in half.
- Fold wing tips upwards and fold shaft tips inwards.
- Twist the 150mm length piano wire into a loop: attach to the wing with Blick Stikkers.
- Unbalanced anemometer wing.
- Thread fishing weight through piano wire and balance (wing horizontal).
- Balanced anemometer.
- Knot length of cotton thread to anemometer and attach completed barometer.
- Balanced device.
- Stitch completed device to hook part of sellotape double-sided Velcro pad.
- Attach loop part of sellotape double-sided Velcro pad as shown.
- Attach completed device to ceiling.

Assembly:
- After making 100-200 individual devices, attach them to ceiling.

Additional notes:
If unable to obtain some components paperclips may be straightened out, plasticine used as counter balance and strong sellotape used to stick the device to the ceiling.

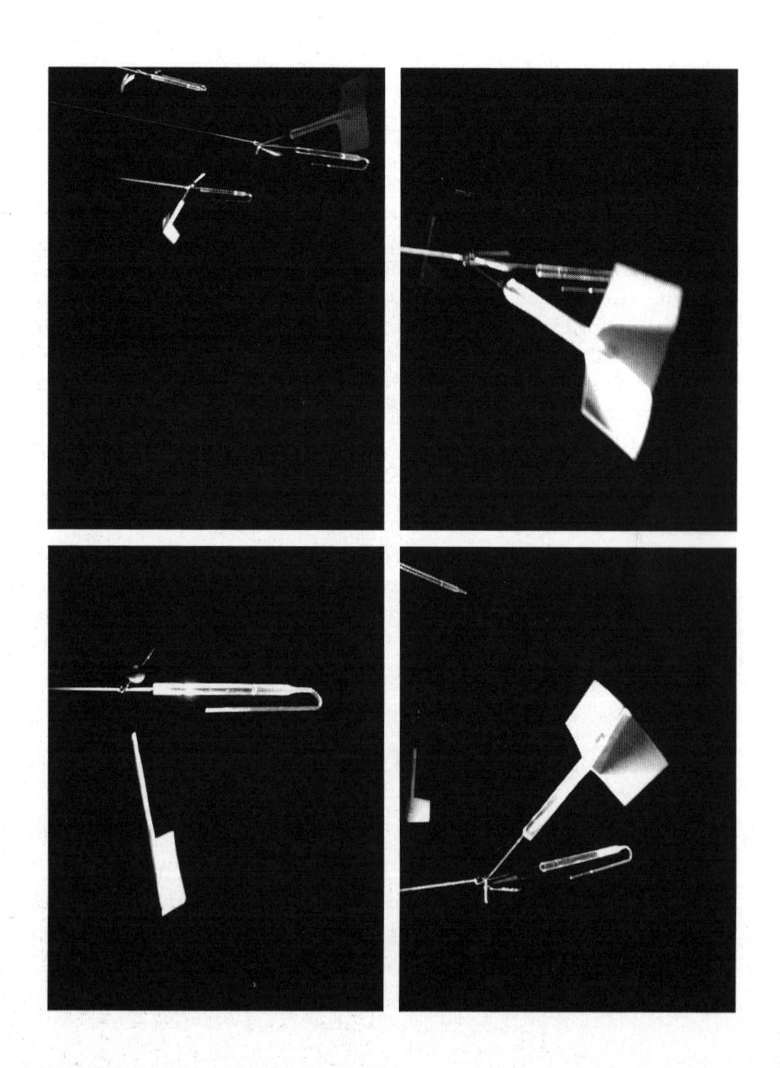

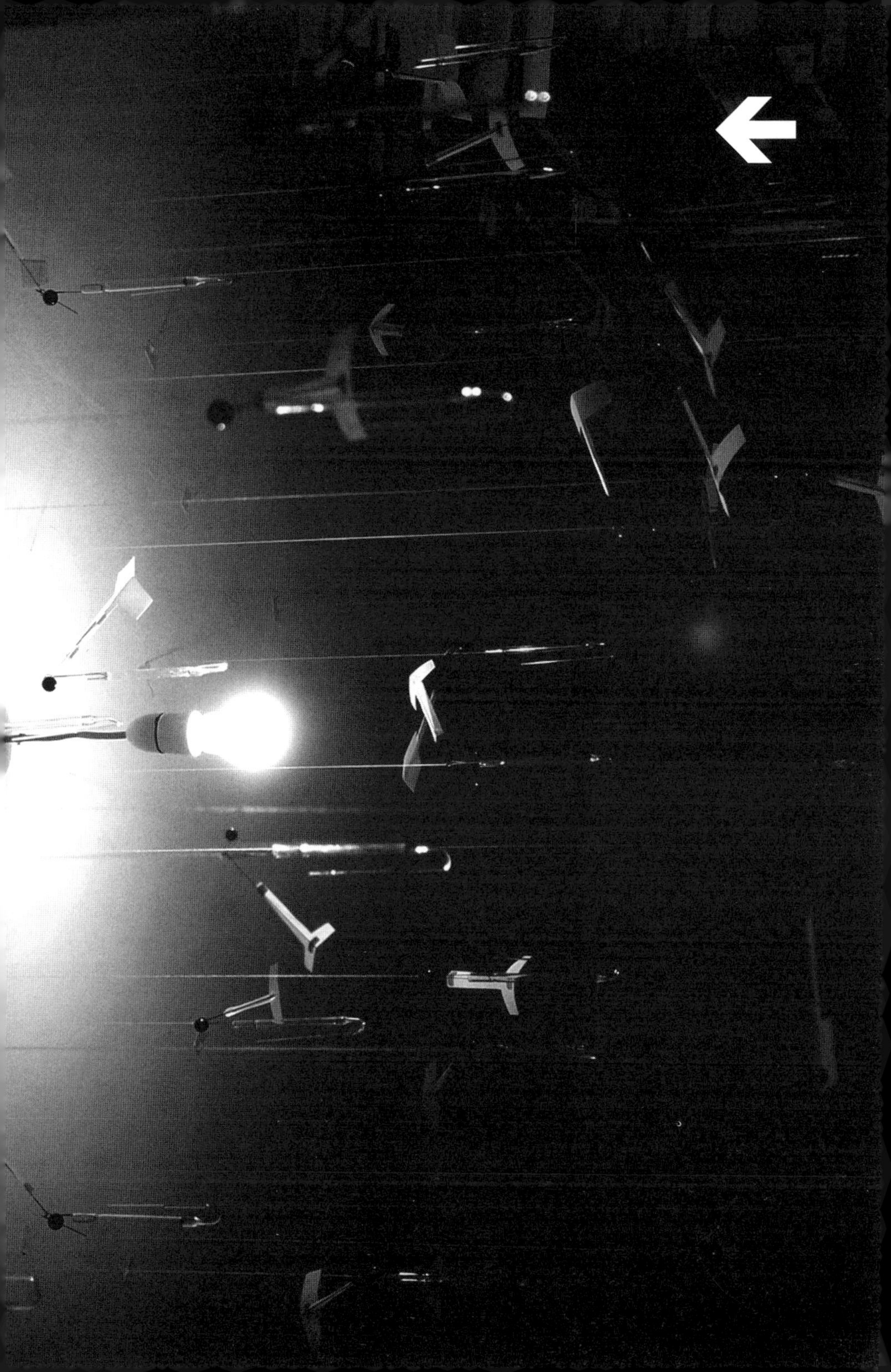

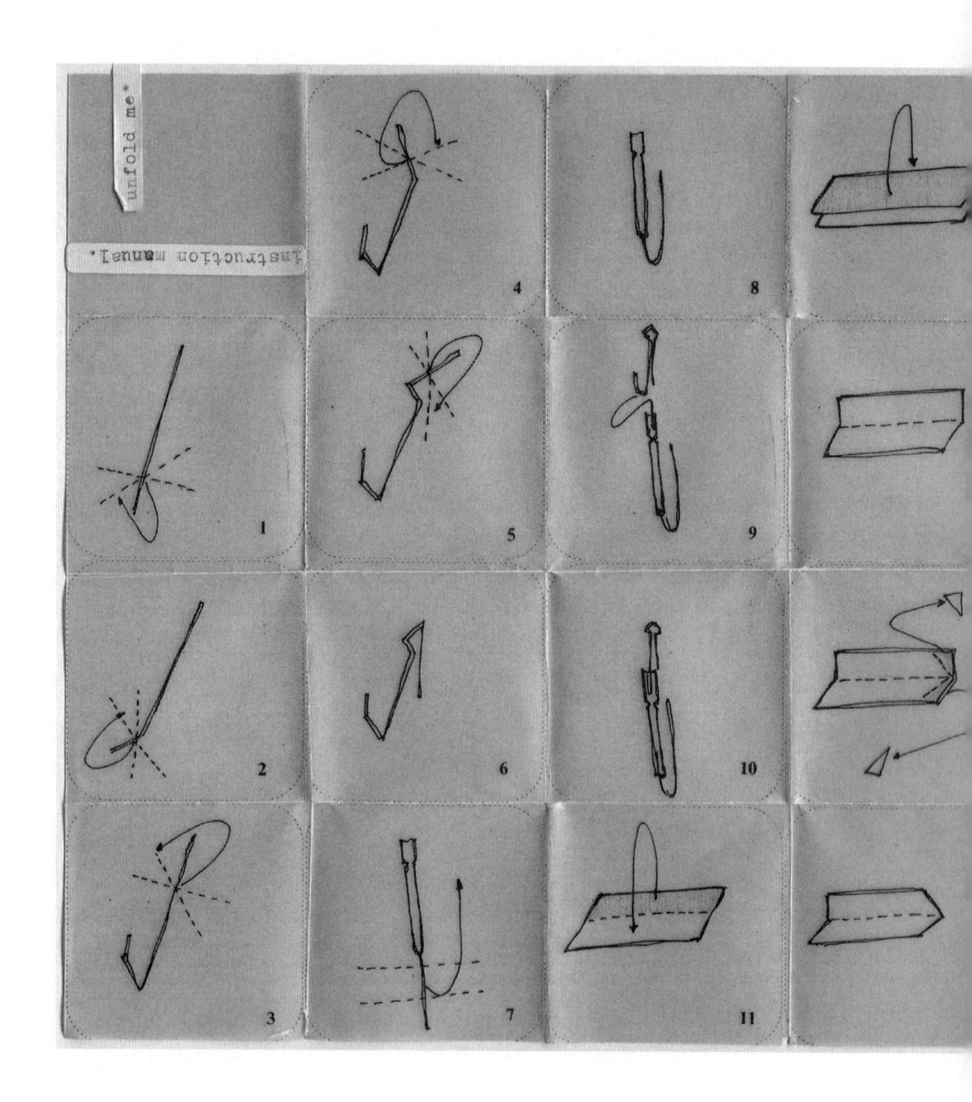
unfold me*
instruction manual.
1
2
3
4
5
6
7
8
9
10
11

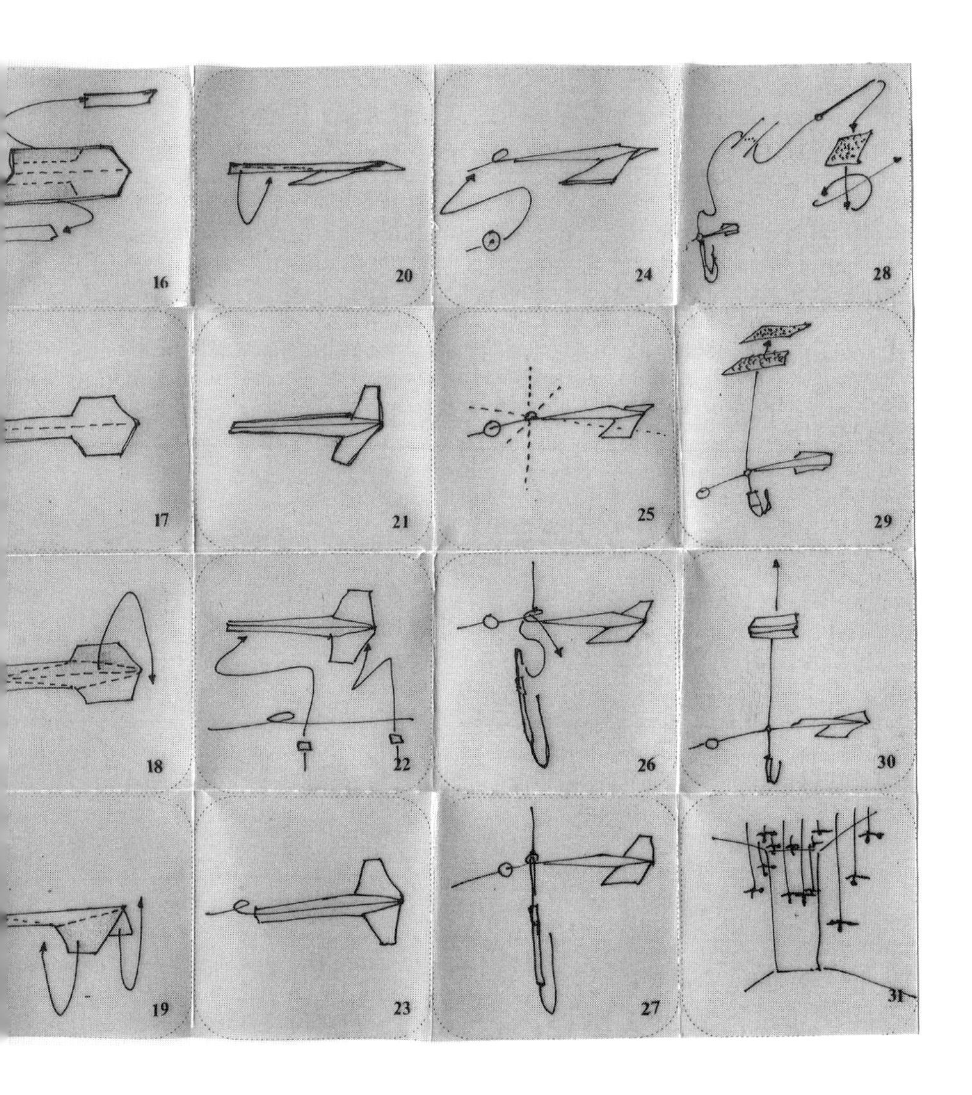
16
20
24
28
17
21
25
29
18
22
26
30
19
23
27
31

Designer: Tom Elliott

Device: Motion of Swarm

Function: Mapping external influence, and interior spatial variations

Concept:
The device is the resulting study of a swarm. Wind, be it natural or controlled, is the applied external force. Each of the wings has independent movement. Multiple forces cause the wings to react differently. However where the forces are equal there is an element of randomness and uncertainty as to the resulting action of the wings. The knock-on effect is apparent due to this constant flickering of the wings. One slight wing movement can disrupt the airflow for the wing behind, resulting in the latter changing position. This process 'swarms' across the device, with each wing adjusting to those around it. The device is to map external forces and its influence towards an internal space.

Dimensions: 540mm (diameter)
140mm (height)

Fabrication time: 56 hours

Assembly time: 5 minutes

Materials:
1no 540mm disc of 5mm clear perspex
1no 540mm disc of 10mm black perspex
3no 140mm lengths of metal threaded rod
12no bolts to fit this rod
3no small rubber discs
73no 87mm lengths of 1mm piano wire
73no metal beads
1no sheet of black cardboard
73no lengths of 0.4mm piano wire
73no 24mm white batons
3no 80mm electric 12V fans
3no sheets of 0.8mm aluminium
9no 10mm bearings
9no 40mm bolts, each with two nuts
3no switches
Electrical wiring
3no 12V batteries

Fabrication:

Perspex container:

- Use a router to cut out two identical perspex discs.
- Temporarily clamp these two discs together and drill 73 holes through the clear sheet, and halfway into the black perspex sheet below. Drill holes 2mm in diameter and in a uniformed pattern, allowing even spacing between all of the holes.
- Drill three larger holes, 8mm in diameter, at even spacing around the outside of the disc, through both layers.
- Cut three tracks into the perimeter of the clear perspex sheet, these tracks should have a 45 degree channel cut between the larger holes.
- Connect the two sheets of perspex together using the threaded rod and bolts, leaving a 78mm gap between the two.
- Attach the small rubber sheets to the bottom of the rod to act as feet.

Internal wings:

- Attach the metal beads to the 87mm lengths of piano wire, 1/3 of the length up, creating the supporting bearing for the wing to move upon.
- Cut the wings out the template in the black card, forming the lengths of 0.4mm piano wire into the correct shape and attach them together.
- Attach the white batons to the top to allow easy viewing, and the ultraviolet light to aid mapping.
- Connect the 73 wings and the previously created supports and place inside the device between the two sheets of perspex.

Fan system:

- Cut and bend the aluminium into forms that hold the fans.
- Drill holes into this sheet metal, then connect the bearings to the fan using the nuts and bolts. This will allow the fans to be moved freely around the perimeter of the device by allowing the bearings to run in the previously cut tracks in the clear perspex.
- Connect the switches to the aluminium frame and wire up,
- Connect the fan to the battery.

Assembly:

- For use with natural wind simply place the completed device, without the fans, in the open.
- For controlled wind use place the three fans on the runners in the main device. Adjust to desired positions, and activate one, two or all of the fans using the switches. The position of the fans can be altered by moving them along the runners.

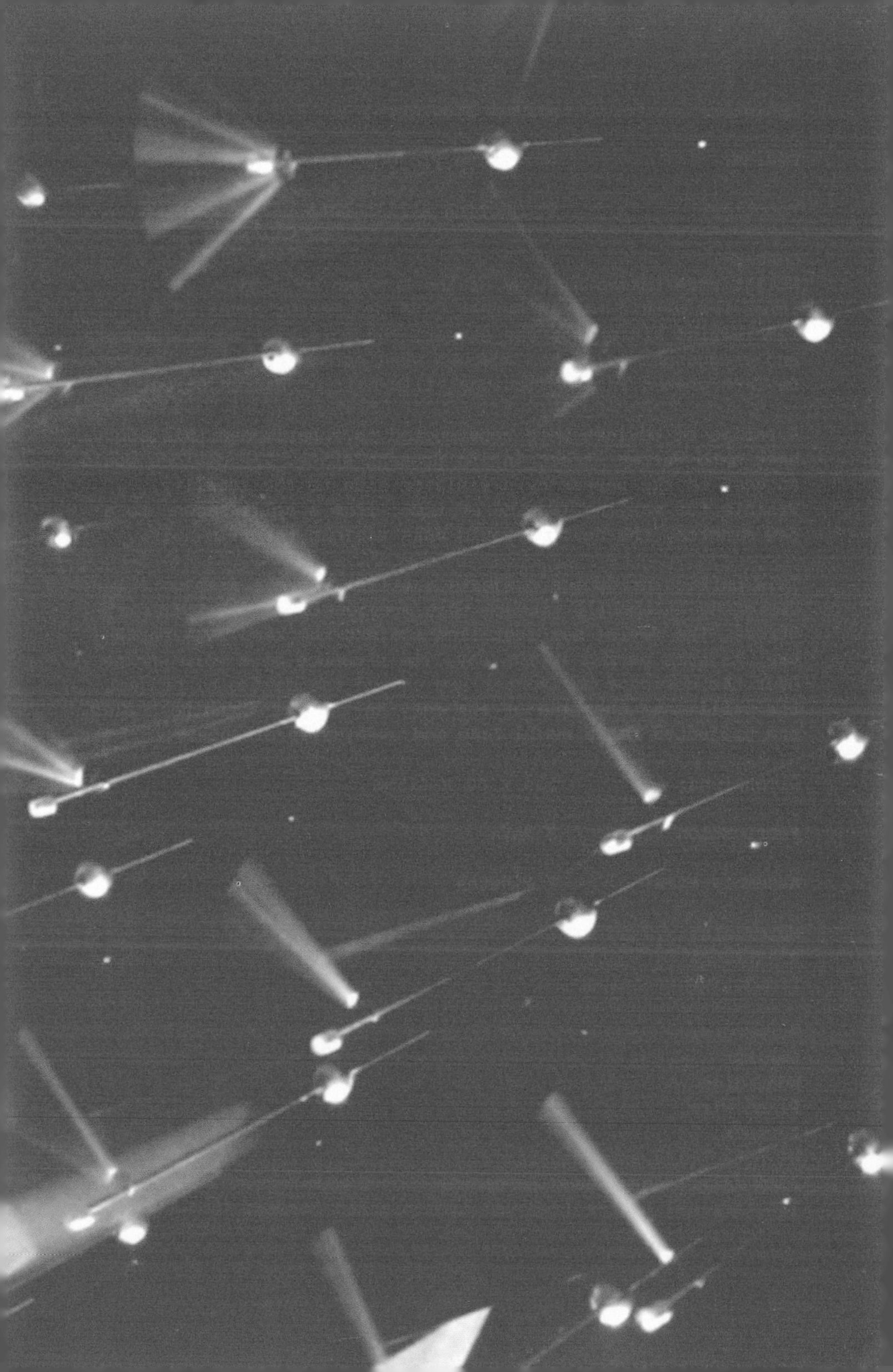

Designer: Andrew Stanforth

Device: Narrative Projector

Function: Projecting stills onto parked cars

Concept:
Whilst undertaking a study of the Borough of Camden, an interview with a Warren Street Café proprietor revealed a fascinating history of the street. The potential embellishments and exaggerations of his account were noted then re-interpreted into a fictional film-noir of Warren Street.

A series of devices were constructed to superimpose this story back onto Warren Street in its present state. The devices would suggest to the passer-by a sinister side to the locality. Visible for varying lengths of time, from a split-second to a few minutes, the devices would make visible the film-noir.

This particular device projects a still from the film-noir depicting automobile traders that previously occupied Warren Street. The device was installed against the kerb in a parking bay. As cars parked in the bay, the presence of a warm engine over the device's horizontal arm caused the device to project the still onto the side of the car. As the car's engine cooled, the projected image would fade and eventually disappear.

Dimensions: 535 x 60 x 415mm

Fabrication time: 3 days

Assembly time: 2 minutes

Materials:
Plasticene
Protective container

Structure:
6mm MDF
Wood-glue
Piano wire
Perspex
M4 nuts bolts and washers
35mm film transparency (cropped)
13A terminal blocks (removed from plastic casing)

Finish:
Spray-paint (canary yellow)
Letra-Line
Dry-transfer text (Helvetica 18pt)

Electronics:
4no AA batteries in holder
Thermistor
Bulb
Stripboard (25 x 10mm)
Relay
Diode
Transistors
Resistors
Potentiometer
Solder

Fabrication:
- Mould plasticene into chosen kerb location in order to generate an impression of the kerb.
- Store in a rigid protective container for transportation.
- Saw and glue 6mm MDF sheet to construct 110 x 60 x 85mm box.
- Compare plasticene kerb impression and draw lines on MDF box so that when cut, it will fit snugly into kerb.
- Sand then prime the box repeatedly.
- Drill holes for thermistor and bulb arms.
- Sandwich film transparency between perspex pieces. Secure with terminal blocks.
- Bend piano wire into shape and solder to bulb. Connect to terminal blocks.
- Solder thermistor to piano wire lengths.
- Push piano wire from thermistor assemblages through MDF box.
- Solder electronics components to stripboard and test.
- Fix stripboard inside box and solder connection to piano wire.
- Spray-paint final coat to box.
- Apply Letra-Line and dry-transfer text.

Assembly:
- Connect battery connector to battery pack.
- Test device by holding thermistor tightly between fingers (body heat should cause bulb to illuminate).
- Calibrate if necessary by adjusting potentiometer.
- Place device against kerb.
- Installation should be performed quickly and discreetly in order to avoid suspicion from vehicle owners. Find a discreet vantage point and wait for car to park over device.

Designer: Nick Browne

Device: Nocturnal Ventilator

Function: Automatic energy storage mechanism (part gun, part bear-trap)

Concept:
Unusually, a flea's knee is capable of storing energy and releases it in one go, producing an extra large hop. The built mechanism attempts to store the thermally induced movement of a wax piston over a day's temperature change. The energy is then used to operate a ventilator at night. The energy is stored in a spring mechanism (rather like an airgun), which cocks between 2.00pm and 4.00pm on a hot day. A series of smaller springs allow the ventilator mechanism to self-open sometime after sunset. Sets of ventilators provided passive cooling of rooms through the lower temperatures of the dark. An hour or so before sunrise the storage spring fires, closing the vent.

Recent building regulations (particularly airtightness standards) have produced a domestic building stock that suffers from overheating during hot weather, and may prematurely become obsolete, as thermal discomfort will occur with greater frequency according to the predicted climatic patterns for the next hundred years. The ventilator is conceived as a potential method for dealing with this problem without resorting to high-energy mechanical methods (e.g. air conditioning systems). An array of ventilators would be retrofitted to problematic dwellings and provide a paired set of inlet and outlet vents for localised (by room) ventilation.

Dimensions: 750 x 300 x 300mm

Fabrication time: 3 months

Assembly time: 2 weeks

Materials:
Aluminium: 3mm plate, 6mm plate, 35mmØ tubular section
Steel: 6mm + 10mm round, 25mmØ tubular section
Brass: 6mm x 16mm solid section, 35mmØ solid section, 6mm rod
Plywood
Mineral wax piston
Various springs (expansion and compression)
One-way clutch bearings x6

Various spur gears and rack (module 1.0)
Various fixings

Fabrication:
A storage mechanism was conceived and appropriate mechanical methods were tested, first diagrammatically and then in quick built test models. Having established a method for adequately storing the movement from the piston in a spring, a prototype ventilator mechanism was then designed and built in the following order:

Spring housing and main structure:
- Cut and mill the steel/aluminium tube and section with 6mm slots to accommodate sliding components.
- Using Cad-cam, make the connecting plates and gearset mounts from aluminium and plywood.

Deploying arms:
- Cut and mill from a 16mm aluminium solid square section.
- Bore to allow M3/M4 threads to be tapped.

Trigger and trigger mounts:
- Cad-cam from aluminium.

Pins/hinges/sliding/rotating components:
- Cut pins/hinges from brass/steel rod, lathe to accommodate.
- Circlips or tap with threads as required.
- Mill hinges to allow setscrew fittings where necessary.
- Cut sliding guides, bore and lathe to size from 35mmØ brass solid section.
- Using Cad-cam produce the Cams and tap with M3 threads.

Assembly:
- Weld steel components comprising main structural armature together as required.
- Fit connecting plates to the aluminium and steel structure with M4 bolts.
- Position sliding components and main spring.
- Fit racks to armature.
- Fit spur gears with clutch bearings and attached to shafts.
- Secure Cams to shafts.
- Fit triggers and gear-sets to main armature and secure with mounting plates.
- Mount wax piston on to armature by connecting plates.

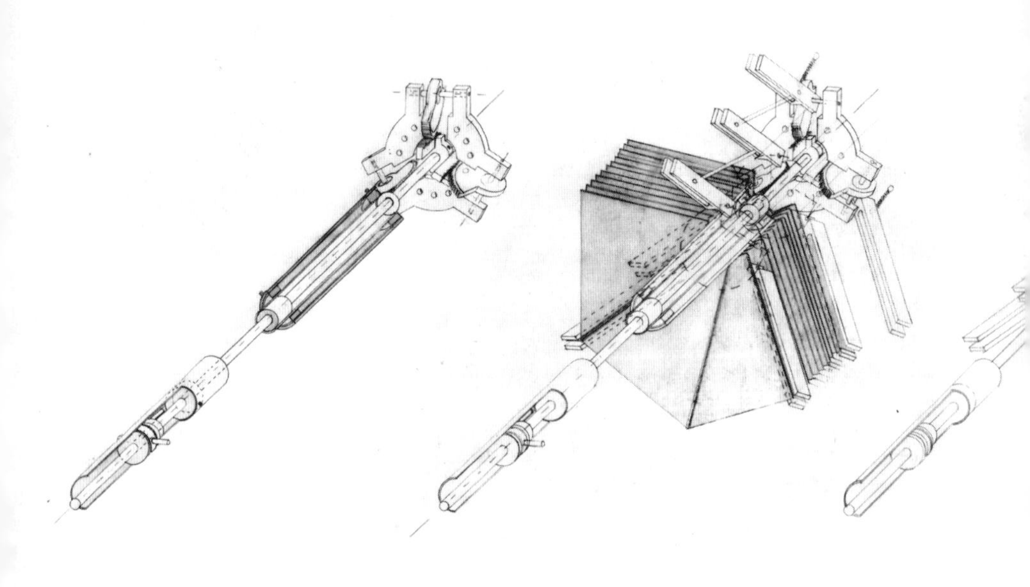

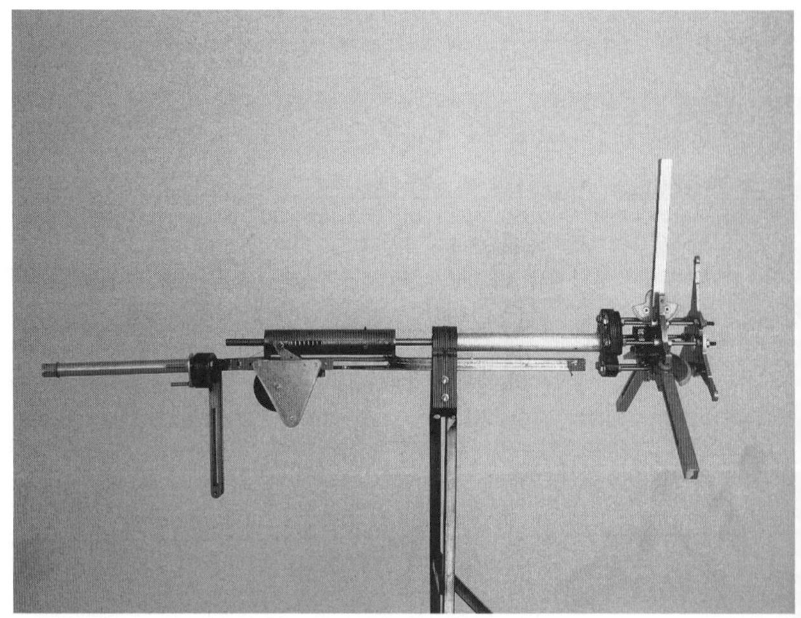

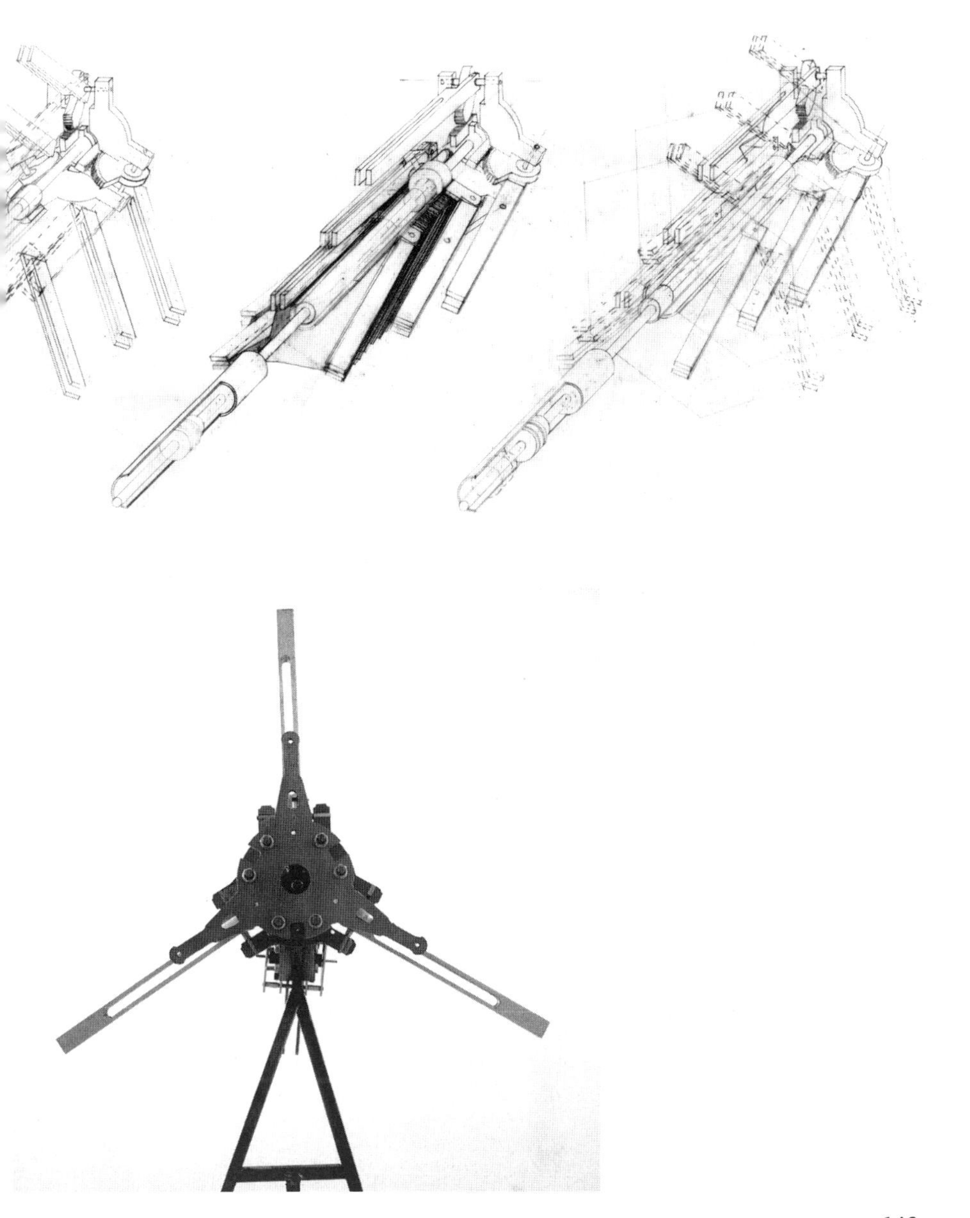

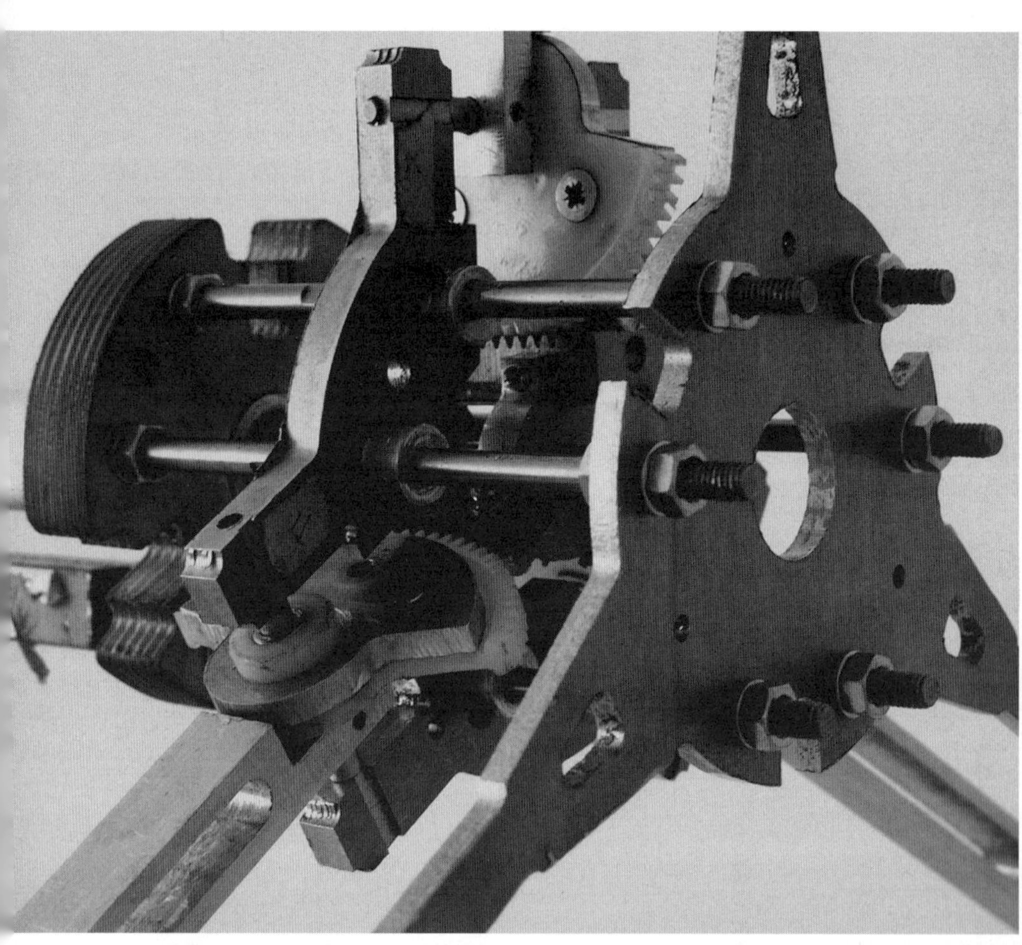

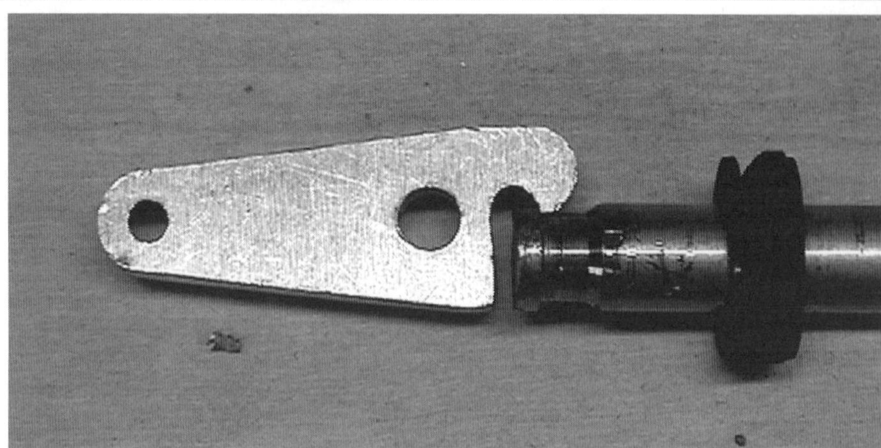

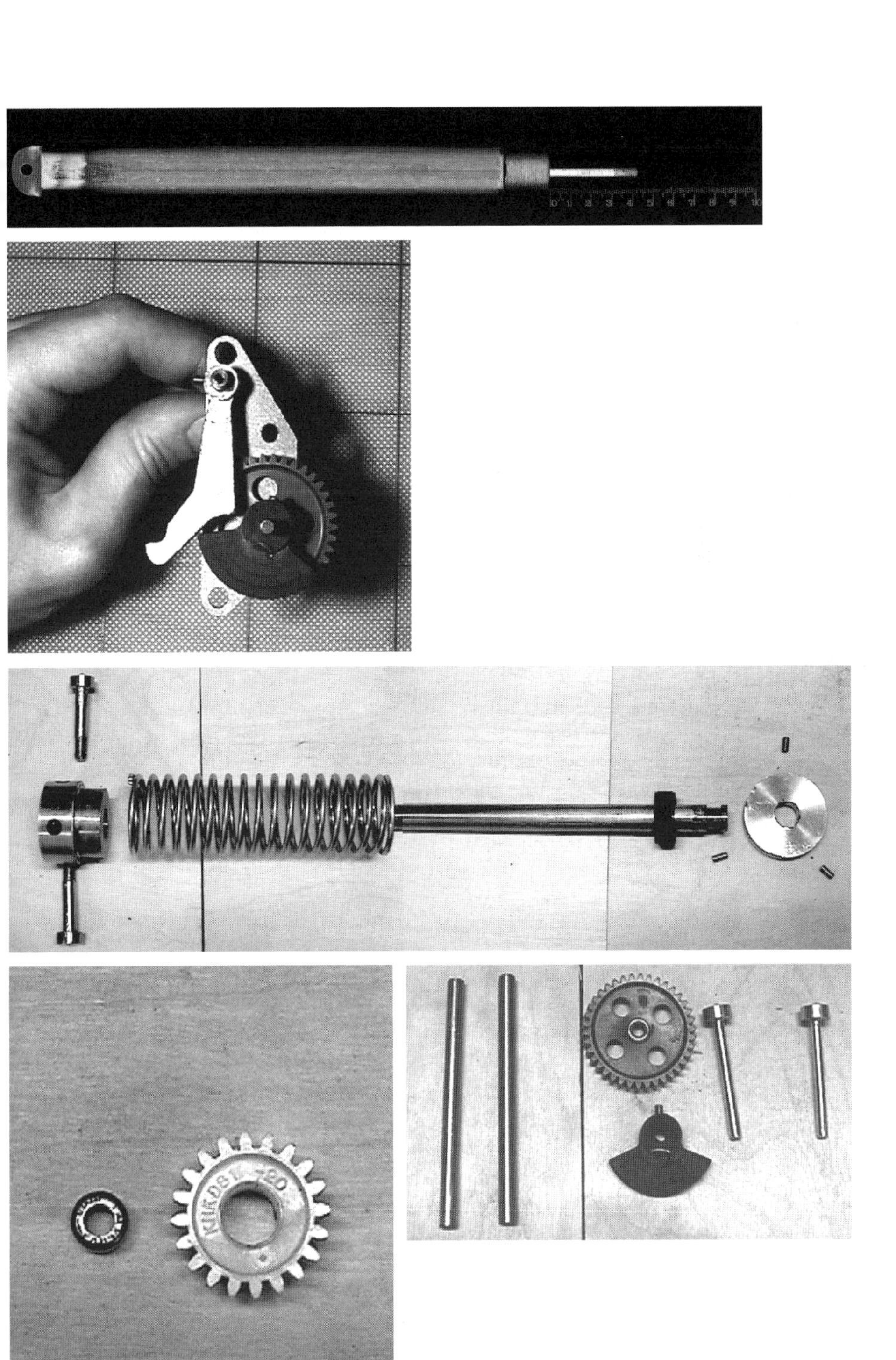
0 1 2 3 4 5 6 7 8 9 10

Designer: Jonathan Hagos

Device: Nostalgia

Function: Embedding memory onto landscape

Concept:
On my journey, my staff acts as a memory device: using a fusion of senses and thoughts I physically stamp on to the landscape. Poppy seeds, which are stored in one of the components, are inserted into the primary shaft of the instrument at the start of each new day and transferred to a depository at the base of the shaft. The second part of the process is the lighting of the incense. An incense stick, also stored within the staff, is inserted at the top of the primary shaft. Once alight, the journey can begin.

Each step brings a fusion of the fallen ash incense with the poppy seeds at the base depository. With each strike of the staff on the earth, the dispersion mechanism comes into effect, depositing the meld into the landscape. The nitrates found in the ash of the incense act here as an emblematic fertilizer, mixing with the seeds and increasing the successful growth of the flower, a symbol of remembrance.

The scent of incense and the ritualistic act of lighting it bring to mind a great sense of nostalgia. I leave behind memories of the past and thoughts of the present, fused with prospects for the future, marking the landscape with my soul.

Dimensions: 1.86m (long) x 30mm (diameter)

Fabrication time: 3 weeks

Assembly time:

Materials:
2m length of 30mm wide pine dowel
1no 55mm compression spring
5no M8 nut plugs
5no M8 screws

Fabrication:
Measuring 1.86 metres in total, the staff utilises a system of plugs and screws and can be assembled easily from its initial six parts.

- Saw a 1000mm long piece of dowel into two along its length.
- Route each side, leaving a channel running along the middle length of the dowel.
- Fix the dispersion mechanism to the base of the dowel. This mechanism is comprised of a 55mm compression spring and bridging rods of aluminium, which together allow each strike of the staff to release the deposits.
- Fix the dowel back together using a wood adhesive, ensuring the dispersion mechanism is in place.
- Connect a 75mm solid piece of dowel to the unattached side of the mechanism. This is the striking base and along with the original piece will make up the primary shaft.

This process is repeated again for the three remaining pieces of the shaft. These pieces are used for storage, thereby the only differing construction point being that a channel is not routed along the full length of these pieces, and that no mechanism is needed.

Of the four pieces now complete, the end piece and the mid piece remain; both of which are solid and do not comprise of internal channels.

Once all the pieces have been completed, insert the plugs to the top of each section; this will allow the pieces to connect. Insert the corresponding screws to the other end of each piece. Finally, fix a 10mm protective steel plate onto the base of the striking piece.

Assembly:
The concept of the device is that it is carried fully constructed from location to location, however this is not always possible and at times requires disassembling.

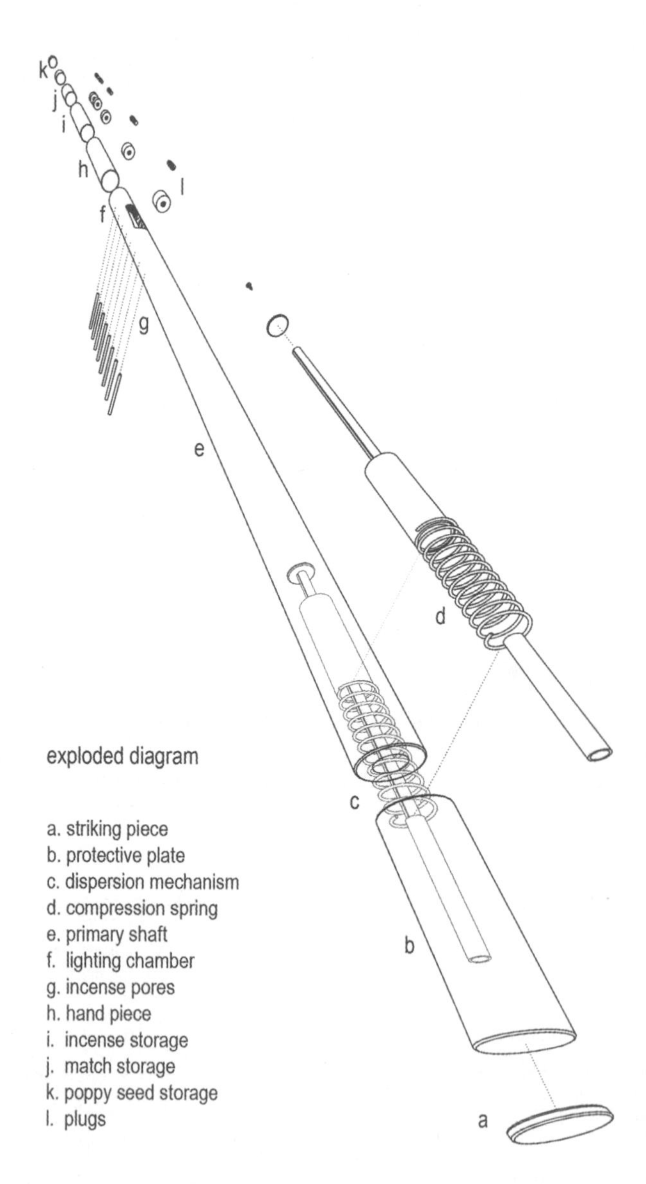
k
j
i
h
f
g
l
e
d
c
b
a
exploded diagram
a. striking piece
b. protective plate
c. dispersion mechanism
d. compression spring
e. primary shaft
f. lighting chamber
g. incense pores
h. hand piece
i. incense storage
j. match storage
k. poppy seed storage
l. plugs

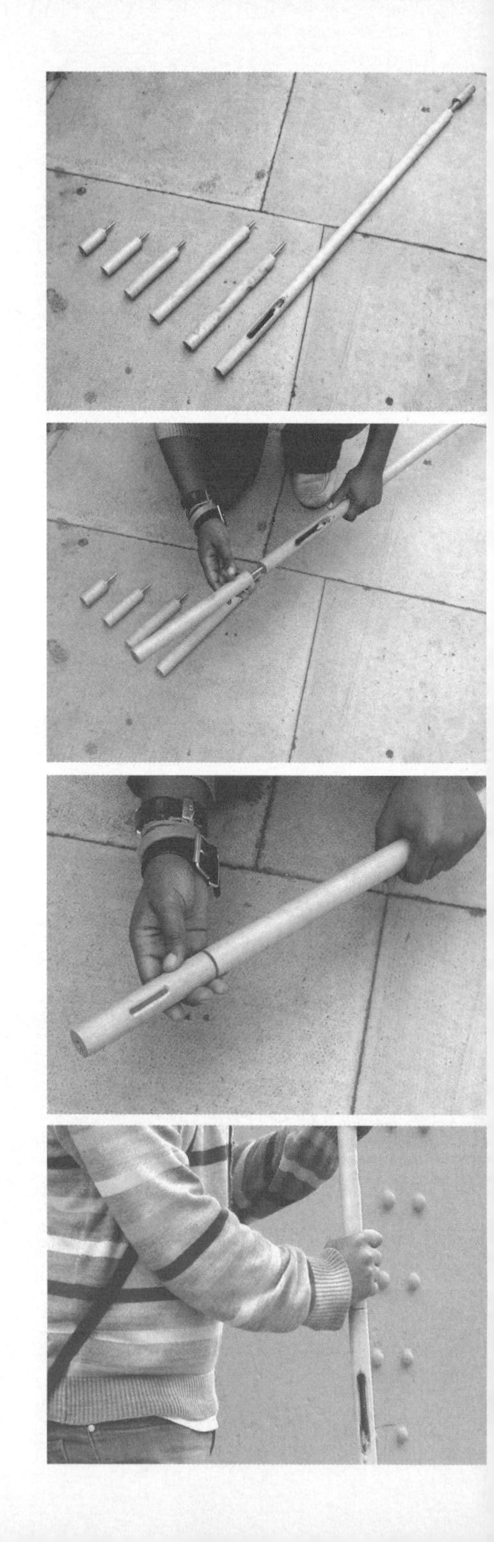

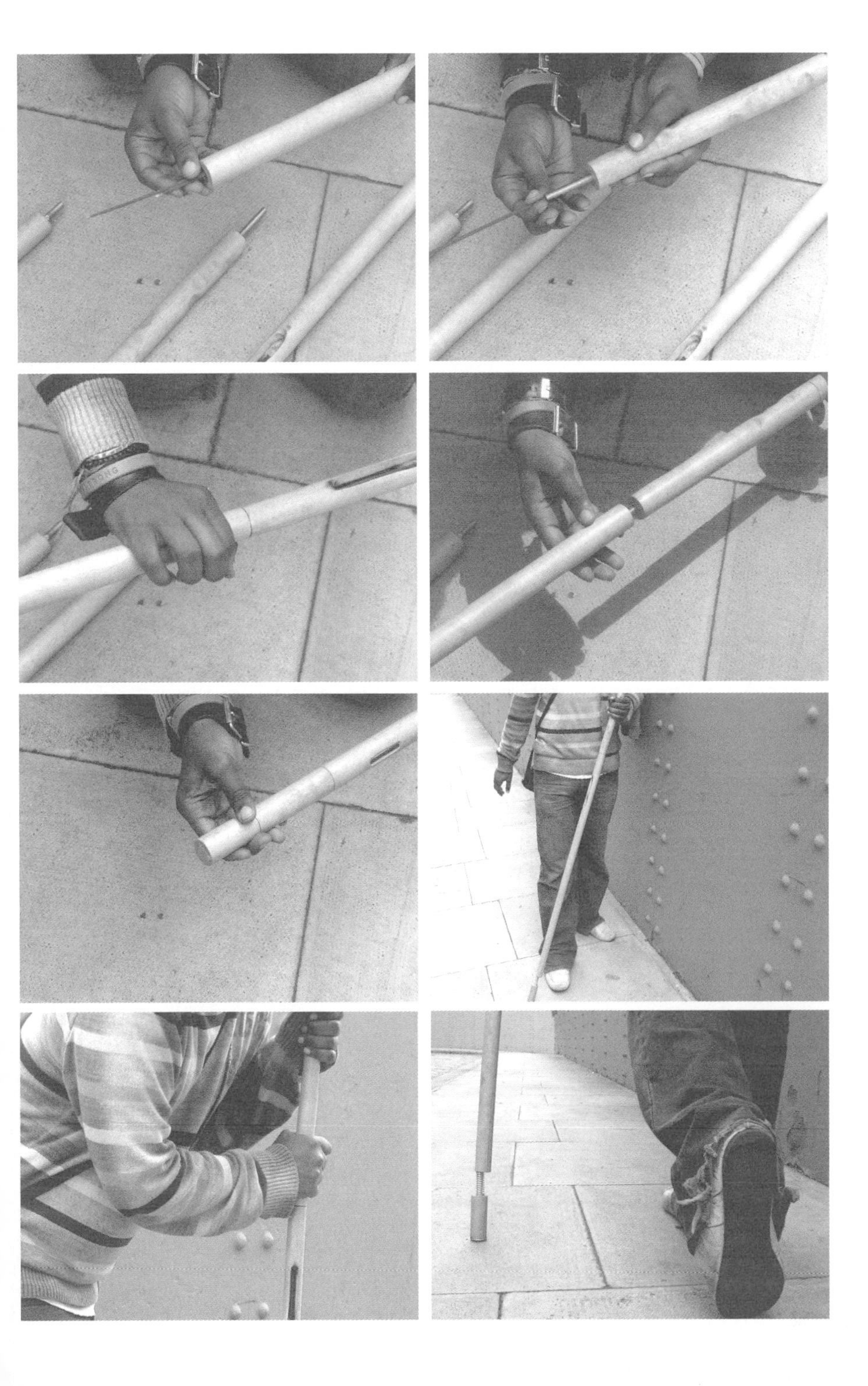

Designer: Julius Klaffke

Device: Pinhole Camera

Function: Representing my visual experience of space

Concept:
The flexible structure of the camera allows independent movement of different parts of the picture plane: towards or away from the pinhole. The infinity depth of field of pinhole cameras is the key aspect to understanding the picture plane as a spatial element: any focal length produces sharp projections.

The pinhole camera is also a design tool. With the camera I take scaled pictures of architectural models. The model anticipates a performance of the camera. The bent picture plane is related to the model space. The two (model and camera) develop an interactive relationship of anticipation.

The picture plane not only represents space but also generates space itself. The bent surfaces of the model take the physical quality of the film from the dark inside of the camera into the real world. The architectural element becomes a picture plane in itself, holding space within its surfaces. The viewer is engaged not only in the space represented on the picture plane but also in its spatial performance.

Dimensions: 10 x 8inch (Picture plane)
12 x 12 x 10inch (Camera body)

Fabrication time: 4 weeks

Assembly time: 0.25 hours in darkroom (per picture)
0.5 hours on site (per picture) to prepare camera for taking a picture

Materials:
Main structure:
Laminated veneer (inner layers: makore, surface: oak)
Steel joint to tripod

Movable arms:
Copper clad circuit board, double sided

Flexible camera body:
Latex

Laminated veneer board
Self-adhesive Velcro

Aperture:
Copper foil, black tape

Template for cutting the film:
Perspex

Additional parts: hooks, screws, clamps

Fabrication:
Main structure:
- MDF mould for lamination
- Laminate veneer frame
- Fine-tune veneer frame

Movable arms:
- Construct CAD drawings
- Cut parts on milling machine
- Solder parts
- Fine-tune and clean structure

Flexible camera body:
- Draw pattern for light-tight bag
- Cut latex skin
- Vulcanise joints
- Fix Velcro in order to form light-tight openings

Aperture:
- Punch hole into copper foil
- Fix black tape to pinhole to close aperture

Template for cutting the film:
- Construct CAD drawings
- Cut parts on milling machine

Assembly:
- Darkroom: cut film in template and load film
- On site: attach flexible camera body to movable structure

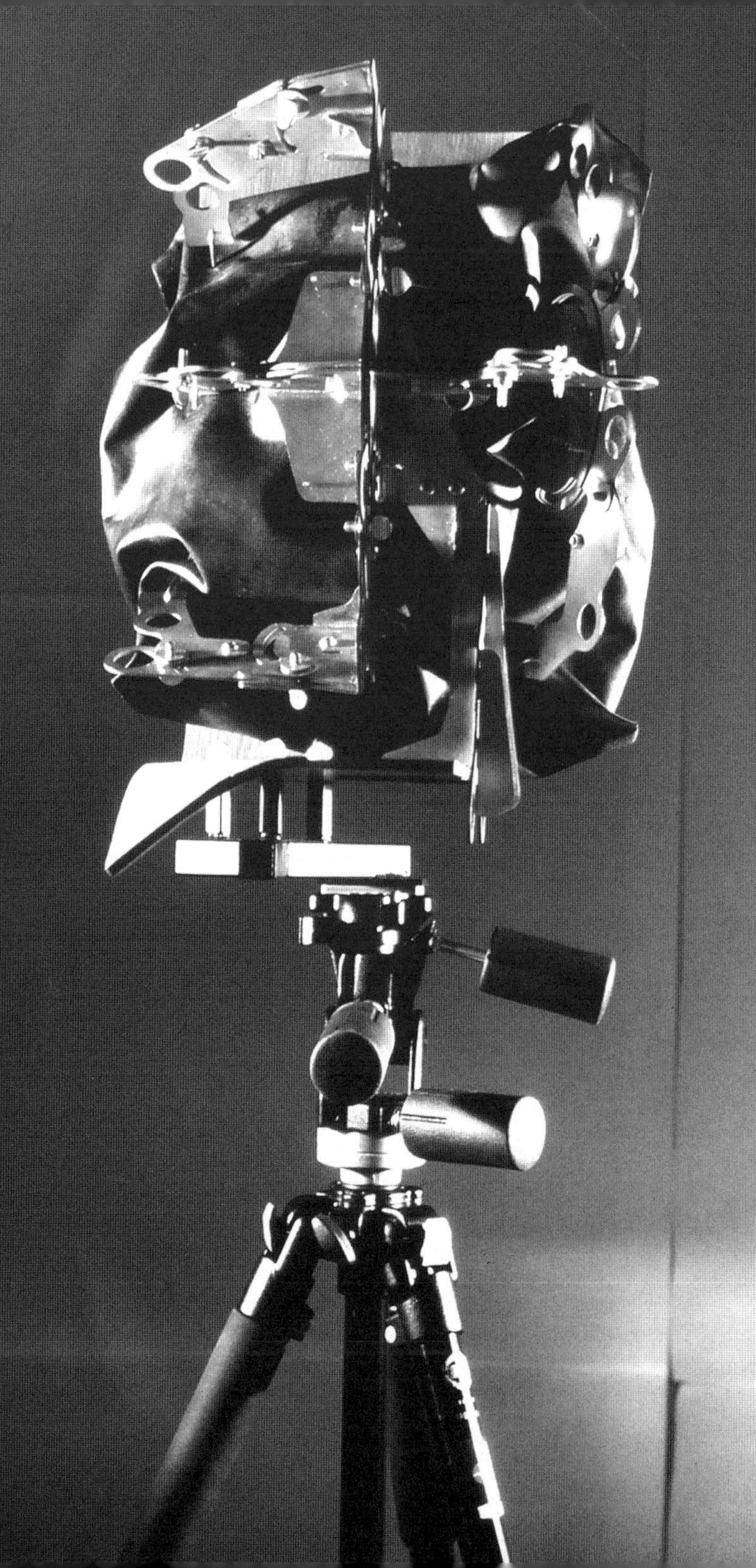

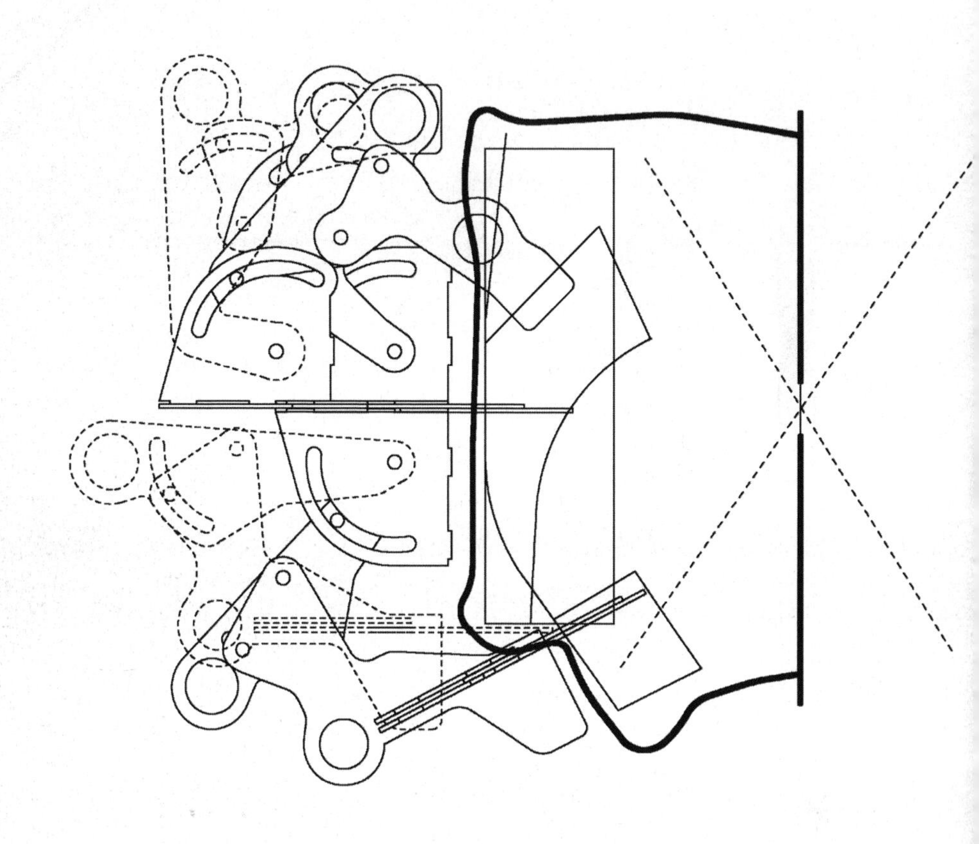

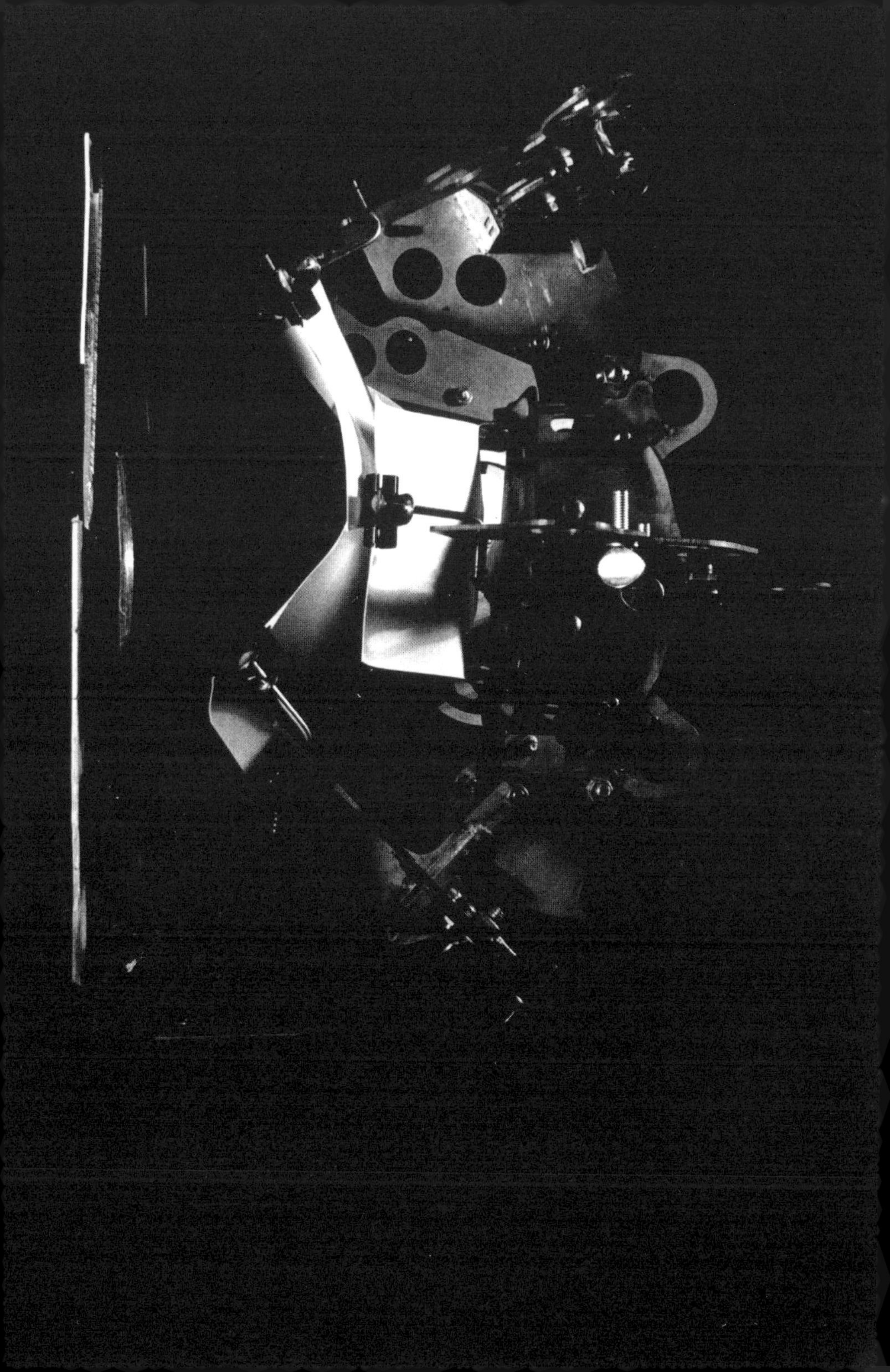

Designer: Pascal Bronner

Device: Smoking Stool

Function: Tobacco lighter

Concept:
This device was inspired by the playful inventiveness of the Victorians and their urge for labour-saving gadgets. Although this device solves few problems, merely saving one from lighting a pipe, it is in line with the Victorian idea of utopia. The stool plays with the idea of extravagance, comfort and boredom – boredom is the luxury of having too much time. This gave rise to new behaviours in society such as the tobacco culture and the crafts industry.

The stool is equipped with a series of mechanisms which are triggered by a person sitting down. The energy driving the mechanism is simply one's own weight, using a vertical compression system to translate the forces across the underside of the seat. A match is struck, lighting a candle which burns tobacco situated directly above the candle's flame. At the same time a balloon-like bag is pumped up with air. This air is released to extinguish the flames when the person gets off the stool. The match-dispenser can be filled with up to approximately 100 matches.

Dimensions: 500 x 500 x 630mm

Fabrication time: 6 days

Assembly time: 30 seconds

Materials:
Timber
Steel (rod, tube, sheet, screws, wire rope, springs, fixings)
Cotton fabric
Cling film
Thread
ENGLISH FLAKE – pipe tobacco
Abrasive strip from matchbox
Matches
Candle

Fabrication:
- Cut and bend steel components for seat and vertical

compression mechanism.
- Cut timber for seat and legs and assemblage of seat, legs and vertical compression mechanism.
- Cut steel components for mechanisms – match lighter, candle holder, tobacco holder, match dispenser and extinguisher-bag holder.
- Assemble the above on the underside of the stool.
- Construct extinguisher-bag. Line the cotton fabric with cling film to ensure the bag is airtight.

Assembly:
- Place stool on site and sit on it.
- Hold the seat firmly with both hands, until a match has been lit and the wig has caught fire.
- Use the belt to strap your leg to the stool.

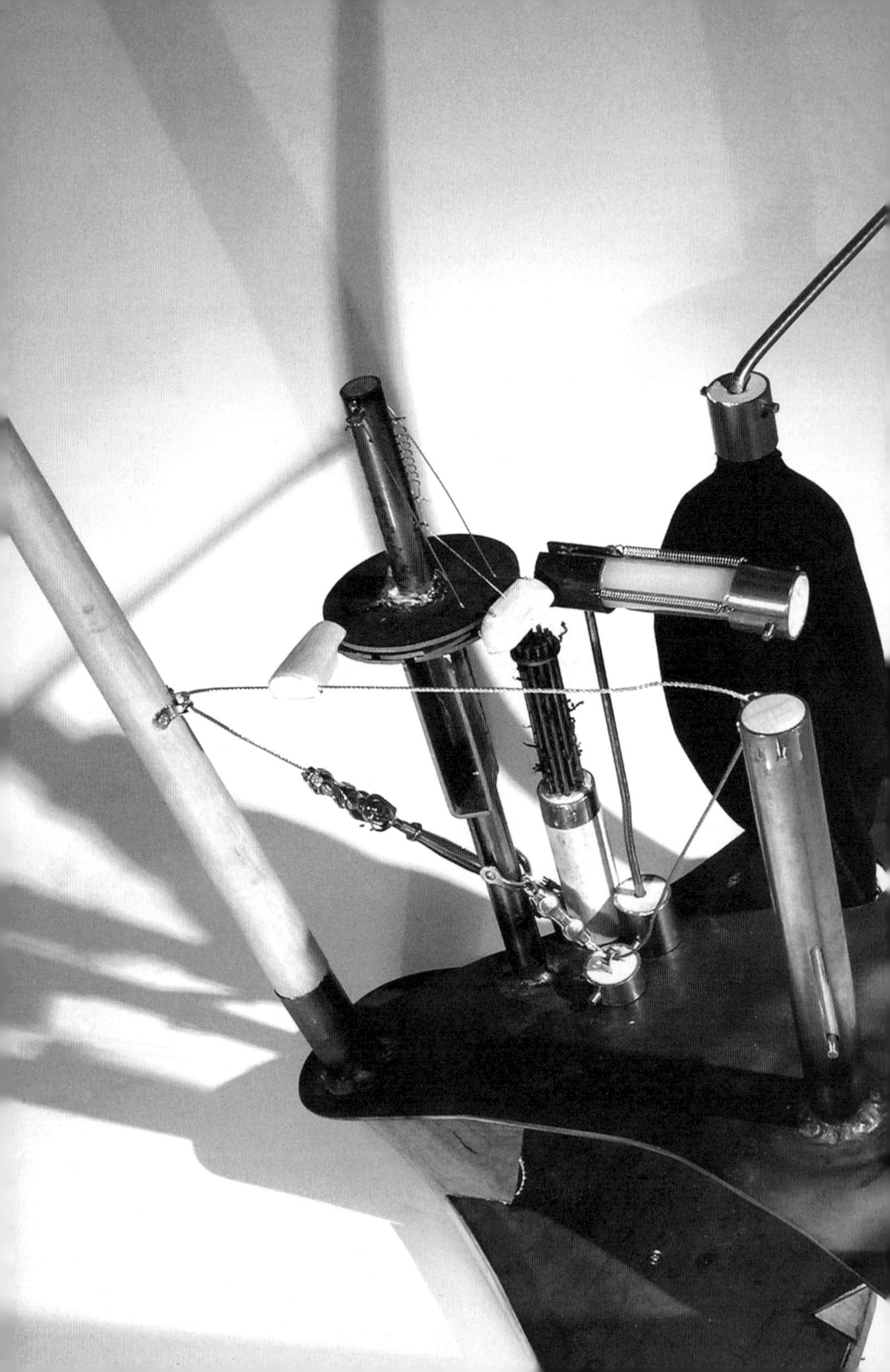

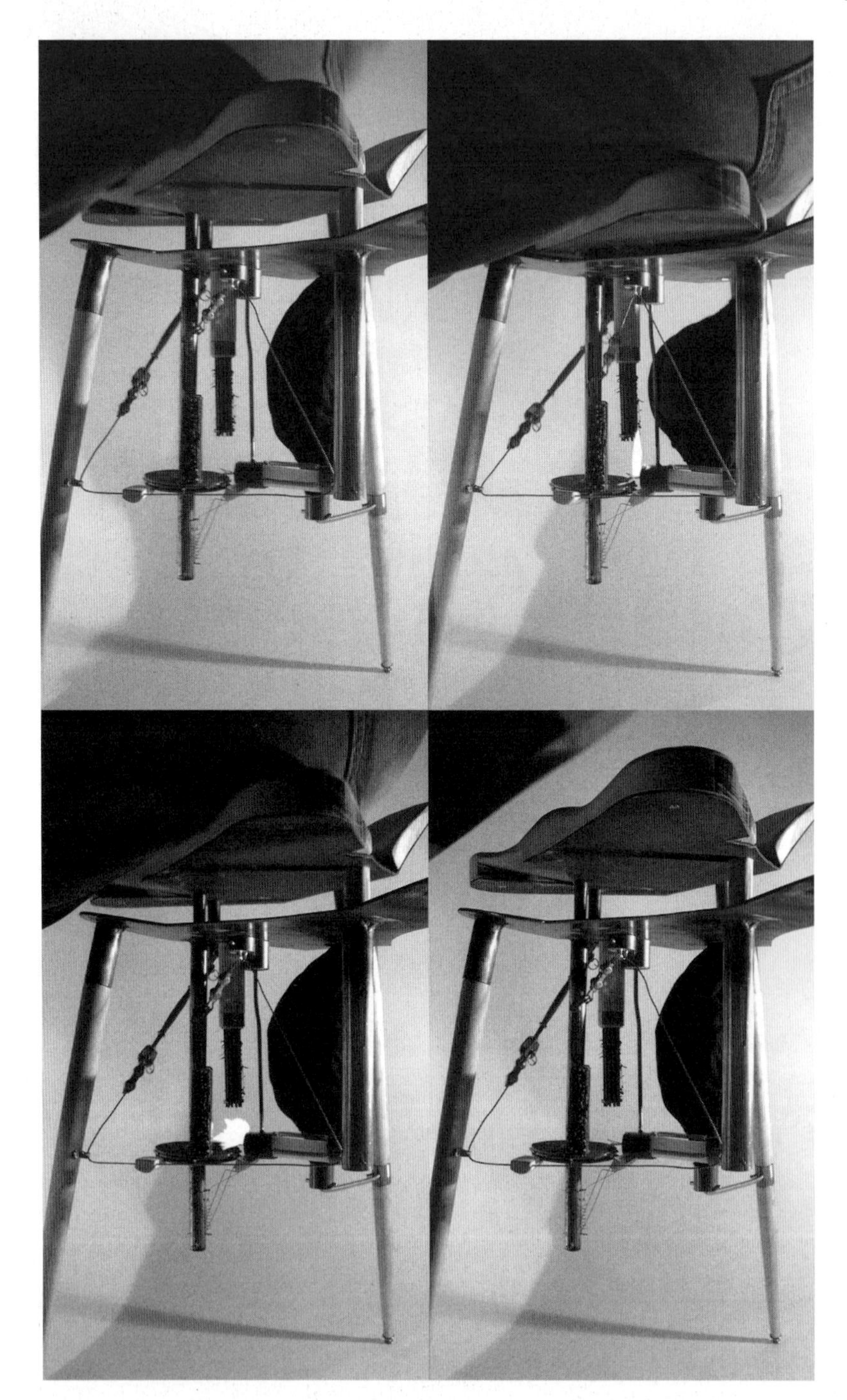

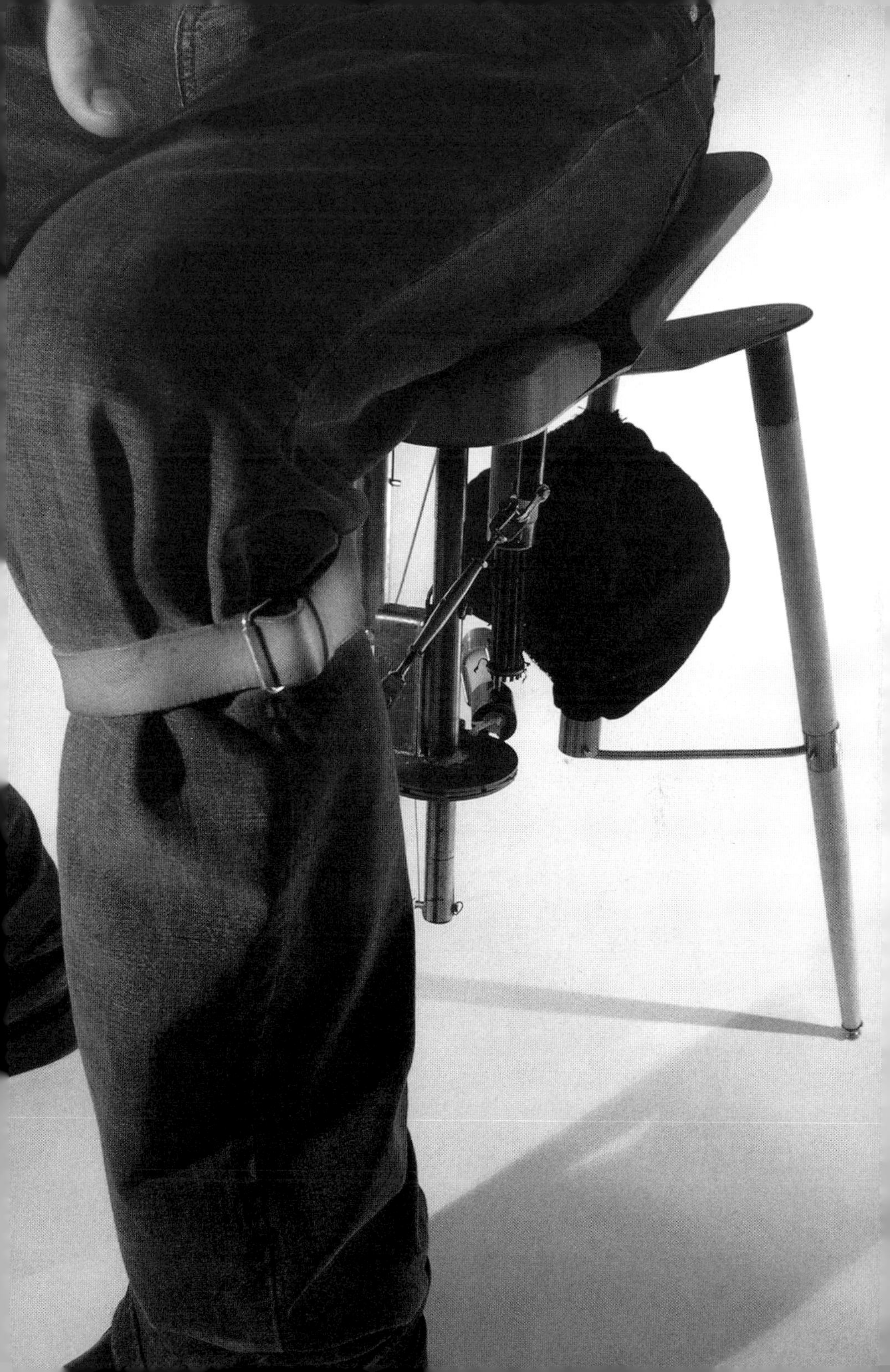

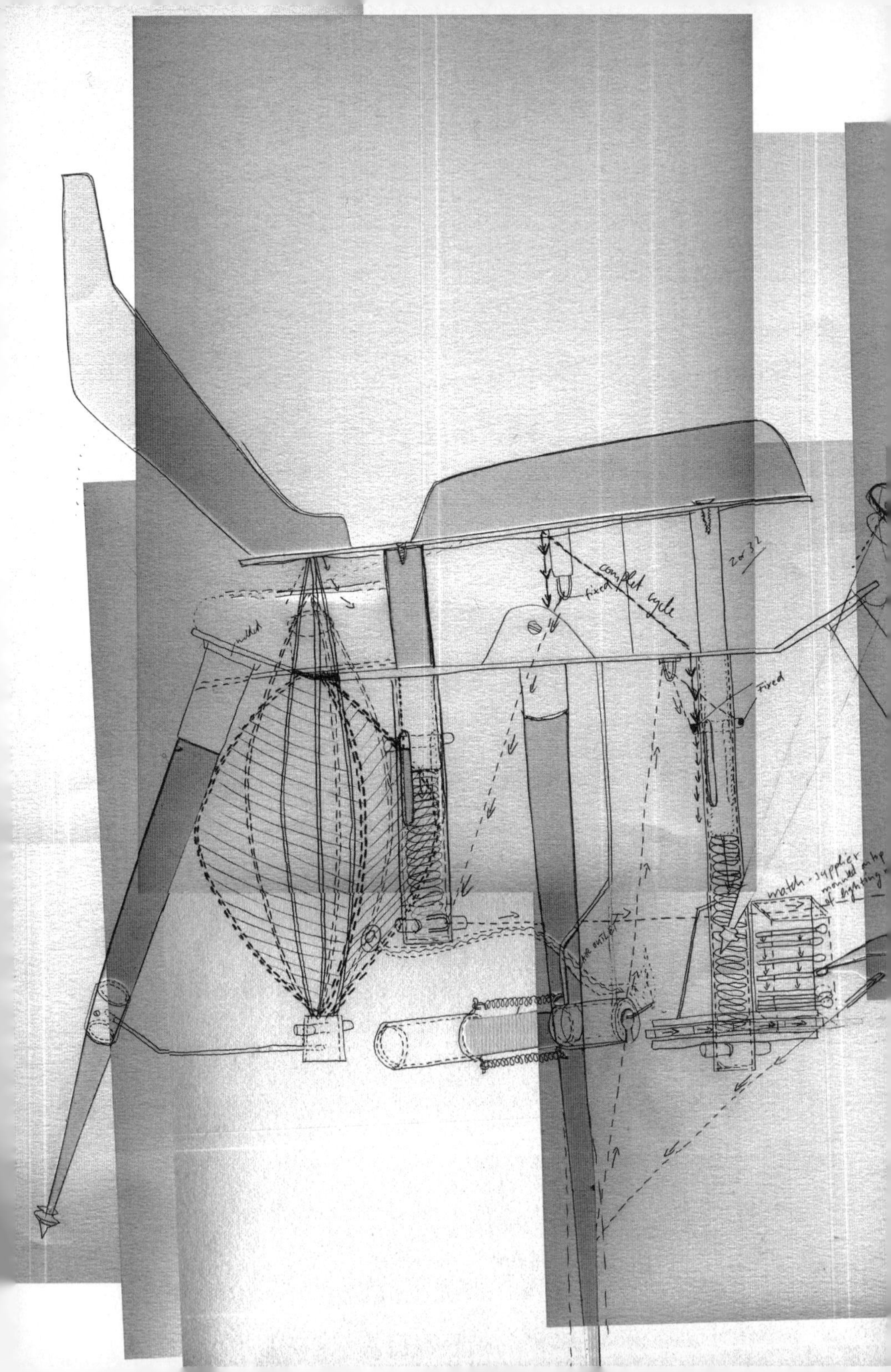
complet cycle
fixed
Fixed
2 of 32
match - supplier
mounted on top
of lighting
AIR OUTLET

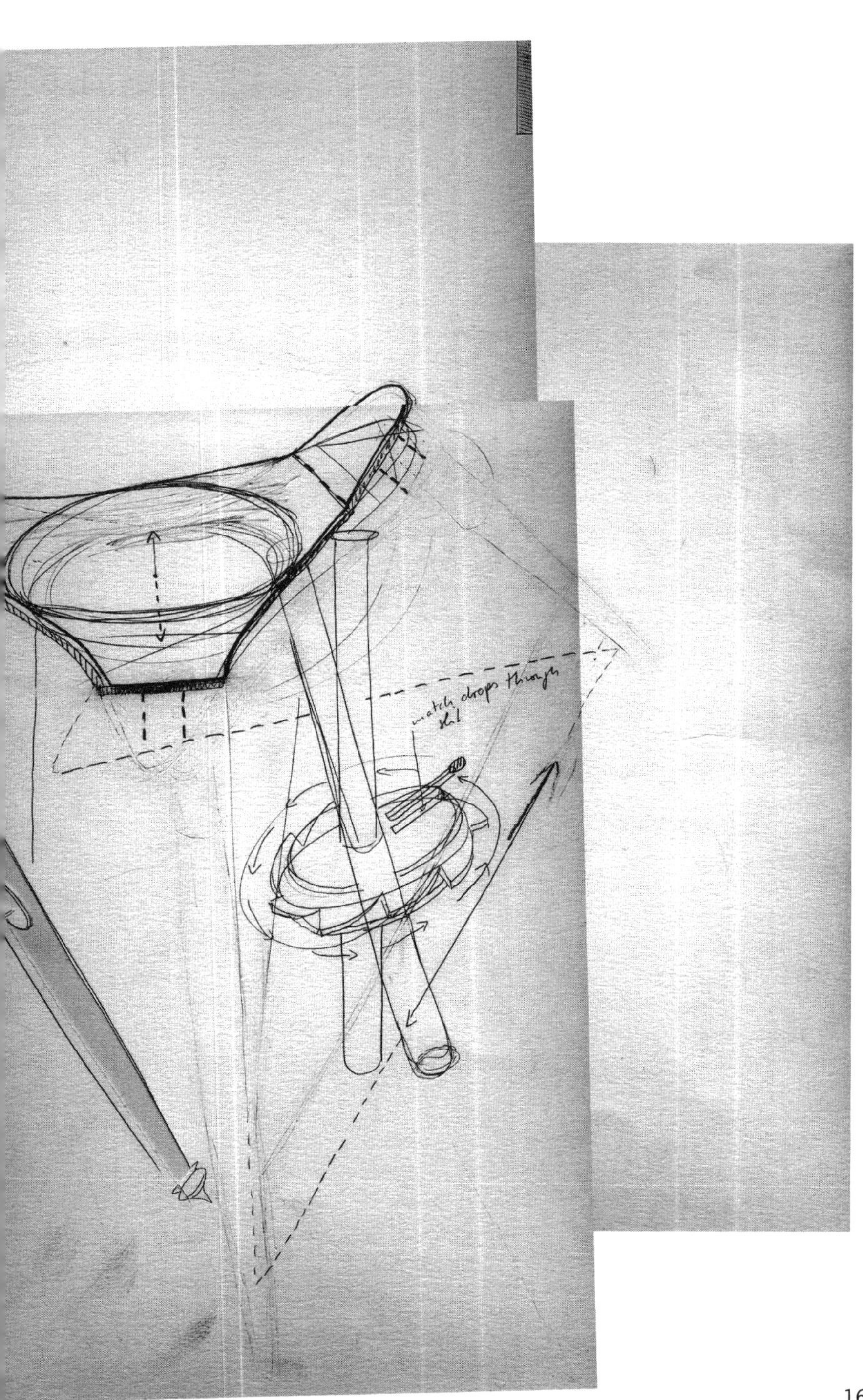
match drops through
slit

Designer: Tony Lau

Device: Spud-master 204

Function: High-speed delivery of mashed potato

Concept:
A portable device that can be used by mobile street-side mashed potato vendors. Hot cooked potatoes with different types of fillings are shot directly at the customer and are instantly mashed on impact. You can shout your order from the 5th floor window of your office, and the food is fired up to you still piping hot!

Dimensions: 1800 x 250mm

Fabrication time: 2 weeks

Assembly time: 1 minute to set up/rate of fire
1 round per minute

Materials:
2″ PVC Pipe
4″ PVC Pipe
2no bell reducers
2no male and female adaptors
Laser pointer
Aluminium bracket
Steel screws
Electrical wiring
Piezo-electric igniter
Wooden handle
Brass rod
PVC solvent glue
Electrical tape

Fabrication:
Cannon Barrel :
- Cut 2″ diameter PVC pipe to size and glue screw adaptor.

Combustion Chamber :
- Glue bell shaped ends to 4″ diameter pipe.
- Glue male and female screw adaptors on.
- Bend brass wires into a triangle and insert into barrel end to form stopper.

Ignition Cap:
- Sharpen screw and bend to shape.
- Bolt onto PVC cap to form sparking contacts.

Trigger and Handle:
- Shape and bolt wood to combustion chamber.
- Mount aluminium bracket with screws and fit Piezo-electric igniter.
- Connect wiring to ignition cap and secure with electrical tape.

Gunsight:
- Cut 2″ diameter PVC pipe to size and insert brass wire for sight.
- Bolt onto combustion chamber.

Assembly:
- Perform ignition test
- Load potato
- Screw gun barrel into combustion chamber
- Spray 1-second burst of propellant into combustion chamber and screw ignition cap on
- Aim and fire

Additional Equipment: (The following items should be worn at all times in the event the potato explodes in the barrel)
- Face shield
- Gloves
- Ear defenders

1. BARREL	(1a) 4' x 2" PVC pipe (1b) 2" PVC male adaptor
2. COMBUSTION CHAMBER	(2a) 2" PVC female adaptor (2b) 2" PVC bushing (2c) Triangular brass wire stopper (2d) 4" to 2" PVC bell reducer (2e) 4" PVC coupling (2f) 18" x 4" PVC pipe (2g) 4" PVC couping (2h) 4" to 2" PVC bell reducer (2i) 2" PVC bushing (2j) 2" PVC male adaptor
3. IGNITION CAP	(3a) Sharped steel screws (3b) Wiring to piezo-electric ingiter (3c) PVC threaded cap
4. GUNSIGHT	(4a) 2" PVC pipe with brass wire inserted for sight and bolted to main body (4b) Laser pointer
5. TRIGGER AND HANDLE	(5a) Hardwood handle bolted to main body (5b) Aluminium trigger bracket (5c) Piezo-electric ingiter
6. BARREL ADAPTOR	(6a) 18" x 4" PVC PVC Pipe

All parts joined with PVC solvents

1216

56

1a

SPUDMASTER204

MASHED POTATO DELIVERY CANNON

IGNITION CAP

COMBUSTION CHAMBER

GUNSIGHT

PIEZO-ELECTRIC IGNITER

POTATO ROUND

LASER SIGHT

PROPELLANT

TRIGGER AND HANDLE

AXONOMETRIC VIEW

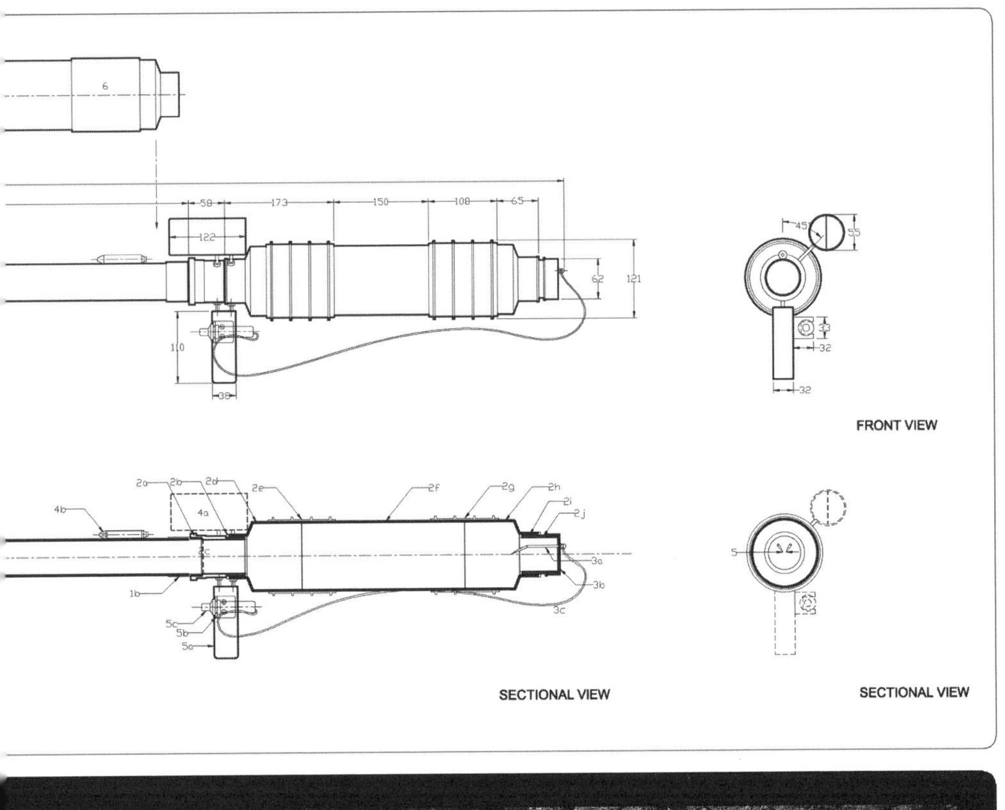
6
59
173
150
108
65
122
62
121
110
38
45
55
33
32
32
FRONT VIEW
2a
2b
2d
2e
2f
2g
2h
2i
2j
4b
4a
3c
3a
3b
3c
1b
5c
5b
5a
5
SECTIONAL VIEW
SECTIONAL VIEW

REL ADAPTOR

Designer: Maxwell Mutanda

Device: Star Gazer

Function: An instrument to watch artificial stars

Concept:
The instrument is designed to attach to a window frame of a building in London, a city where light pollution means that stars cannot be seen either through the naked eye or telescope. As a response to this, the instrument's intended use is to find artificial stars in the sky by deploying the grid of an old tennis racket to break up the sky into small sections making it easier for the user to plot the positions of moving objects in the sky. The device is modelled against perspective grids once popular amongst artists and draughtsmen as well as the childrens's game, Battleships. Two grids work together to create this perspective grid that is subsequently viewed through lenses positioned to create a telescope, which magnify the object in the sky.

Dimensions: 800 x 350 x 1100mm

Fabrication time: 2 weeks

Assembly time: 7 minutes

Materials:
American walnut
Aluminium shaving mirror holder
Dunlop tennis racket
Armchair castor wheel
6 x 3mm brass bolts
Nuts and wing nuts
Felt pads
Florist wire crosshairs
White colour plan card
2no brass door hinges
Brass rod
Magnifying lens
Spectacle lens
Expanding double scissor jack arm

Fabrication:
- American walnut is planed into uniform sections to create adjustable sliding arms.

- The sliding arms are then embossed with marks to establish units along their length.
- The head of the tennis racket is separated from its handle to create the larger perspective grid and a handle. Felt pads are placed on the exposed ends that rest on the walnut.
- The dismantled head and handle of the tennis racket are hinged to the main walnut sliding arm.
- A smaller perspective grid is made from the aluminium shaving mirror frame using florist wire as crosshairs and white colour plan card.

Assembly:
- The three sliding arms are connected to each other using brass bolts and wing nuts.
- The tennis racket head is locked into position using a threaded brass rod.
- The instrument is secured into position on the window frame and locked in place with a wedge above the radiator.
- An additional handle is extended from the main walnut piece to hold the mirror section.
- The double scissor jack arm is connected to the walnut frame to hold the lens.

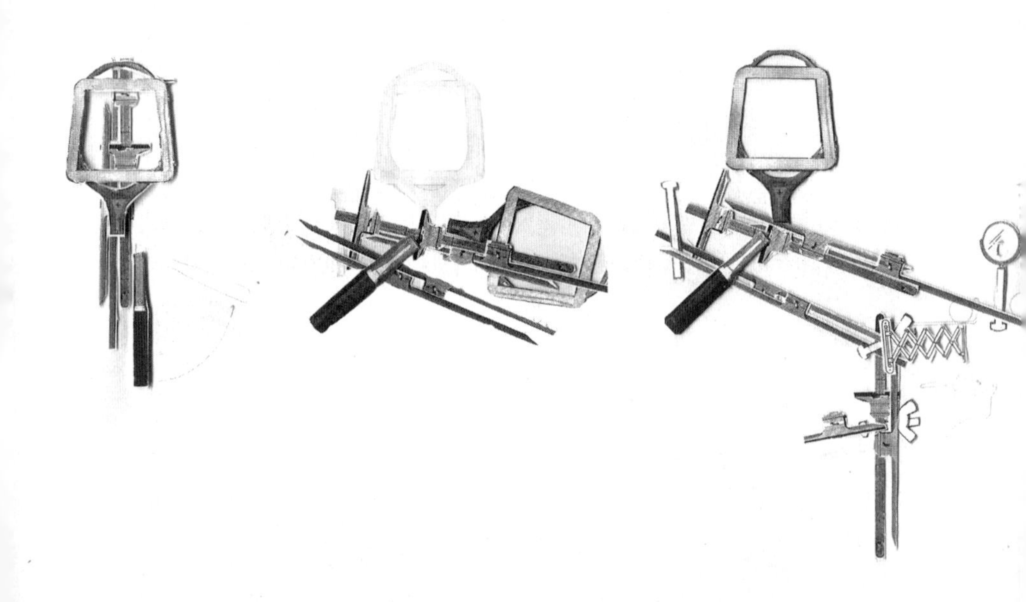

Designers: Mark Shaw + Ursula Thompson

Device: Storm Topography

Function: Reading metaphoric storm

Concept:
The daily 'storm' is a great inconvenience and once it has occurred a sense of relief prevails. The device is a metaphoric representation of these conditions before and after the storm.

The device is worn as a body suit or prosthetic while undertaking a tour of a given 'site' and making a film recording of the 'event'. The design of the suit restricts body movement and impedes the progress of the wearer. The eyepiece restricts sight and vision. The neckpiece restricts head movement and the knee pin prevents the knee from bending making walking difficult.

The 'event' is triggered by a sensor which picks up fluctuations in differing predetermined environmental conditions. When this occurs, a balloon, connected to the suit, inflates with helium gas and lifts up into the air. As it raises it disconnects pins in the knee and the headpieces. This allows the knee to bend and the head is suddenly released from its fixed position allowing the wearer to look up and watch the balloon rise. The leg piece becomes a seat, allowing the wearer of the heavy and cumbersome suit to rest during the event.

As the balloon rises, it releases the camera from the steel leg. The camera is tethered to the suit by a nylon thread. The resulting film describes the transformation from a repetitive monotonous study of the ground surface to a fascinating air-borne survey giving an extraordinary panoramic view of the site.

Dimensions: Human scale

Fabrication time: 4 weeks

Assembly time: 30 minutes

Materials:
Winding mechanism
Pin release
40no fixings
Digital video camera
Helium gas

Met balloon
Balloon bung
Mount board
Velcro
Aluminium
Steel
100m of nylon thread
3mm opaque perspex
Red weather balloon
Helium gas, pipe and fixings
3mm black neoprene
Stainless steel Allen headed bolts

Fabrication:
- Select person to model suit.
- Mark shapes required on the body using paper.
- Cut shapes out of card.
- Attach card to body, redefine shapes until happy.
- Proceed to final suit.

- Draw required flat shapes on perspex and cut.
- Heat over bar heater and bend into desired shape.
- Attach neoprene and trim to shape with scalpel.
- Drill small holes in edge of perspex and attach aluminium clips for Velcro straps.
- Make 40 aluminium fixing bolts by taping and threading 8mm aluminum rod to take 6mm bolts.
- Fix aluminium rods to perspex pieces with fixing bolts.
- Lathe wooden stopper for balloon and attach steel fixing for nylon threads.
- Weld steel leg piece and fix to seat piece with fixing bolts and aluminium rods.
- Make perspex and neoprene cradle and attach camera with bolt into tripod hole on camera base.

Once suit is constructed:
Climb into suit, charge gas cylinder with helium, switch on sensor device and begin tour of site.

During tour of site:
- Stop when balloon begins to inflate. Rest on the seat leg.
- Wind balloon back down when nylon is fully extended.
- Remove stopper to release helium when balloon comes into reach. Fold balloon back into pouch on front of suit, place camera back into position on steel leg and continue journey around site until the next event.

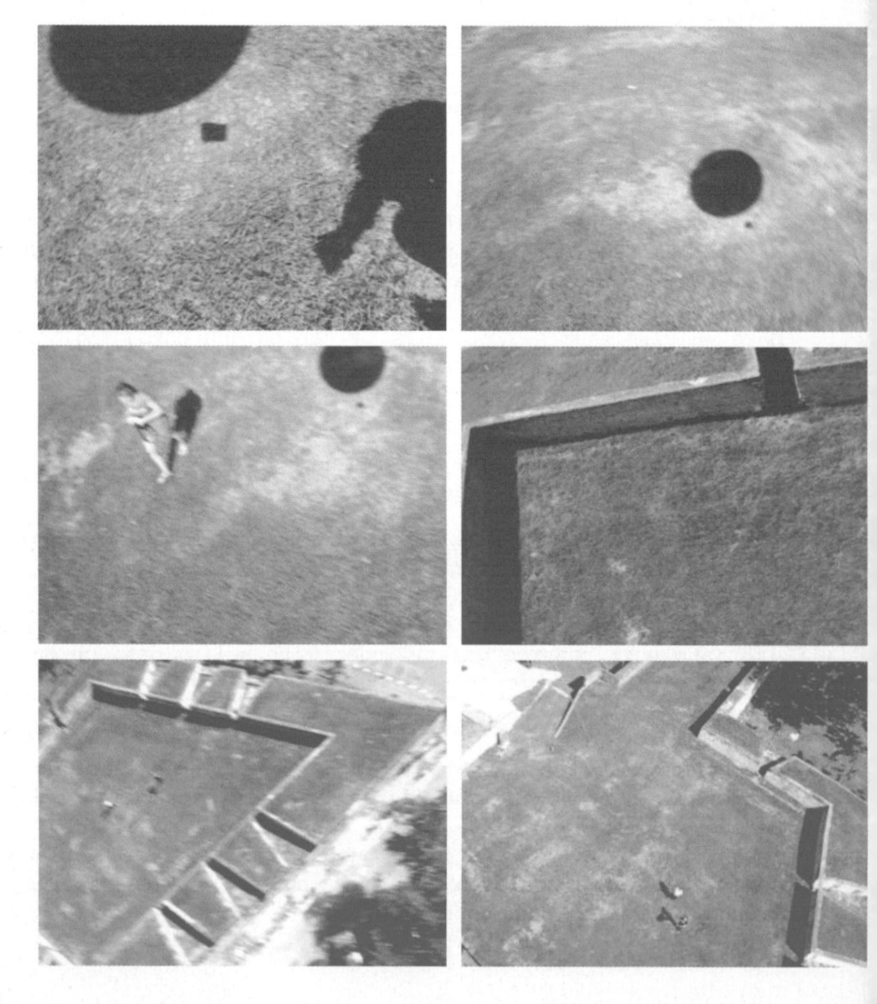

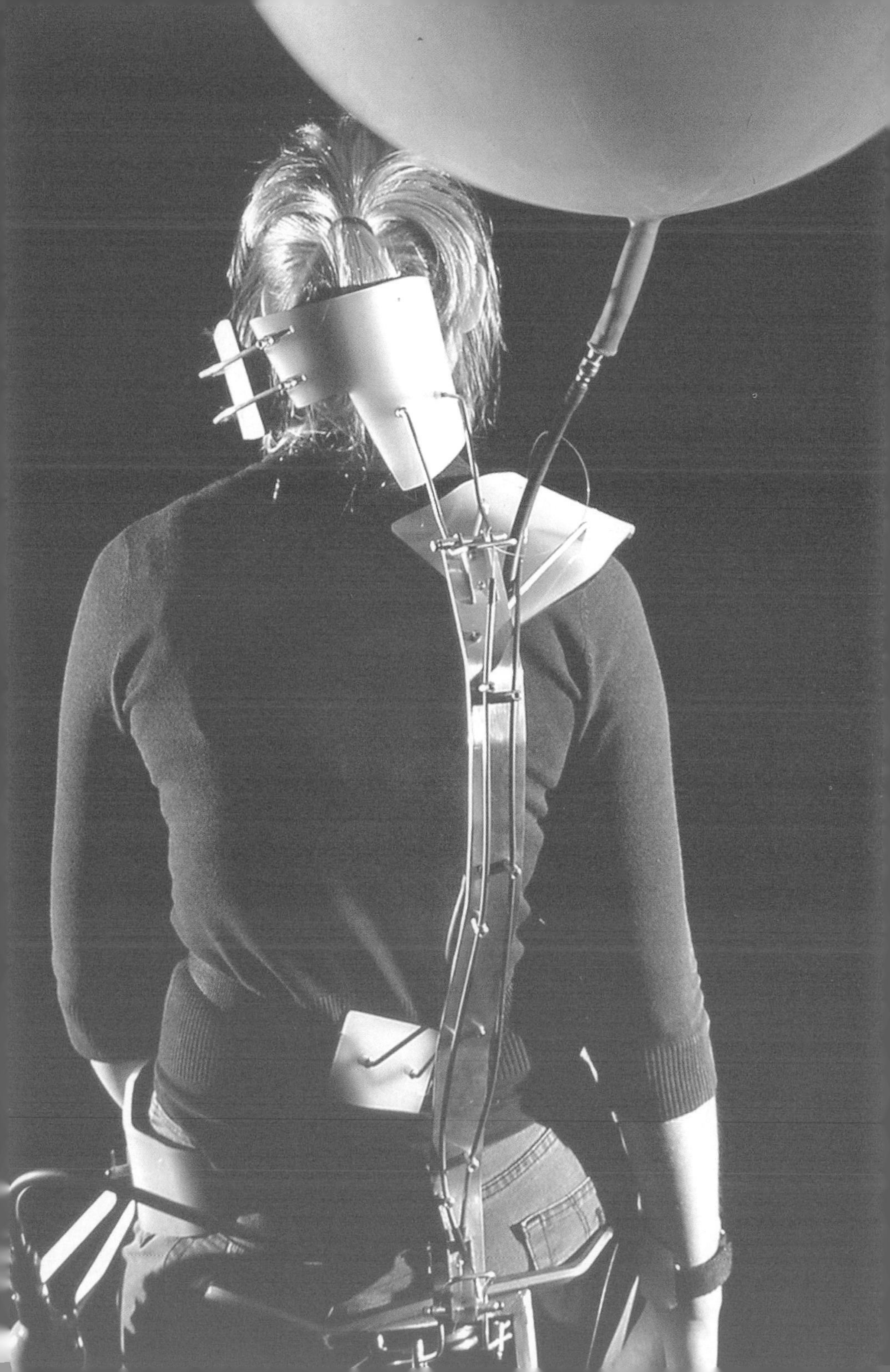

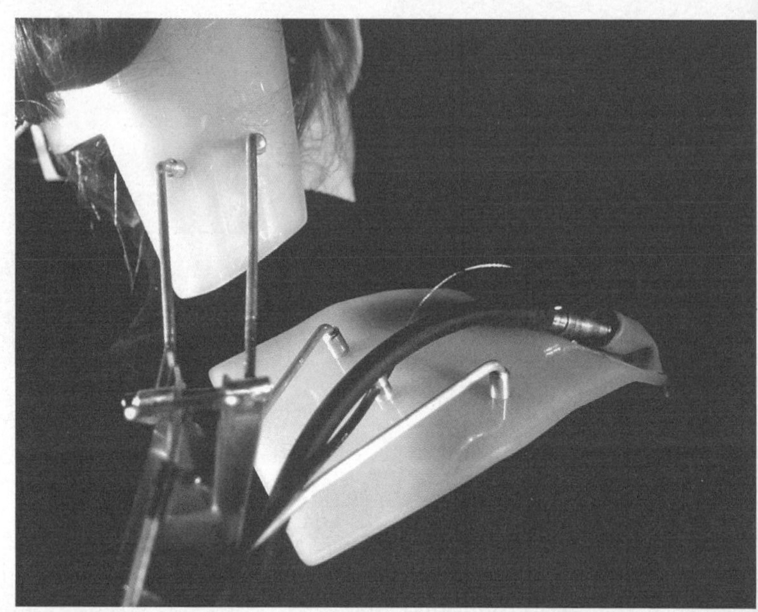

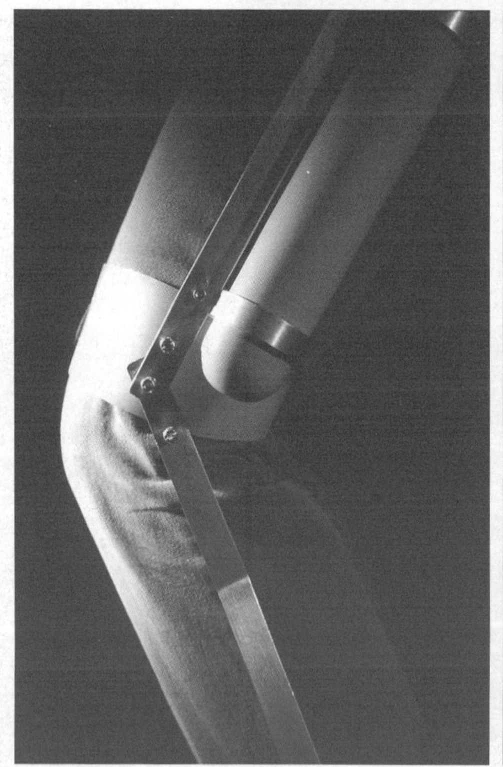

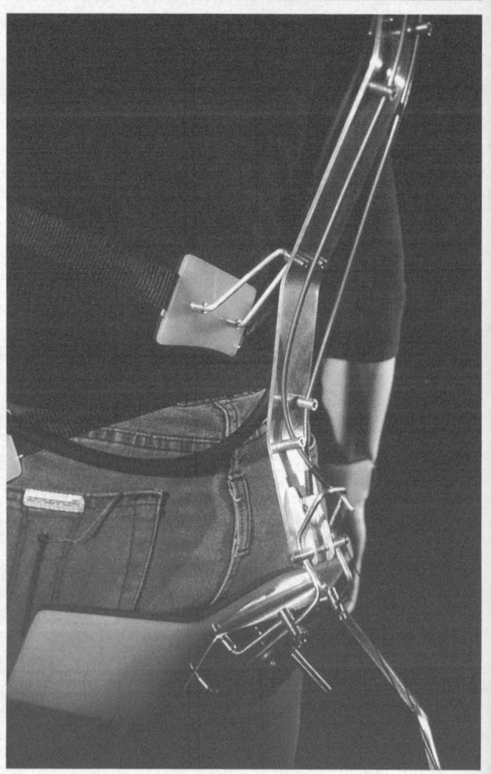

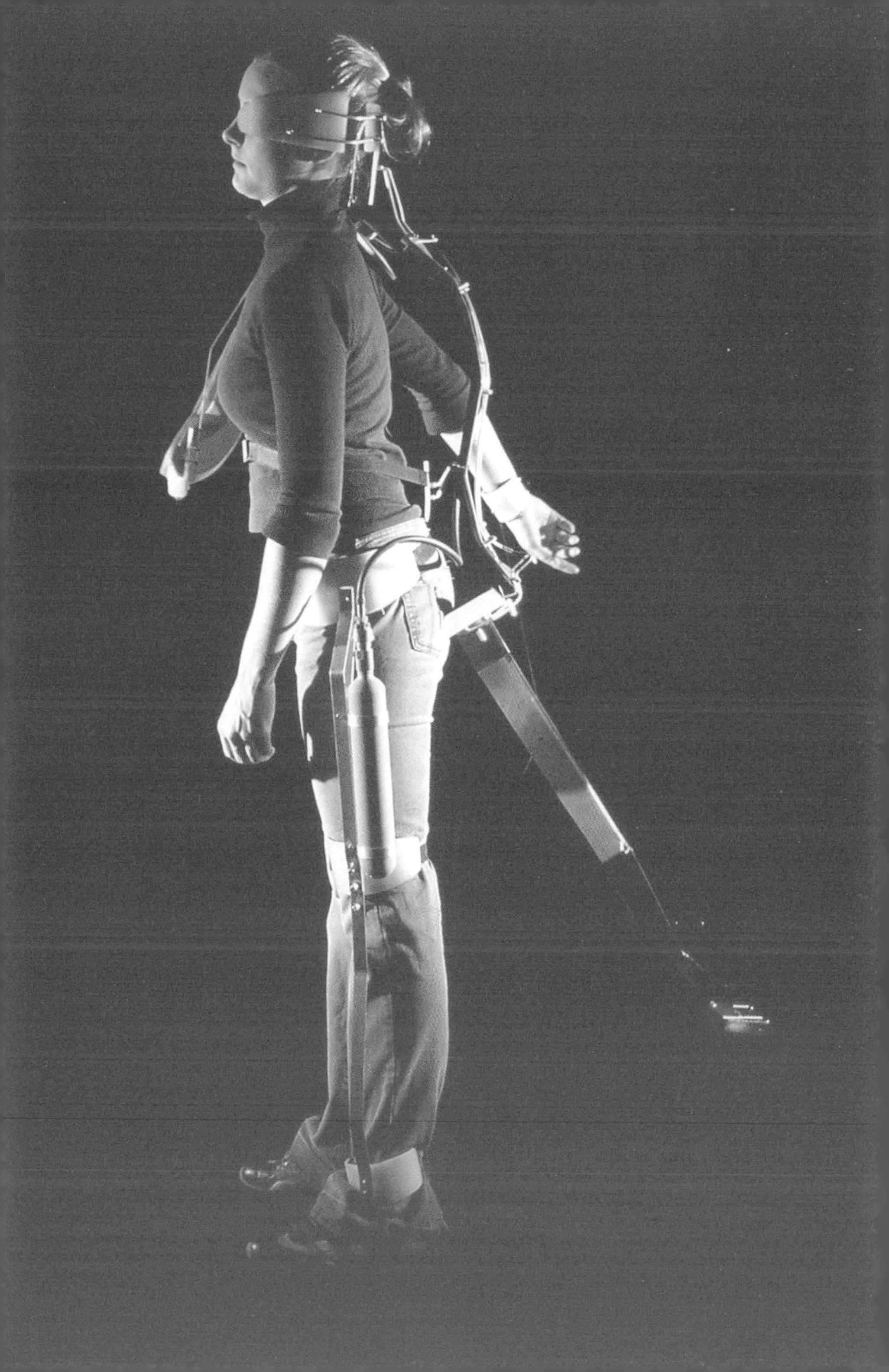

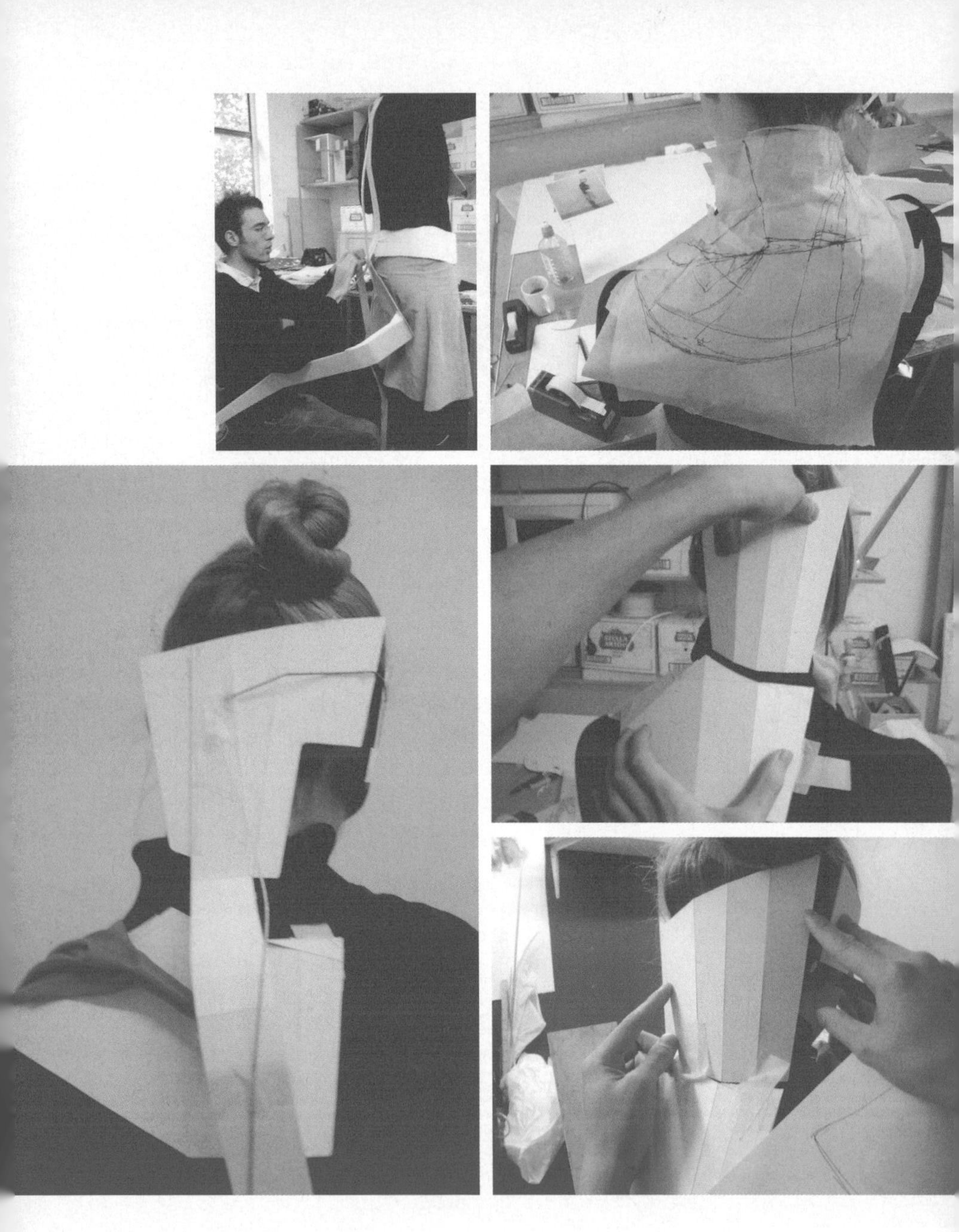

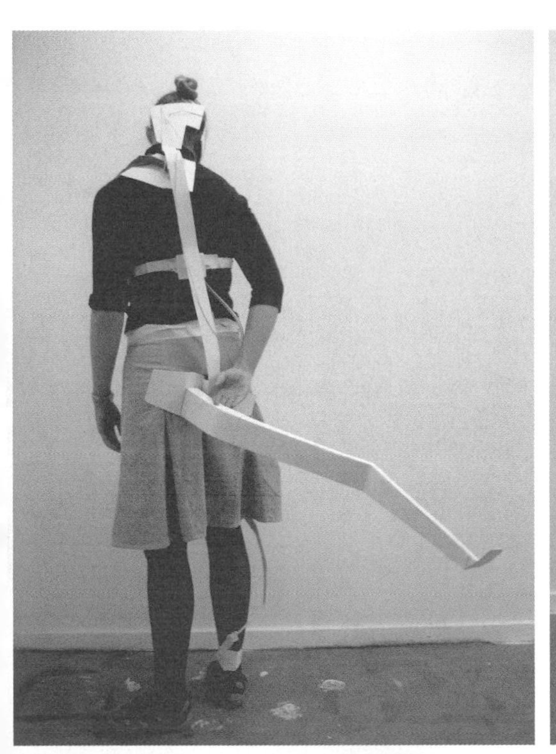

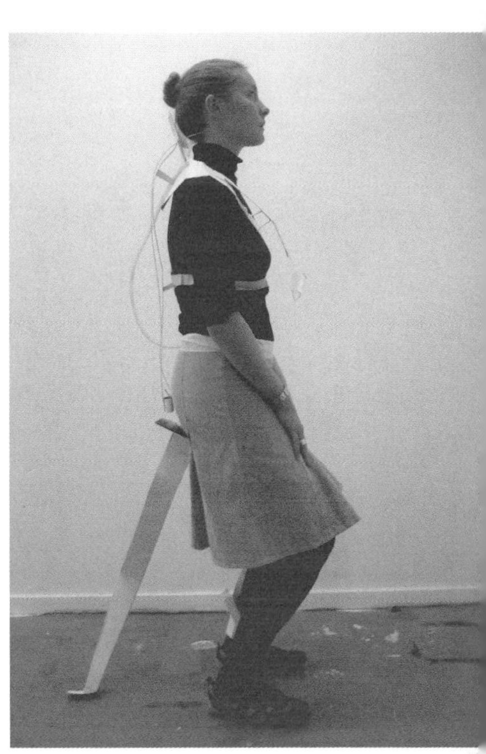

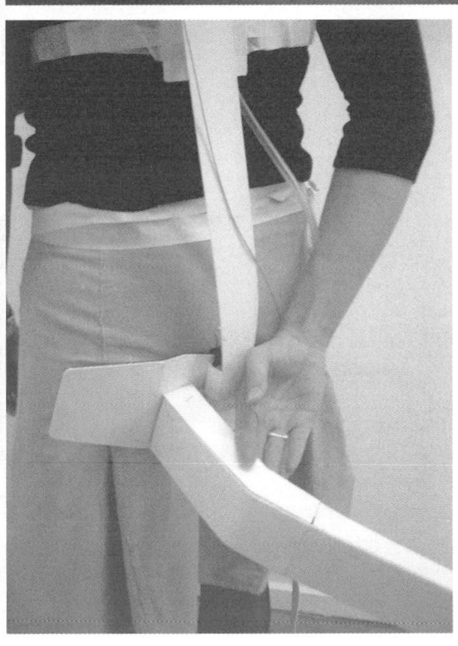

Designers: Alina White, Rene Nedergaard + Ed Lipton

Device: Talking Feathers

Function: Recording conversations

Concept:
The air movements of a conversation are captured by a matrix of feathers, causing varying degrees of movement. The device responds to intimate conversation from two persons to a lively animated group debate. Louder conversation includes movement in a greater number of feathers, in turn triggering sensors which convert the movement into electric impulses. At this point, pumps activated by the impulses hiss cold water onto a hot plate to create steam. The condensation of steam turns the clear perspex surface into an opaque image plane; shadows of feathers captured, an abstraction of the conversation is recorded.

Dimensions: 350 x 680 x 1100mm

Fabrication + Assembly time: 2 weeks

Materials:
18no white feathers between 240 and 280mm length
11no rigid metal rods 0.8mm diameter 600mm length
4no threaded rods 12mm diameter 180mm length
9no metal beads 6mm diameter
9no metal rings 25mm diameter
9no DC motors, cogs and fins
9no small lead weights
9no night light candles
3no perspex sheets 350 x 400mm
1no perspex block 50 x 35 x 300mm
1no water tray 350 x 90 x 50mm deep
1no metal sheet 500 x 350 x 0.6mm
1no 9V battery pack
Metal flat 3 x 20mm cut to varied lengths
Metal box sections 20mm cut to varied lengths
Plastic tubing
Copper tape
Copper solid core electrical wire

Fabrication + Assembly:
Feather Matrix:
- Group and tie together feathers into 9no sets.
- Solder metal beads to centre of 9no metal rods.

- Insert rods to feather stems.

Frame:
- Weld frame and rivet metal flats to box sections.

Hot Plate:
- Drill holes for rubber tubing and rivets.
- Bend metal sheet to drawn fold-lines.
- Attach bent sheet to main frame with rivets.
- Insert night lights onto lower shelf of metal plate.

Image plane:
- Drill holes at top corners of perspex sheets.
- Bend remaining 2no rods, 50mm from end to 72 degree angle and 20mm from end to 90 degree angle.
- Insert rods into main frame.
- Hang image plane on rods.

Mechanisms + Electrics:
- Drill holes in perspex sheets for suspension fixings.
- Drill holes for rods in upper sheets, rings in lower sheet.
- Stick copper tape in three parallel strips across rod holes, attach copper wire to create negative connection to battery.
- Insert metal rings into holes in lower plane.
- Solder positive wire connections to each metal ring.
- Attach perspex sheets to main frame using threaded rods.
- Insert feather rods through holes in two perspex sheets.
- Attach lead weights to bottom of rods.

- Drill pump chamber and water flow holes in perspex block.
- Attach cogs and fins to motors, insert pump chambers into block.
- Cut rubber tubing into 9no 600mm lengths.
- Attach rubber tubing to water flow holes.

- Attach water tray to main frame.
- Lower perspex pumping block into water tray.
- Tread rubber tubing through holes at top of hot plate.
- Make electrical connections to motors.

Additional notes:
- Fill water tray with water, connect power pack and switch on night lights 5 minutes prior to use.
- The sensitivity of the device can be altered by adjusting distance between upper and lower perspex sheets or lead weights on the feather rods.

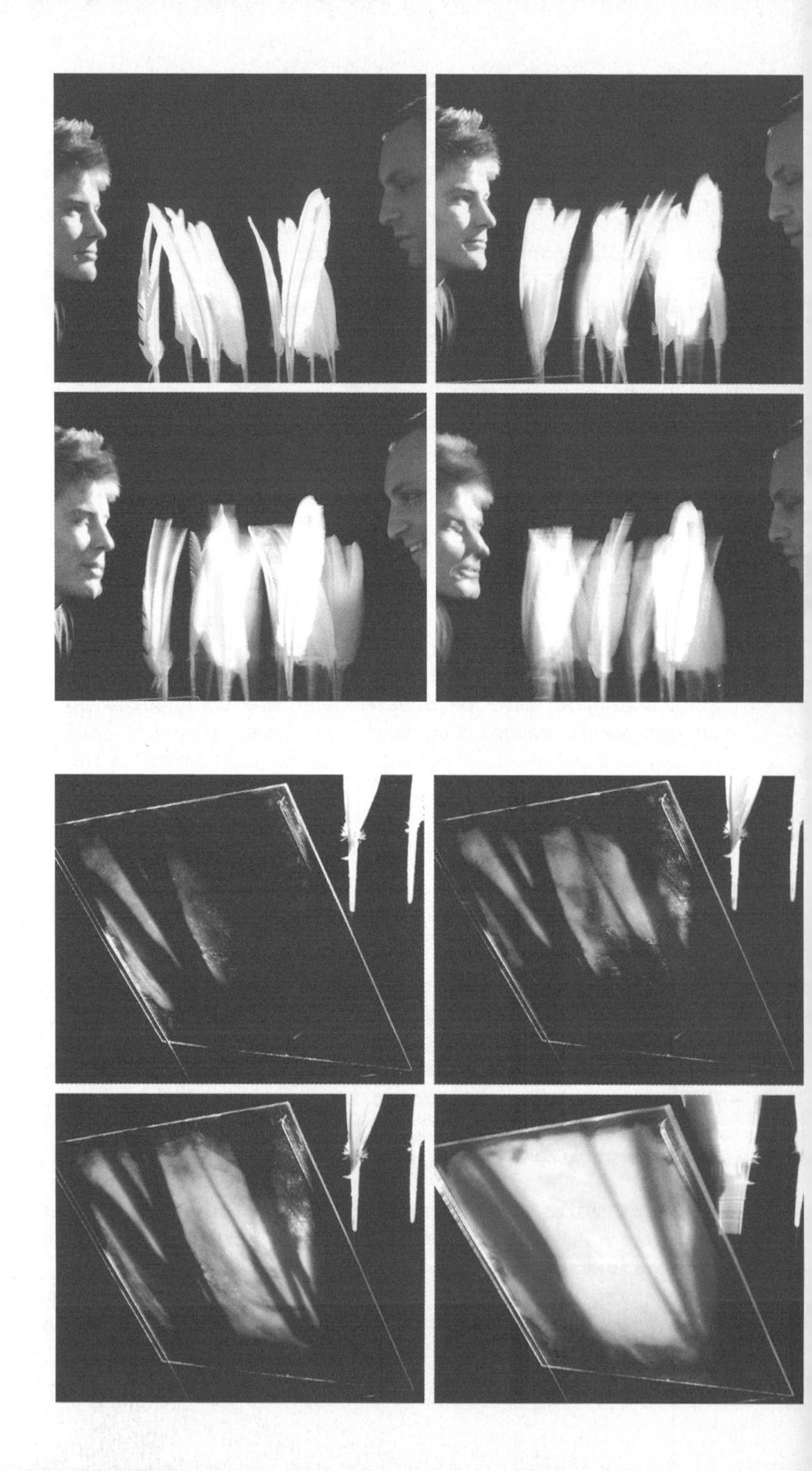

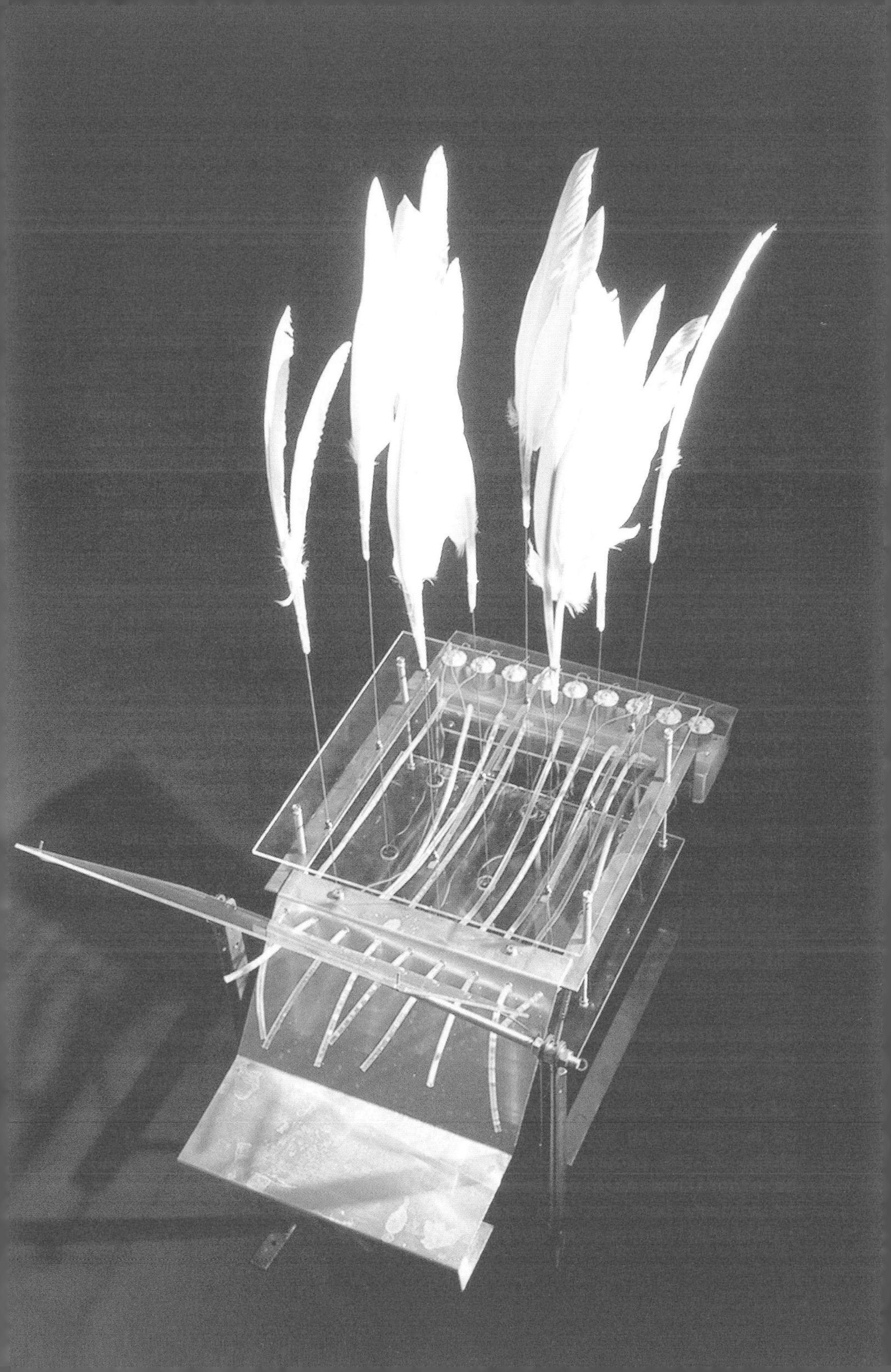

Designer: Rachel Bethan Cruise

Device: The Dry Stone Waller

Function: Stone data input device for the virtual construction of a dry stone wall

Concept:
The Dry Stone Waller is a suggestive piece of software that was written to investigate designing with construction components that have an accepted range of properties. The measurement rig was constructed to digitise the individual characteristics of the construction components for the design program. The nature of data the measurement rig provides, influences the decisions made in generated design proposals. The Dry Stone Waller uses the three-dimensional description and the weight of each stone collected to make decisions about the order of assembly and positioning of the given materials.

The Dry Stone Waller was written as a way of creating proposals that simulate the design and construction decisions made by a traditional dry stone waller. It was not written as an 'expert system' to find optimum design solutions, but as a design procedure that follows a certain methodology of fabrication. The Dry Stone Waller is governed by constraints in the physical world through which a design proposal is created in reality. The design proposal itself then becomes a simulated outcome of the fabrication steps needed to physically make the proposal.

The craft of dry stone walling is the skill of choosing and placing stones to achieve a particular aesthetic and structural outcome. The act of carrying out design decisions and the act of construction are the same process. In making a wall the Dry Stone Waller is solving design decisions that act over two different scales but both are resolved by the choice of a particular stone and its placement in the wall.

In all instances except for the choice of the very first stone the Dry Stone Waller has to consider how a potential stone will fit into the given gap in a partially completed wall. This decision is based on local information about the shape and size of neighbouring stones that create the gap and the size and shape of the proposed stone or stones. This has been described in algorithms as a consideration of how surfaces will interact to achieve best-fit and stability. The second decision that influences the choice of stone is the overall desired shape and size of the completed wall and these are set as design goals given by the user of the design software.

The choice of stone determines both the relationship to neighbouring stones and how it contributes to the achieved height, width and length of the wall. Both decisions vary in importance depending on the location of the gap in the wall. The final stone and to a lesser degree the penultimate stone, in any length of coursing, will be critical in determining the precise length of the wall.

The Dry Stone Waller's approach relies on the understanding of differences between construction components. This design process uses these differences, the sequential or 'tactical' selection and the positioning of components in rows and courses in order to create a proposal that achieves the desired objectives.

Dimensions: 500 x 1500 x 1800mm

Fabrication time: 9 months (fabrication and programming)

Assembly time: 0.5 hours
(frame setup and laser calibration)

Materials:
3D scanner:
Mechanical fluid dispenser's gear box and motor – reclaimed from a skip outside UCL Medical Department
Clock cogs - Old Father Time Clock Centre, Portobello Road
Low voltage laser module - Maplins
USB mini web camera - Maplins
Stepper motor - reclaimed from an Epson printer
Aluminium bar and rod – The Metal Centre, West Midlands
Mild steel bar – The Metal Centre, West Midlands

Scales:
Cast-iron Victorian weighing scales - Camden Passage Antique Market
Clock cogs - Old Father Time Clock Centre, Portobello Road
Carbon track potentiometer - Maplins
perspex - Dean Street, London
Microphone - Maplins
Stepper motor – reclaimed from a skip in Birmingham

Striker:
Brass door bolt - Camden Passage Antique Market

Clock spring - Old Father Time Clock Centre, Portobello Road
Brass flat — The Metal Centre, West Midlands
Mild steel bar and rod — The Metal Centre, West Midlands
12V Solenoid - Maplins
Basic stamp - Parallax

Rig frame:
Aluminium rectangular hollow section - The Metal Centre, West Midlands
Solid square aluminium section - The Metal Centre, West Midlands
Grubscrews - Clerkenwell Screws Ltd. London
Bolts - Clerkenwell Screws Ltd. London

Programming software:
PBasic compiler - Parallax
MatLab version 5.0 - The MathWorks Ltd

Assembly:
The measurement rig combines three instruments held in specific positions on an aluminium frame. The instruments are used to make measurements on stones and the data from the three instruments is read into the stone input program, which is part of the Dry Stone Waller software.

The first instrument is a three-dimensional scanner that uses a laser controlled by the basic stamp and a camera connected to the pc USB port, to measure distances. The instrument is based on a gear box and motor that is used to move the laser in a vertical direction. The stone input program, through the basic stamp, controls the scanner's steeper motor to position the laser at a known angle from the camera and the camera is triggered to take a picture of the laser beam on the surface of the stone. The position of this bright spot is detected in the image by the stone input program. Any changes in the distance between the stone surface and the laser is calculated from the apparent shift of the laser beam detected in the camera image.

The second instrument, the scales, rotates the stone in front of the scanner. The stone input program, through a basic stamp, controls a stepper motor in the scales to rotate the stone a predetermined angle and the laser distance measurement is repeated. Once a complete circumference of the stone has been measured the laser head moves to measure further circumferences to build up a three-dimensional profile of the stone.
The scales are a modified set of cast-iron scales whose original dial was removed and replaced with a series of cogs and

a potentiometer to convert the motion of the dial mechanism into a varying voltage. This signal is read by the Dry Stone Waller via the basic stamp and used to calculate the stone's weight.

The third instrument uses the mechanism of a brass door bolt as a striker to produce a sound from the stone, giving a qualitative parameter that is used to decide the material used in the wall. The stone input program electronically triggers a solenoid in the striker causing the door bolt to tap the stone. A clock spring returns the solenoid armature returns from the surface of the stone to prevent damping of the resulting sound. A microphone is held in the centre of the scales platform, just below the stone, which relays the stone's sound back to the program for analysis. If the sound recorded is above a particular amplitude the stone is accepted by the Dry Stone Waller.

The function of each instrument requires a particular spatial arrangement. The scales' three feet are located in milled out slots in the base of the aluminium frame and the stone to be measured is placed on the scales weighting platform. The size of the stone will determine the height at which the striker is positioned above the stone, and the height at which the scanner is bolted to the opposite side of the rig's frame.

The Dry Stone Waller's stone input program is then run. The program requires the distance from the laser module in the scanner to the centre of the scales' rotational platform in order to calibrate the measurements taken by the scanner. The stone is firstly tapped by the striker and if it is found acceptable a weight reading will be taken and the three-dimensional data collected. Once the process is complete the three-dimensional data and the weight of the stone are stored as variables amongst data from many other stones. The weight and three-dimensional data is used to select a particular stone for positions in the virtual construction of a dry stone wall.

Additional notes:
The Dry Stone Waller software was developed alongside the construction of the measurement rig. In order to develop the software, virtually generated stones were used to test the algorithms. Once the rig was completed data from the measured stones replaced these algorithmically generated stones.

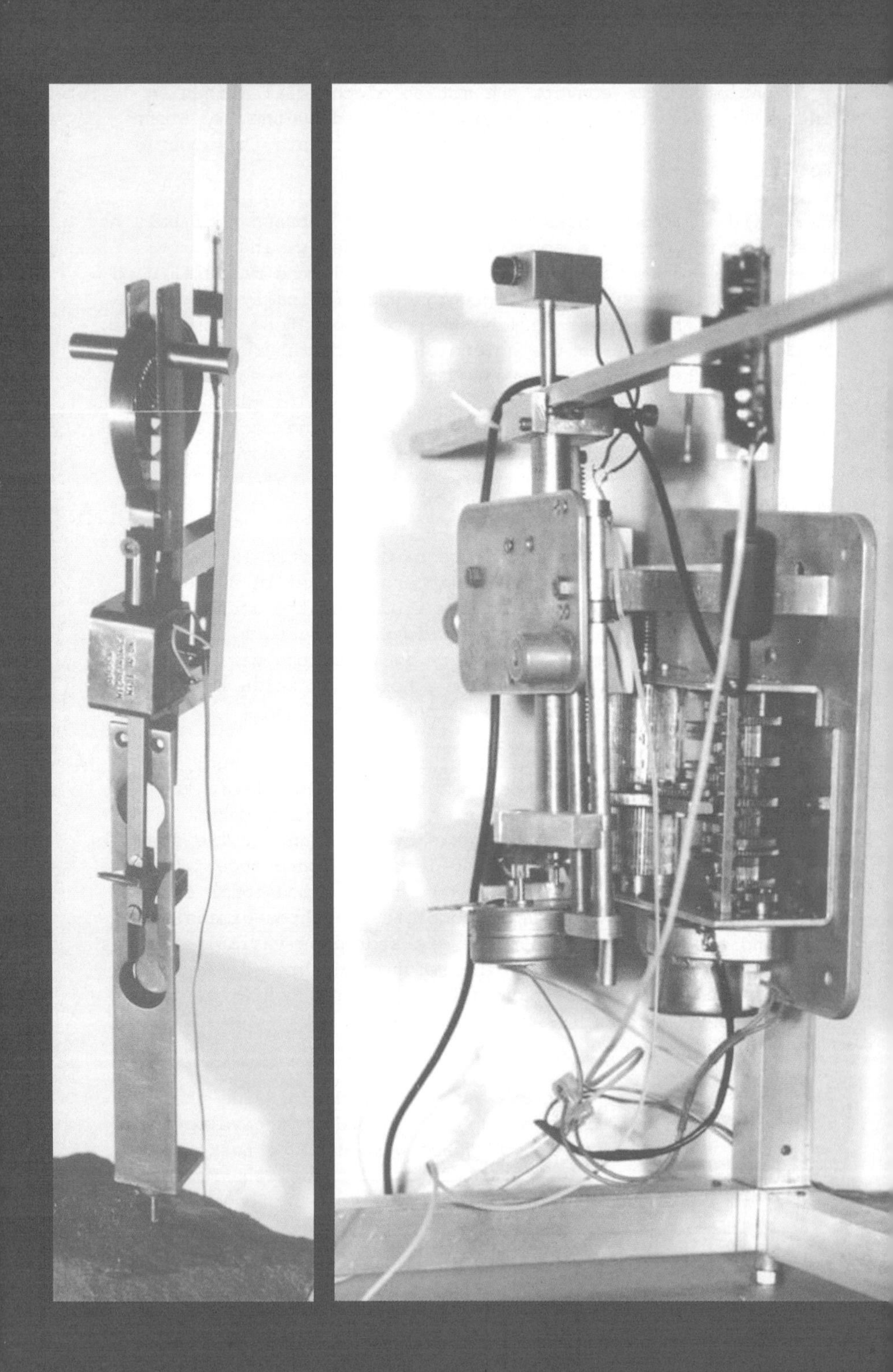

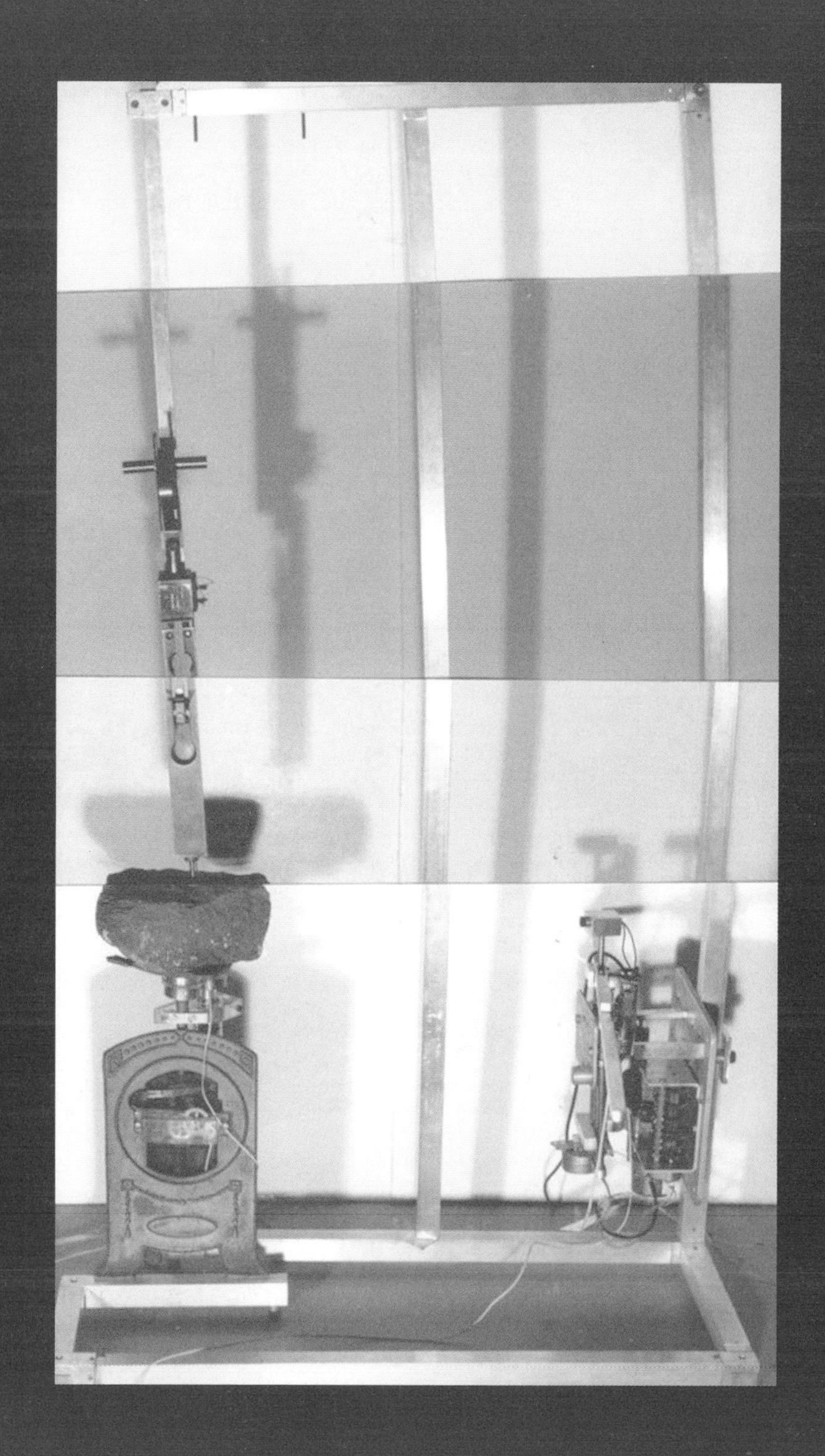

Designer: John Craske

Device: The Shipping Forecast

Function: Transposing the shipping forecast

Concept:
The device is generated from the postal communication between designer, 'a conceiver of ideas', and assembler, 'the recipient of instructions and parts'. The recording device is thus a transposition of both the enigmatic shipping forecast and the irrepressible disparity between designer (intent) and assembler (realisation). Each component of the device represents a different strand of the shipping forecast and is sent in the post, accompanied a day later with instructions, to the assembler. Despite the burdens associated with such a delay, the fabricator endeavours to assemble the machine to the best of his abilities and in doing so reveal a 'truer' understanding of the shipping forecast. The forecast however resists such an interpretation and represents the unfathomable, a set of infinite codes and combinations, modelled only incrementally and never conclusively.

At 5:07 and 12:48 I sit at the machine, listen to the ensuing forecast read from Radio 4 and press the corresponding keys. The machine plots the recording onto a graph that, along with incidental ink stains it receives on the way, is also sent by mail. Each key, or representative, is attached to a point on the curtain of my bedroom window and moves accordingly. Light from passing traffic or the sun at dawn is filtered through this interface and thus the conditions of my room become dependant upon the conditions of the shipping regions. Funded by a glow from inside, passer-bys are exposed to my curious behaviour.

Dimensions: 960 x 362 x 158mm

Fabrication time: Endless. Currently 168 days, equating to 1080 hours labour working 9 hours a day, 5 days a week.

Assembly time: Endless plus 1-2 days (or the time it takes for a package to be received).

Materials:
Piano base
Piano pedal base and pedals
Wooden royal mail package support frame

2 empty cans of baked beans
1 wooden clock with mechanism
1 metre of wooden dowel spacers
1no paint roller
1no end of a mop
Piano hammers
Piano levers
Piano keys (both whole tone and semitone)
2 metres of string
2 wooden bed wheels
4 blackboard pulley wheels
1 pen
1 curtain rail
3 springs
2 doorknobs
35 brass screws
20 brass nuts
16 brass wing nuts

Fabrication:
Many of the articles employed are used in their unrefined state. Before they are parcelled to the assembler however, they are labelled and prepared with the necessary holes, fixings or hooks. Upon hearing the forecast the conceiver may wish to fashion a key with a particular turning span or stiffness, relative to whatever it is he wishes it to model. All articles before being sent in the post are packaged appropriately and subject to the correct stamp fee.

Assembly:
- Construct a base from two parts of a piano.
- Join together with two lengths of timber onto which wind an old parcel frame.
- Attach the clock, or engine, to the rear of this frame and wind into the baked bean cans and paint roller.
- Fasten the clutch to the spring-loaded piano lever over the bed wheel and up to the spring release in the clock.
- As subsequent keys arrive fasten with screws and join to components or mechanisms as delineated in the instructions.

Additional notes:
All materials were sourced from skip on Frognal Lane, dumping area on West End Lane, miscellaneous spring and hook collection in small drawer of wardrobe, window mechanism on 2nd floor of house, cleaning cupboard and draining board.

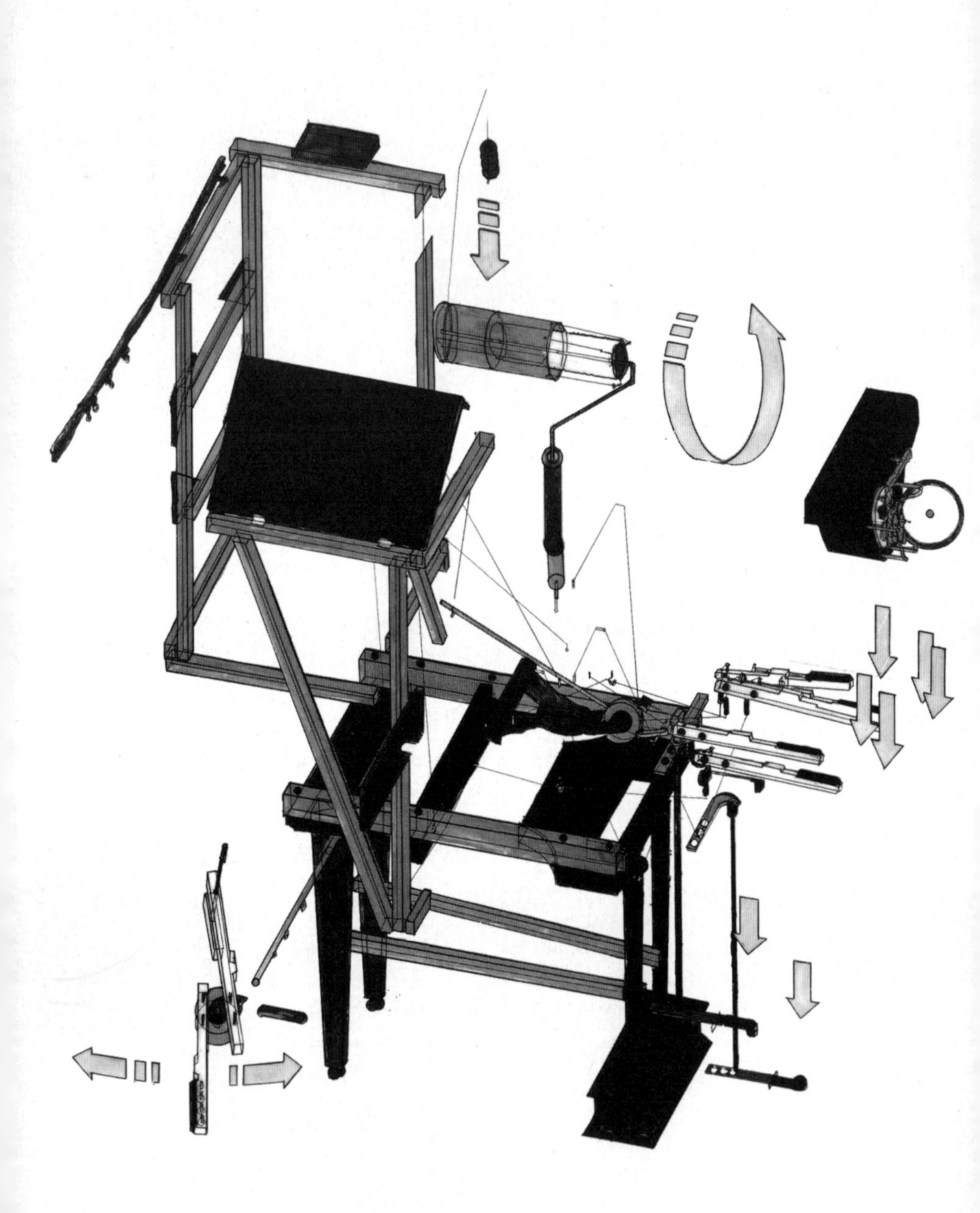

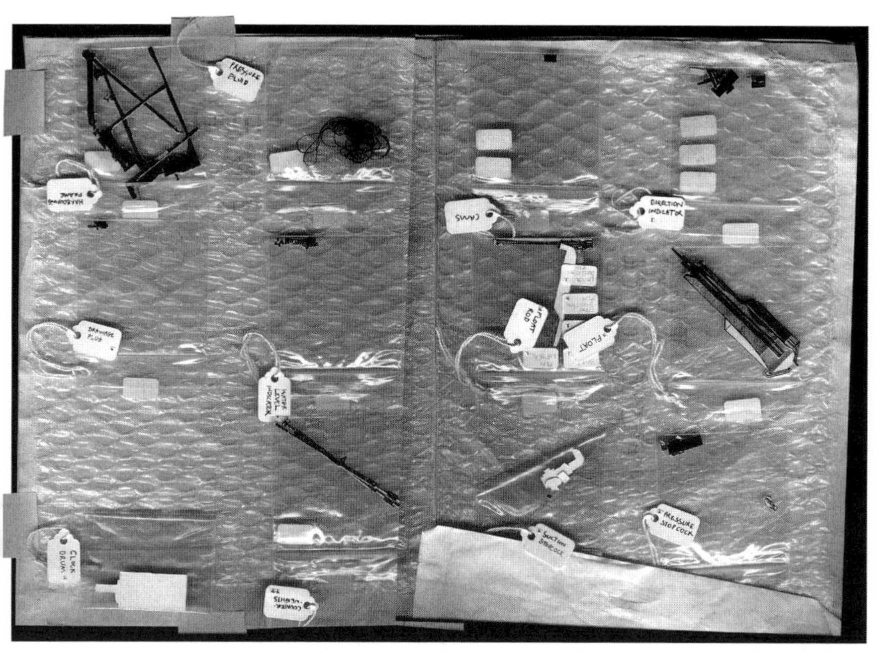
PRESSURE PLUG
HARROWING FRAME
CAMS
DIRECTION INDICATOR
DRAINAGE PLUG
FLOAT ROD
FLOAT
WATER LEVEL INDICATOR
CLOCK DRUM
SUCTION STOPCOCK
PRESSURE STOPCOCK

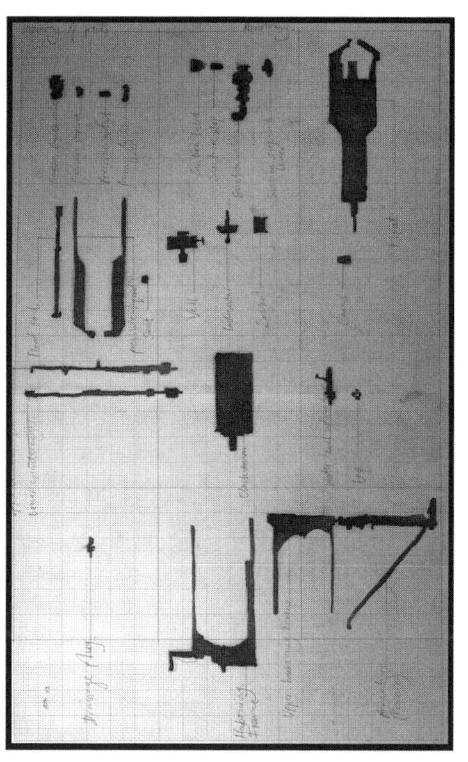

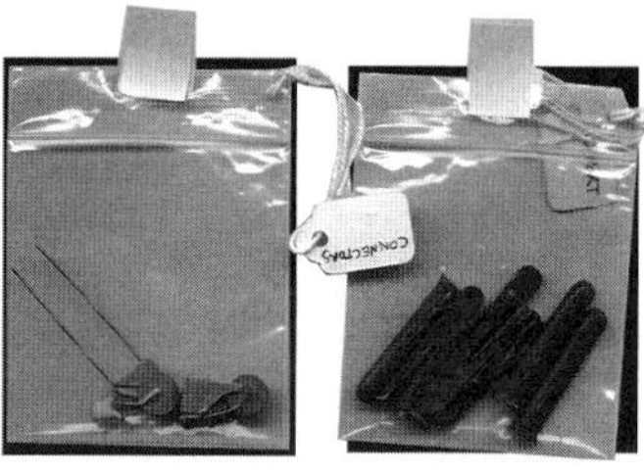
CONNECTORS

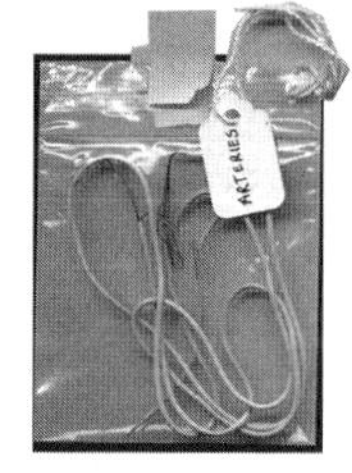
ARTERIES

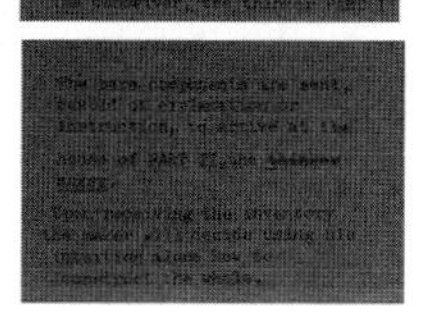

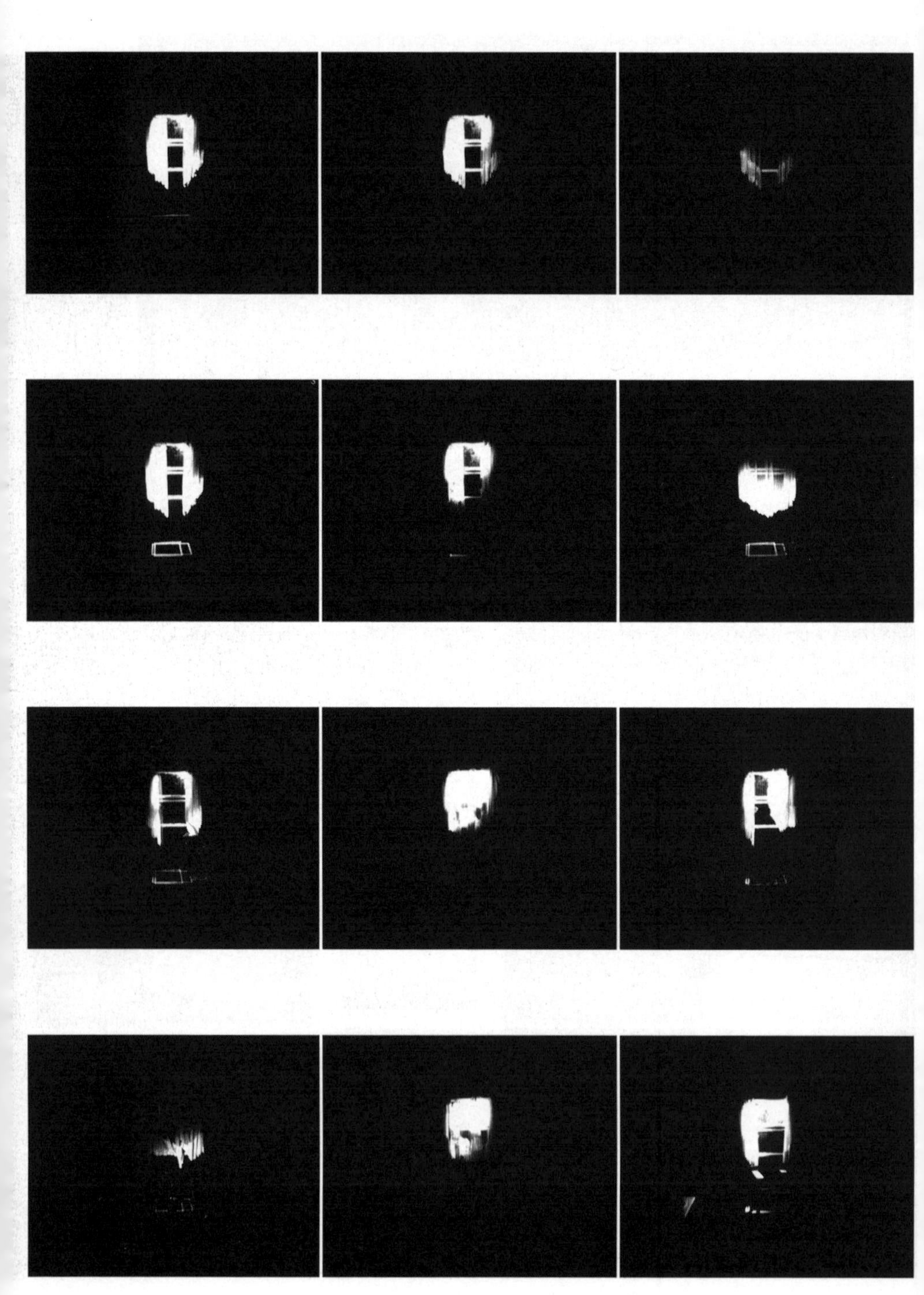

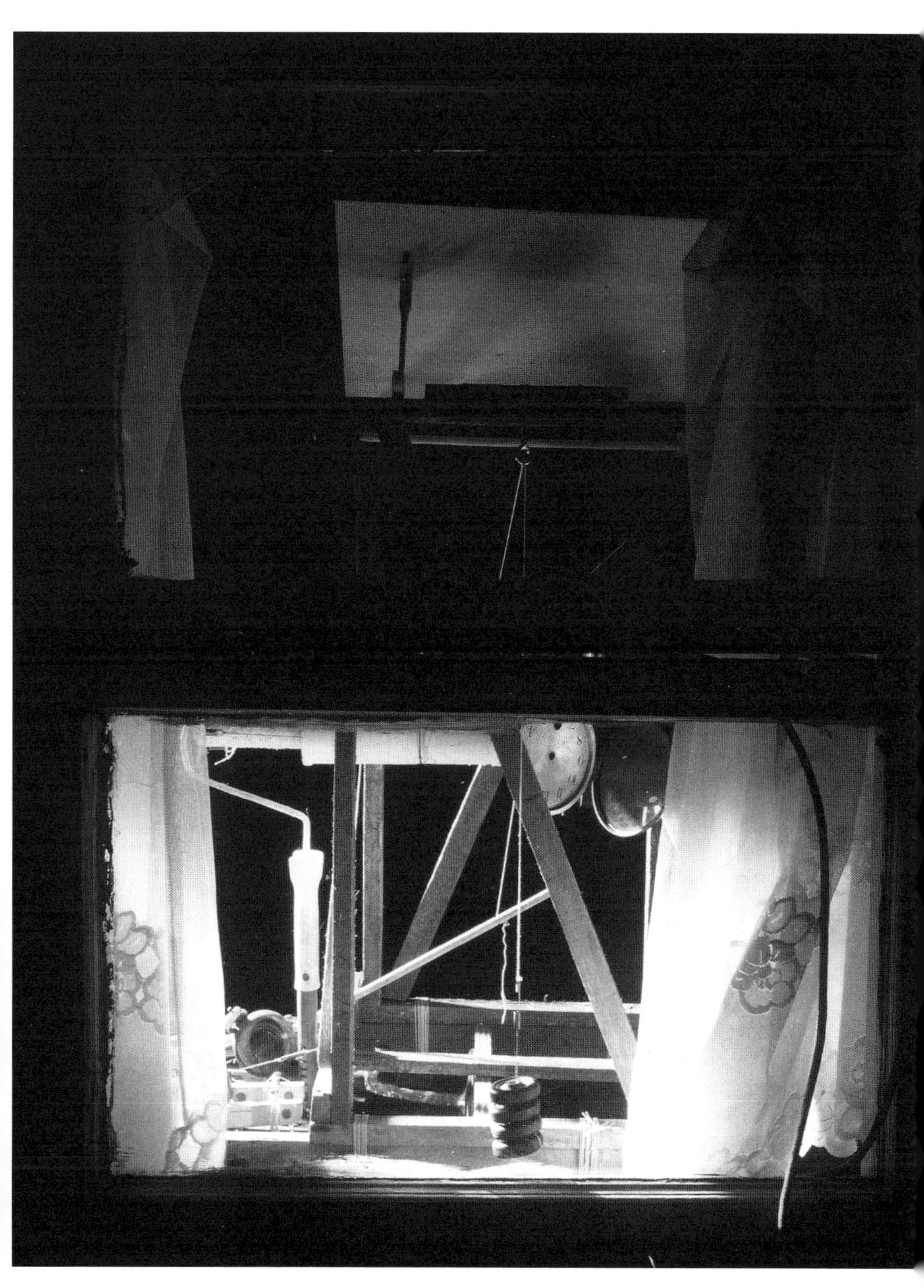

Designer: Neil Tomlinson

Device: Thorax Cybernation

Function: Self-designing temporal space machine

Concept:
The attraction to Fruit Fly Drosophilia Melanogaster was its ability, through the pre-programming of its components, to bring forth strange monsters known as Homeotypic Mutants - a newly hatched fly, for example, have antennae where legs would conventionally grow or genitalia where its head should be.

This concept proved most engaging in a spatial sense because while biologists have produced these monsters in an attempt to further their knowledge of the automatic ordering process during growth, the unpredictability of mutants produced using essentially the same kit of parts will literally bring billions of possible working, living and moving dynamic combinations. If this process could be transferred to human scale construction, then a machine could be produced whose physical dynamic, although very finitely controlled at component level, would produce an array of completely unpredictable overall structures: essentially a self-designing machine whose individual elements and universal junctions have been previously carefully designed, therefore ensuring a perfectly finished construction.

Dimensions: 1410 x 870 x 764mm

Fabrication time: 73 days

Assembly time: 3.5 hours

Materials:
200 x 110 x 4mm aluminium plate
5m stainless steel flexible cable
1200 x 1200 x 6mm clear perspex
1200 x 1200 x 3mm clear perspex
12no Martonair 15mm diameter pneumatic cylinders and 4mm t connectors
2no Martonair 25mm diameter pneumatic cylinders and 4mm t connectors
36no 22mm, 3mm diameter low resistance springs
60 brass male/female straight shaft hinge connectors
4no 74mm, 5mm medium resistance springs

46no M4 stainless steel bolts with nuts and sprung steel washers
6no 12mm black rubber tap washers
6no chromium eyes
4no stainless steel 40mm x 20mm hinges
36no M5 bolts stainless steel bolts with nuts and washers
12no 10mm brass electrical connectors
4no 1000mm carbon fibre rods
4no 1000mm fibre glass rods
8no 120 degree polypropylene 4mm kite connectors
8no rubber boot 4mm kite stop ends
6no M8 Hex head stainless steel bolts
6no chromium 12mm internal diameter ball-bearing race rings
8no stainless steel U brackets
4no yacht pulley reels
10m long grey 3 core electrical wire
3m long white single core electrical wire
3m long brown single core electrical wire
1no roll of black insulation tape
1no Mitsubishi sequence controller
1no custom-made solenoid valve field bus
10m clear nylon pneumatic tube
12no Excell 22M-48M493/2 sub-base solenoid valves
1no compressor unit rated 4 bar.
4no 100 x 100 x 500mm blocks of aluminium
1no 20 port electric connector

Fabrication:

- Perspex vacuum formed thorax shell components are cut to required size and shaped to form the main three thoracic body assembly units.
- Digitally milled aluminium components to form wing brackets and reassembly sections.
- All components are then bolted to thoracic floor and shell components to form the complete twenty-one separate units.

Assembly:

- Assemble each of the twenty-one separate components in any one of over 18 billion combinations.
- Connect field bus to compressor and power up the compressor to fill cylinder reservoirs.
- Connect and switch on sequence controller to allow the cylinders to expand and retract in sequence with the walk and fly pre-programmed muscle movements.

34
7

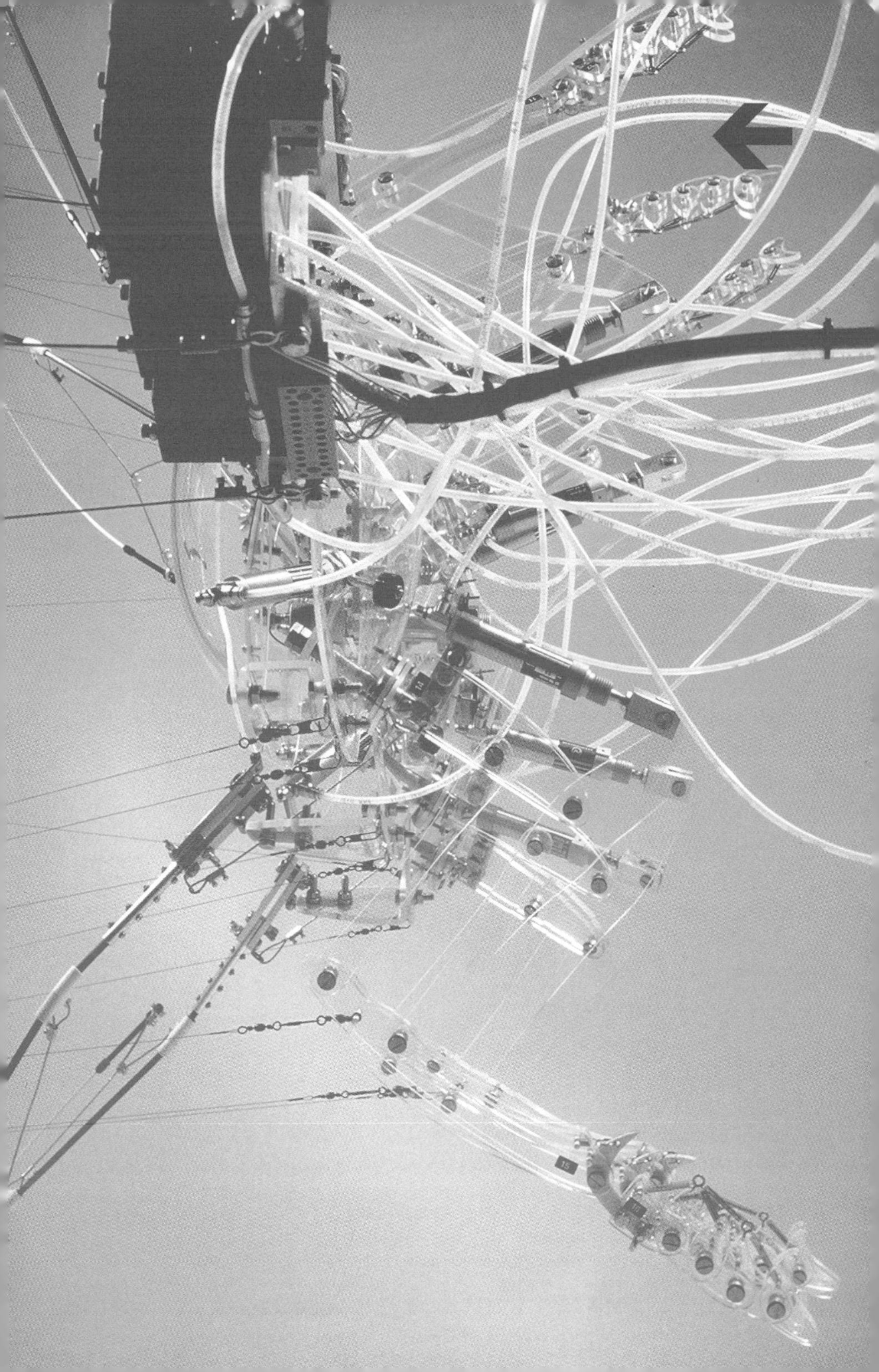

Designer: Jimmy Kim

Device: Through the Looking Lens

Function: Transforming a window into a lens

Concept:
The lens serves to alter the window interface, magnifying the exterior view perceived through the glass.

Through a series of cavities in an acrylic block the device alters the view through a window. Each block of acrylic is affixed using suction cups that temporarily allow the device to be carried to other sites.

A series of bags of water and a pulley system fill each lens through a siphoning effect. In effect the lens grows through an increase in water contained within it. The device was modelled on the observation of bacteria growing on petri dishes, the transparency of the surface being of particular interest. After a period of time the water gradually evaporates off the device, in effect 'killing' the growing lenses, reducing the magnification of the window.

Each set of lens cavities was considered as a colony of bacteria growth: some lenses were very large, others fed off each other, some did not have any access to water so therefore existed only as cavities. Over a period of time these cavities leaked water and the leakage fed other lens cavities. This produced a viewing device that was both subtle and unpredictable in its nature; no two experiments were ever the same.

Dimensions: Differing dimensions, its space is limited to the size of the window. Maximum diameter of lens cavity 30mm.

Fabrication time: 1 week

Assembly time: 5-7 minutes for window 2 x 3m (this can vary)

Materials:
Acrylic slab 25mm
Drill bits machined from existing drill parts
Transparent plastic used to create bags
Acrylic screws (machined using 10mm and 5mm dowel)

Transparent 20lb fishing wire
Transparent nozzles to affix to lens cavity holes
Transparent piping 0.2mm diameter (approx 6m)

Fabrication:
Tools:
- Mark a circle on the ends of routing bits using a pencil, on both sides.
- Using a grinding machine reduce each bit to its desired shape.
- Chamfer the edge of the drill bit tip to ensure that it can cut in a clockwise direction.
- Polish each drill bit and harden the newly formed tip using oxy-acetylene torch.

Lenses:
- Mark on acrylic block points to drill lenses.
- Using tools created, drill into acrylic block ensuring plenty of oil to lubricate and cool acrylic block during drilling.
- Using a 5mm drill bit drill into acrylic block vertically through the side of the block, a length adjacent to the lens drilled.
- Using a 0.9mm drill bit drill through the lens into the adjacent 5mm diameter hole using plenty of oil and much care.
- Repeat for a desired number of holes and lenses.
- Drill holes on back of acrylic block (approx 10mm deep) for the suction cups to be attached to.
- Using superglue fix suction cups ensuring they are level with the back of the acrylic block.

Acrylic screws used to fix acrylic sheets:
- Using a tap and die set and plenty of oil.
- Carefully thread the dowel to create a screw.
- Ensure that the screws are able to affix to the acrylic blocks and hold them tightly together (ensuring water tightness within the lens cavities).
- Cut screws to desired length (approx 35mm) and create a small cut into each end for a screwdriver to be applied.
- Using oxy-acetylene torch polish the screws making them transparent.

Pulley system and water bags:
- Using polythene bags and a plastic heat strip machine.
- Cut bags to desired size (approx 15 x 10mm) and heat ends to enable it to hold water.
- Affix eyelets to each of the four corners.
- Cut a semicircular piece using 10mm acrylic block.

- Polish and then affix onto suction cups (20mm diameter).

'Lab' box:
- Using MDF 0.7mm thick create box.
- Compartmentalise the interior using foam core.
- Glue felt into compartment covering entire interior of box.
- Attach brass hinges and apply veneer.
- Polish exterior and apply a coat of varnish.

Assembly:
- Affix pulley system on window using suction cups.
- Attach fishing wires to water bags and to pulley system.
- Arrange colony of lenses on window using suction cups.
- Affix nozzles to lens colonies and transparent piping to water bags.
- Fill system methodically with water ensuring that a siphoning effect is achieved with the lenses.
- Allow system to reach equilibrium.

Additional notes:
The device itself weighed about 4kgs.

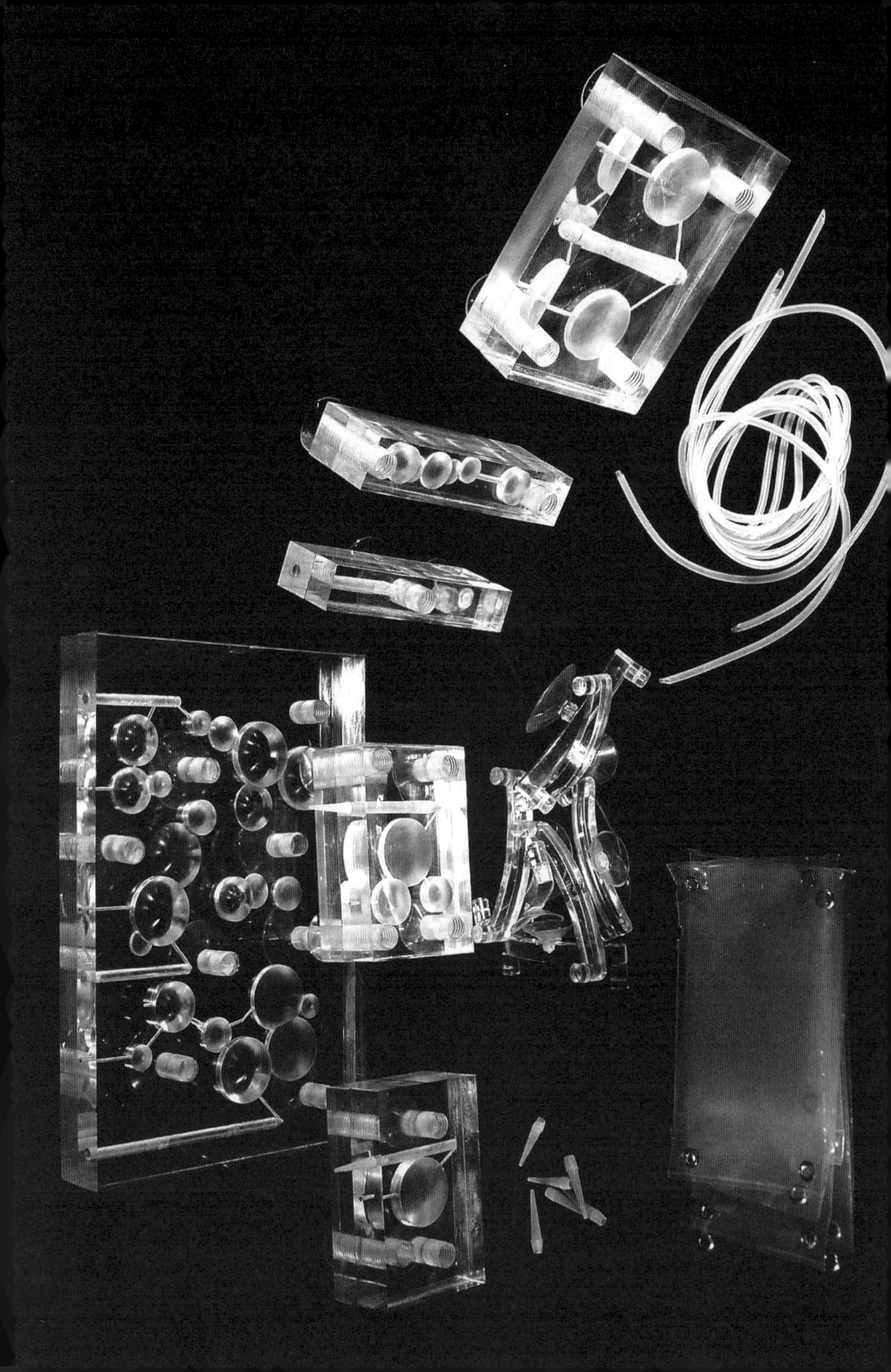

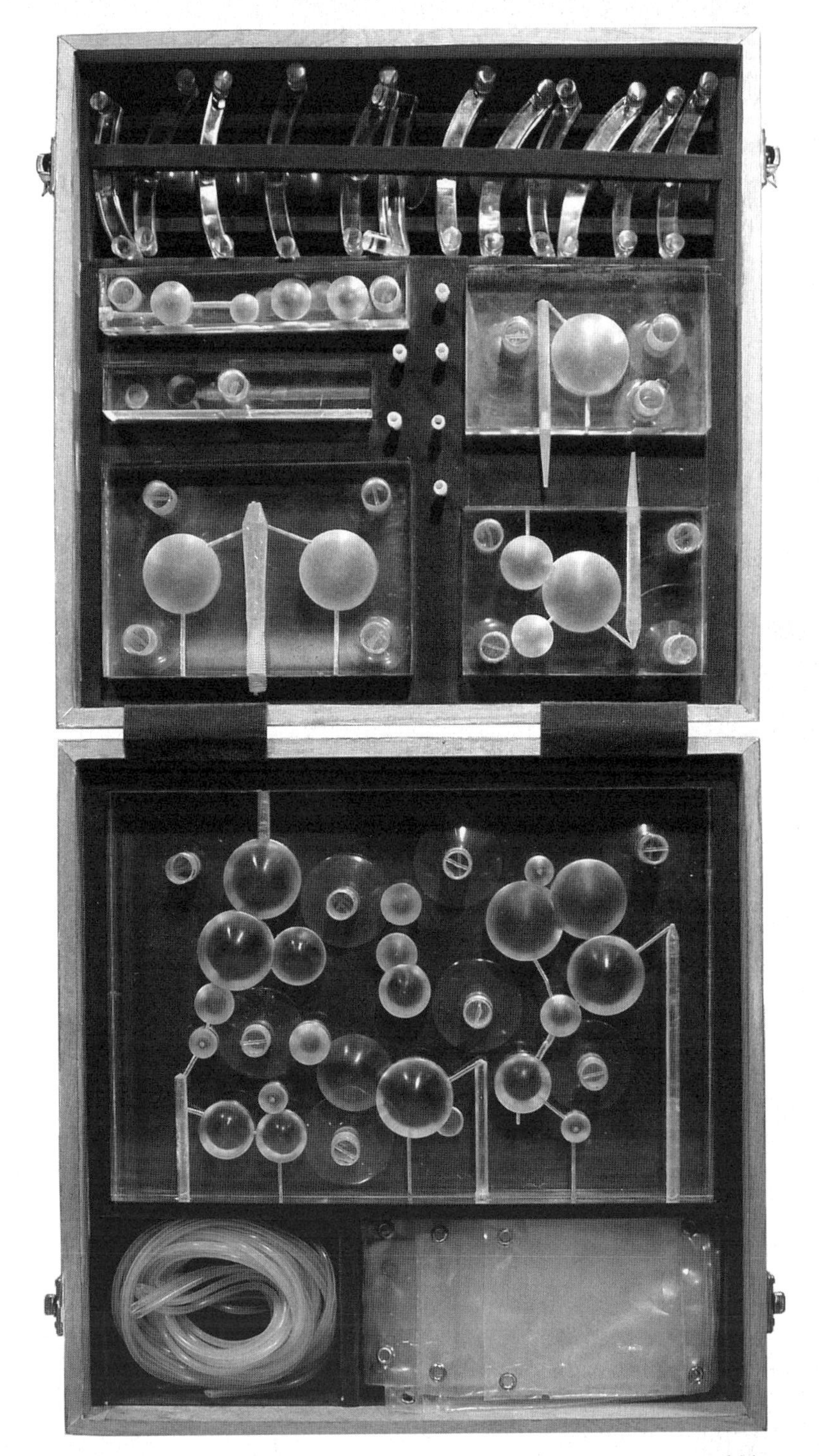

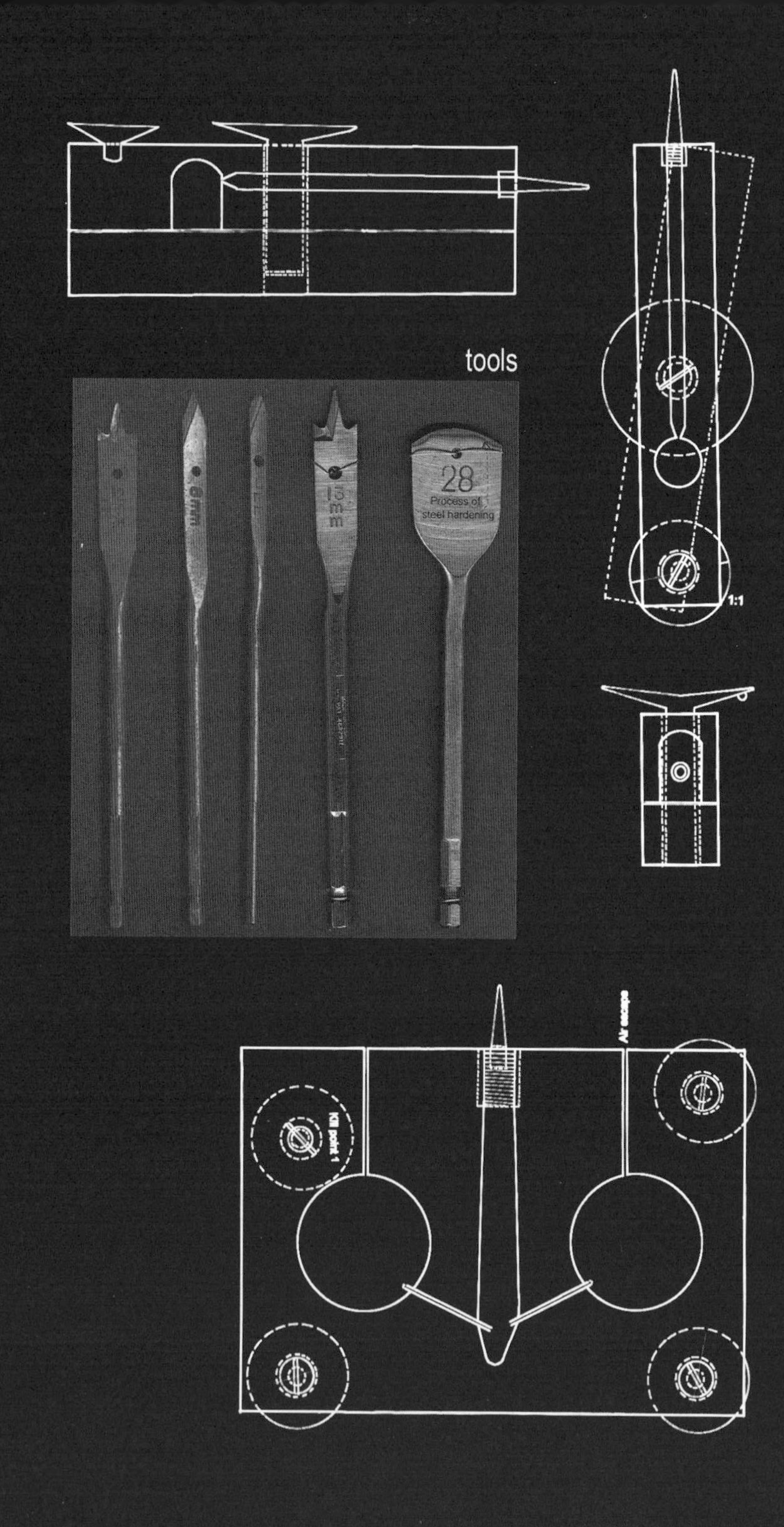
tools
6mm
13 mm
28
Process of
steel hardening
1:1
Air escape
Kill point 1

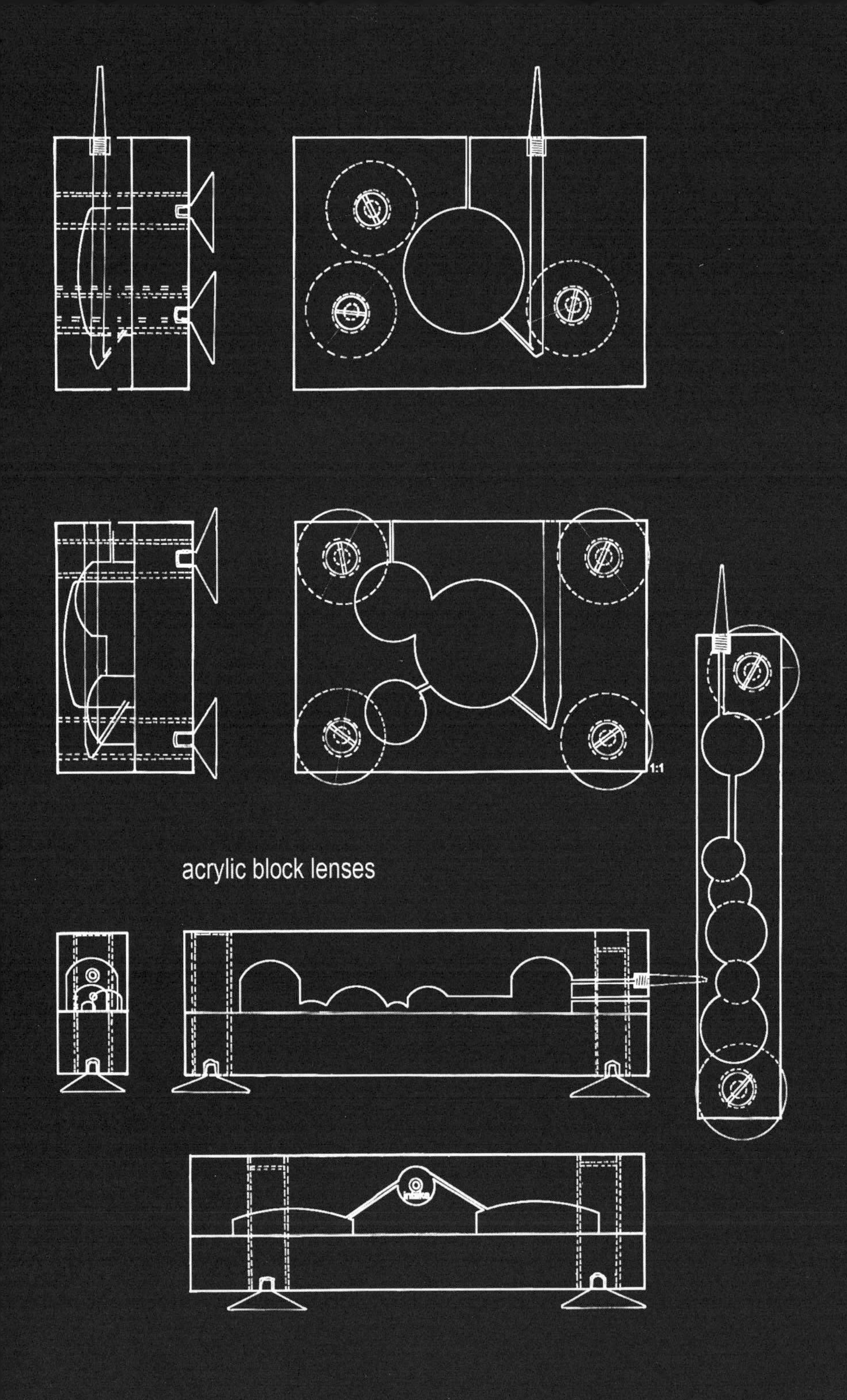
1:1
acrylic block lenses

Designer: Geraldine Holland

Device: Transient

Function: Creating constant and random movement with light

Concept:
The device investigates the making of transient spaces. Pendulums swing arbitrarily, constantly moving through space. They are attracted and repelled by magnets on the end of steel pins. This movement can be manipulated by moving these pins around the grided perspex plate and repositioning them at different heights. LED lights are attached to small batteries positioned on the end of each pendulum. The batteries act as weights for the pendulums. They are also attracted and repelled by the magnets. The pendulums swing with only a gentle touch to create constant and random images of light reflections. In order to visualise the transient movements, the performance has to be recorded through long exposure photography.

Dimensions: 800 x 600 x 300mm

Fabrication time: 1 week

Assembly time: 5 minutes

Materials:
1no clear perspex sheet @ 800 x 300 x 10mm
2no steel flatbar @ 25 x 3 x 1000mm
4no steel piano wire @ 1000 x 3mm, 5 x 1000 x 2mm
4no brass piano wire @ 1000 x 2mm
4no brass sheeting @ 20 x 80 x 0.25mm
4no steel screws 20 x 3mm
4no small 3mm white LEDs
4no small round batteries: C1200
40no cylinderical magnets 3 x 3mm

Fabrication:
- Keep perspex protective film on at all stages of fabrication.
- Mark chosen shapes and cut out using a Band-saw.
- Mark a 20mm square grid on film and drill with 2mm drill bit hole through perspex at each point in the grid.
- Drill holes in perspex for steel legs attachment.
- Sand down edges of perspex with wet and dry paper.
- On top face of the perspex, mark and cut out of film shapes of

surface to be sandblasted.
- Sandblast exposed perspex surfaces.
- Remove film and etch pattern into surface with scalpel.
- Mark up steel for legs and cut ends at angle so as to meet parallel to the perspex edge.
- Cut steel and weld at an angle to achieve a bend.
- Drill a 3.5mm hole through the steel at 10mm from the ends in order to attach to perspex.
- Drill holes for pendulum arms to pass through.
- Bend steel on slight diagonal with bending machine.
- Polish steel legs and piano wire with wet and dry paper.
- Cut 2mm steel piano wire into 10mm strips with pliers and sand ends.
- Cut and bend 3mm steel piano wire with pliers for pendulum.
- Cut and bend 1mm brass piano wire for the pendulum.
- Trim one arm of the LED short enough to hold battery yet not protrude from edge of battery (to avoid circuiting).
- Using long nose pliers loop longer arm of LED through brass piano wire pendulum and neatly bend the brass piano wire around to create a link to the LED.
- Cut pieces of the brass sheet nearly halfway from both sides (do not cut full in half).
- Fold one side in half, both ways and unfold to give small dent in centre for the end of the pendulum to sit.
- Fold the remaining sheet around end of 3mm piano wire arm.

Assembly:
- Screw steel legs to the perspex.
- Fit the 3mm steel piano wire arms through the holes in the legs and glue the ends in to the steel legs.
- Fit the 2mm steel piano wire strips through holes in perspex.
- Attach magnets to piano wire strips.
- Fit the LED around the battery.
- Place the pendulums on brass sheet holder on piano wire arms.
- Place mirrors below at angles.
- Swing pendulums and turn off the lights and watch.
- For recording light movement, photograph with a tripod with the camera set on very long exposure.

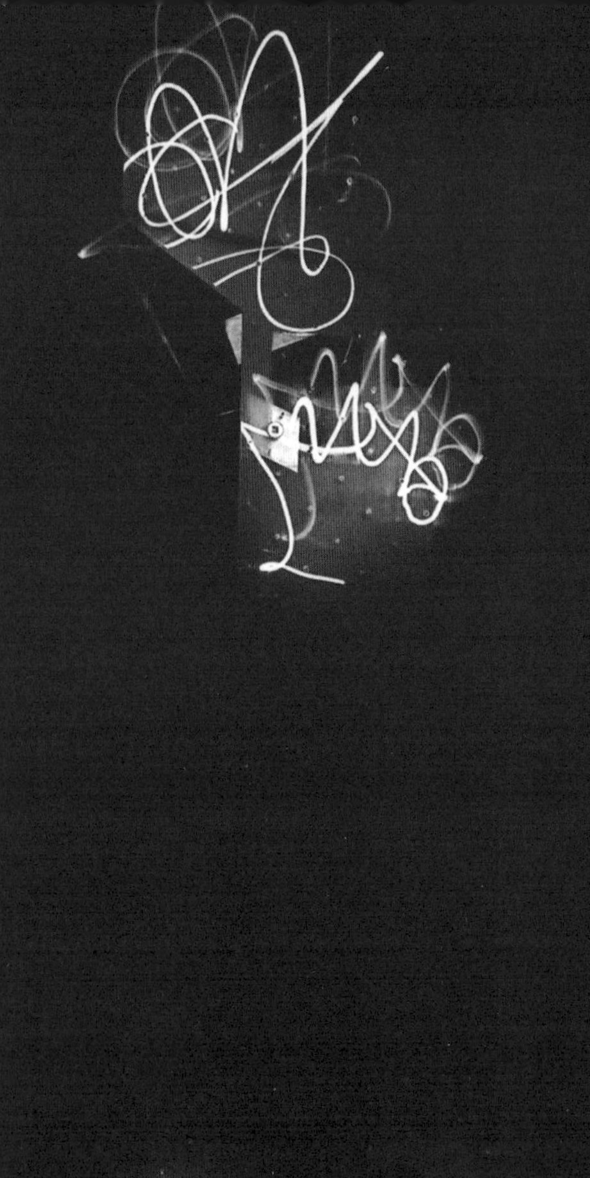

Designer: Edward Liu

Device: Untitled

Function: Controls and transcribes motion into a series of back-projected images

Concept:
The installation is a response to the phenomenological experience of occupying an unfamiliar derelict house without the sense of sight. Three image-maps were made tracing these explorations in the dark, which were then internally back-projected into a slim 1250mm high black perspex box located in the centre of a room.

The minimal intervention of extending retractable steel cables from the black box to the perimeter of the room at different heights render the room unfamiliar in a blacked-out environment, engendering uncertainty in the mind of the interloper/explorer.

As the interloper/explorer moves around the box in a path semi-prescribed by the cables, infrared beams from strategically located motion detectors are broken, setting off motorised reflectors within the box.

The back-projected images distort and overlap, transcribing the interloper/explorer's movement in a palimpsest of fragmented light, existing only until the room's next occupant enters and recharts his predecessor's path.

Dimensions: 900 x 200 x 1250mm

Fabrication time: 4 weeks and 3 days

Assembly time: 2.5 hours

Materials:
4no 20 x 20 x 1200mm extruded aluminium tee sections
4no 20 x 20 x 900mm extruded aluminium angle sections
4no 20 x 20 x 200mm extruded aluminium angle sections
2no 1200 x 900 x 6mm dark grey mitred perspex panels
2no 1200 x 200 x 6mm dark grey mitred perspex panels
1no 900 x 200 x 6mm dark grey mitred perspex panel
1no 182 x 882 x 20mm MDF
2no 150 x 30 x 20mm mitred MDF
2no 850 x 30 x 20mm mitred MDF

Drafting film
Magnetic tape
Dichloromethane
Superglue

10no 100 x 100mm perspex clamp plates
5 steel spring coils extracted from tape measures
5no lengths 4m stainless steel cable
5no lengths of 25mm diameter steel CHS
5no audio cable pin connectors
40no screws
5no pressed sprayed aluminium wall brackets
10no black countersunk wall screws

3no IR beam detectors
3no IR beam emitters
3no electronic circuits
3no 12V motors
6no battery holders
32no AA batteries
3no 200mm lengths M3 threaded rod
6no M3 nuts
3no pin connector clips
3no 120 x 80mm mirror panels (plastic-backed)

3no slide projectors
3no slides
6no 400mm lengths M6 threaded rod
12no M6 nuts
4 point power cable

Fabrication:
- Construct of aluminium frame:
- Assemble base and power unit.
- Attach motors + cranked armatures holding reflector plates.
- Attach infrared motion sensors.
- Install projectors.
- Assemble and install motion circuits.
- Assemble and install retractable cable units.
- Apply film to interior face of perspex.
- Attach perspex to aluminium frame.

Assembly:
- Locate device in room, align + fix motion detectors.
- Fix retractable cables to room walls.
- Black out room and turn power on.

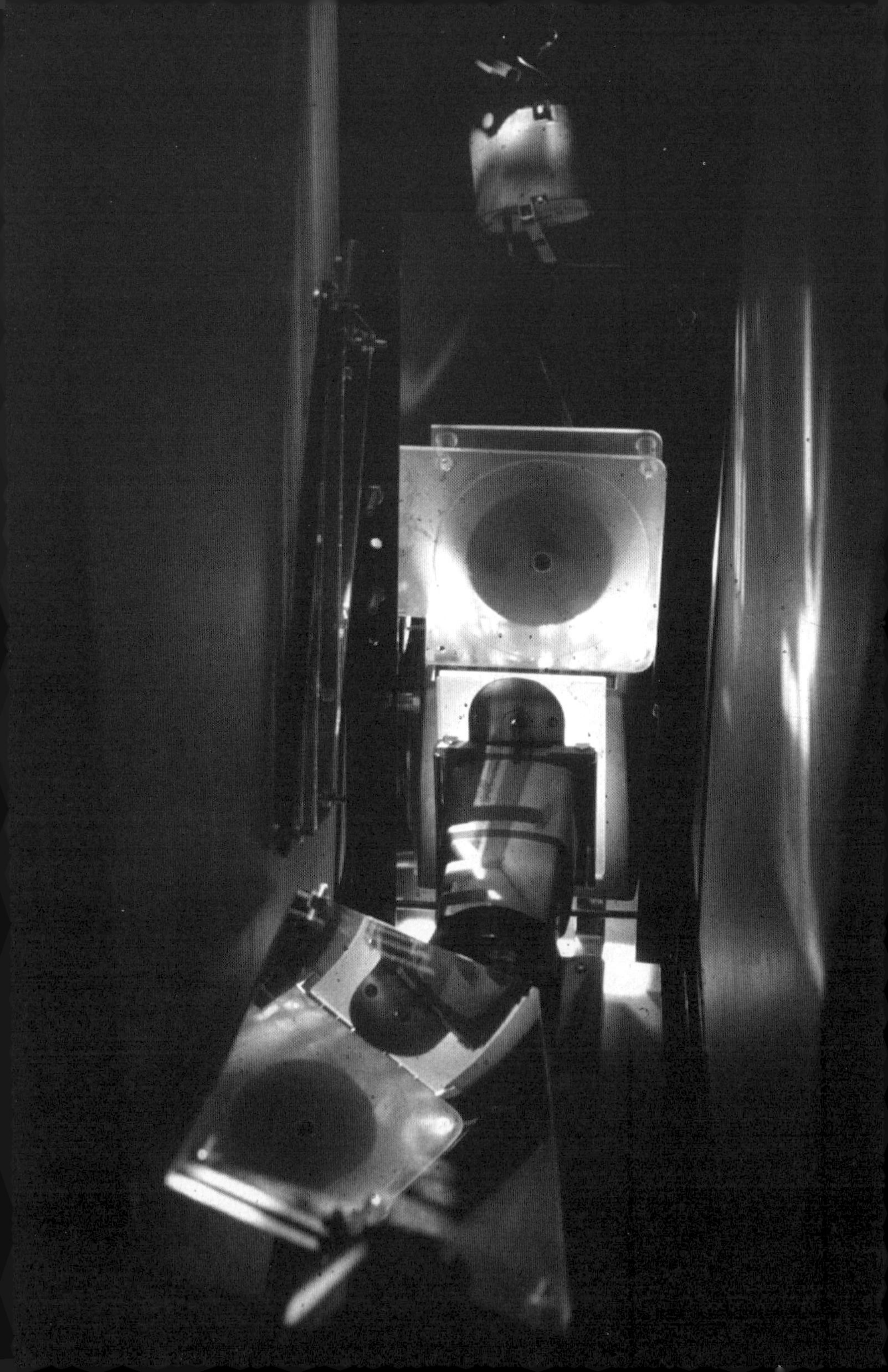

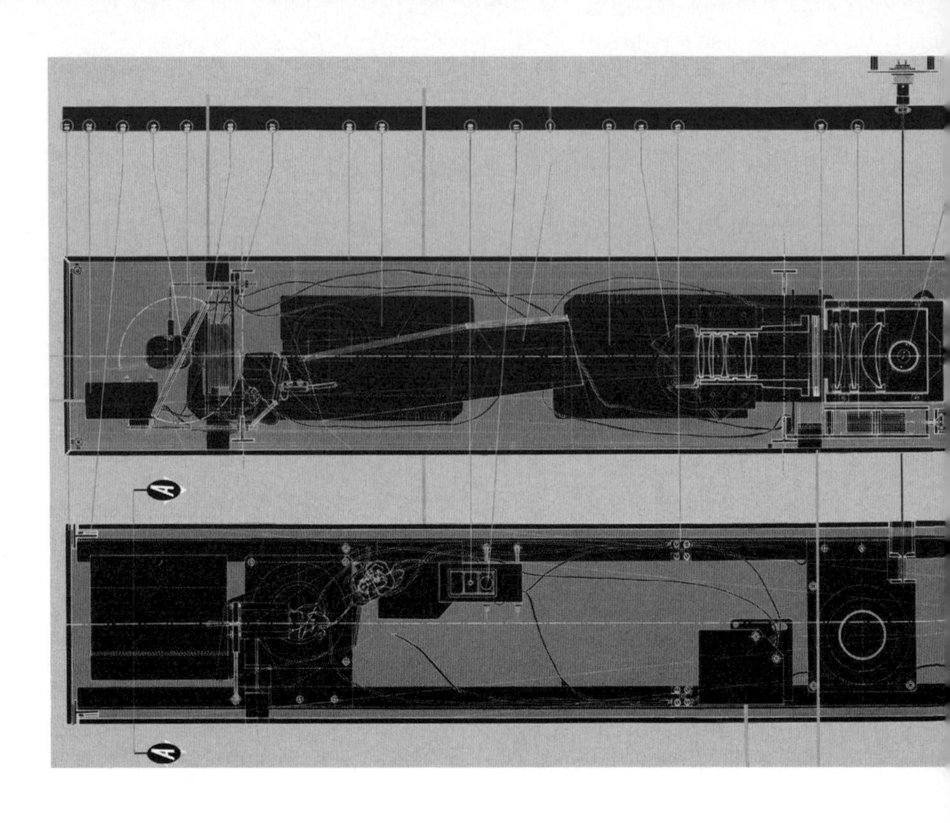

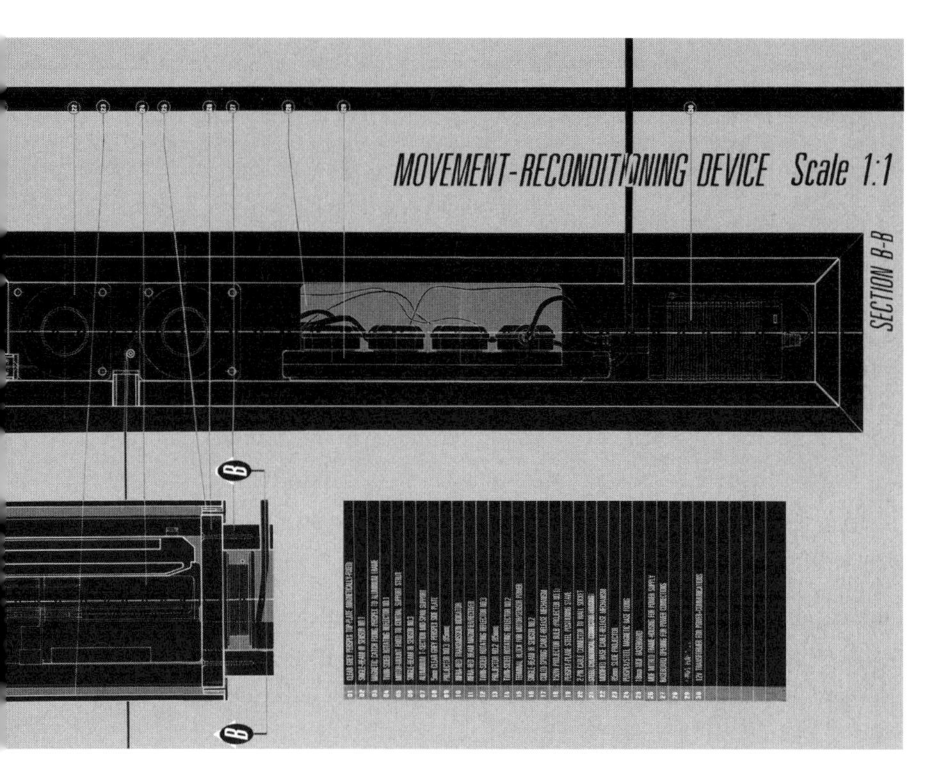
MOVEMENT-RECONDITIONING DEVICE Scale 1:1
SECTION B-B
B
B

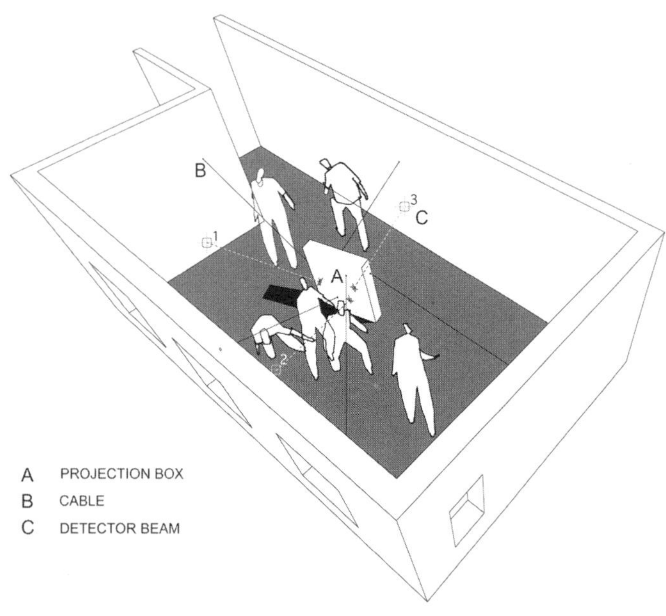
B
1
2
3
C
A
A PROJECTION BOX
B CABLE
C DETECTOR BEAM

Designers: John Oliver, Alex Tucker + Lawrence Wong

Device: Urban Diviner

Function: Revealing the presence of hidden subterranean River Fleet

Concept:
Traditional water divining techniques are used as an analogy for the device to perform: stationary, flickering and then the final dramatic display. The unseen water of the atmosphere is collected in the form of condensation. Varying levels of condensation produce a range of responses in the device demonstrating the differences in microclimates within the site.

The three vessels are positioned around the entrance to no.2 St Bride Street. One of the vessels is static while the other two run along tracks allowing them to disperse and pass through the various microclimates of the site. The various microclimates allow the devices to exhibit different behaviour and responses to atmospheric conditions within a relatively small area, highlighting the delicacy and precise circumstances of the process of condensing water vapour from the atmosphere. The saturation of both vessels results in revealing the presence of hidden subterranean River Fleet.

Dimensions: 33 x 4m (Installation)
2.5 x 0.55 x 0.45m (Individual diviner)

Fabrication time: 2 weeks

Assembly time: 11 hours

Materials:
Bespoke 3mm glass vessels
35 x 50mm hollow steel frame
2.5mm square section steel
Single and double 3 axis arken pulleys
Various electrical components
2mm + 4mm hollow plastic tubes
3V GOW bulbs 2mm white plastic sheeting
1.2mm piano wire, 10 x 1.5mm flat bar steel
12mm rubber tubing
95m of steel cable
12no small gauge electrical cable ties

3no spring
Projector
Generator

Fabrication:
- Cut all materials to size.
- Weld rectangular sections to form frames.
- Attach all pulleys and MDF supports.
- Attach and wire salt pad lights to the upper section of the bespoke glass vessels.
- Attach vac-formed ventilation gates to both the upper and lower openings of the glass vessels.
- Insert wooden armature and screw to the raw steel conducting plate.
- Thread glass spikes into the individual backing brackets and attach to the vertical pulley system.
- Attach the upper battery pack circuits to the satellite vessels.
- Connect all conversing electrical systems.
- Prepare all protective packaging for travel to site.

Assembly:
- Connect all frame components and bolt securely together.
- Position frame within doorway and extend both the upper and lower footpads until frame is securely fixed.
- Attach parasitical fastenings to both existing posts.
- Thread the steel wire through the pulley system and tighten using arken twine grips.
- Attach the preassembled glass vessels to the two runs of wire and then retighten the system using the central anchor points.
- Attach the preassembled projector, cantilevered arm and screen to the riverside traffic sign.
- Wire all on-site electrics and connect projector to the portable generator.
- Set up time laps video camera.
- Start system and ensure public safety.

Additional notes:
The system was installed on site on the 27th of November 2004 for 24 hours and displayed the behaviour that we had predicted following a series of tests performed in a synthetic environment.

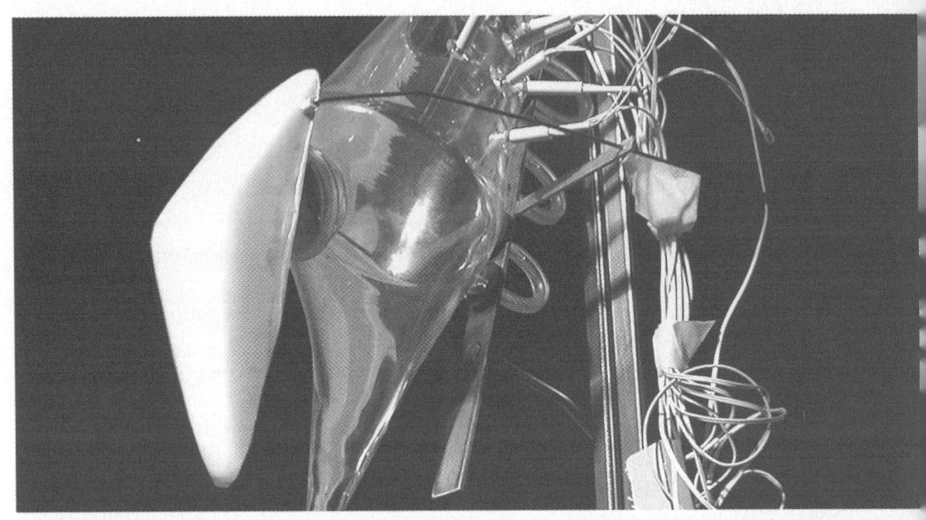

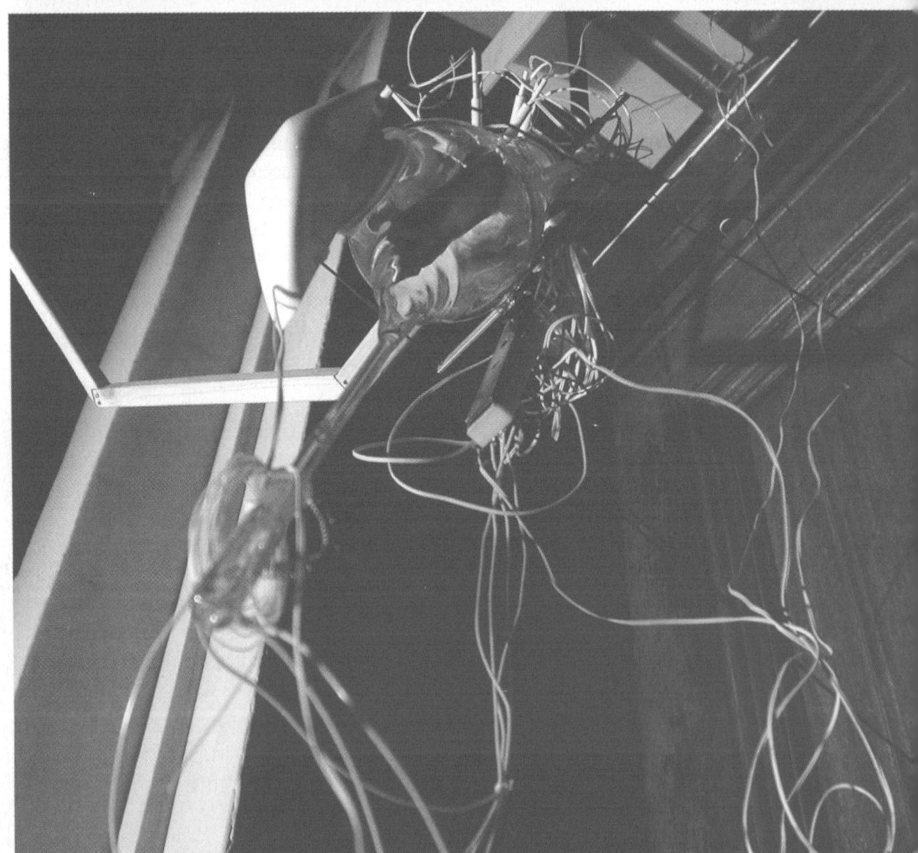

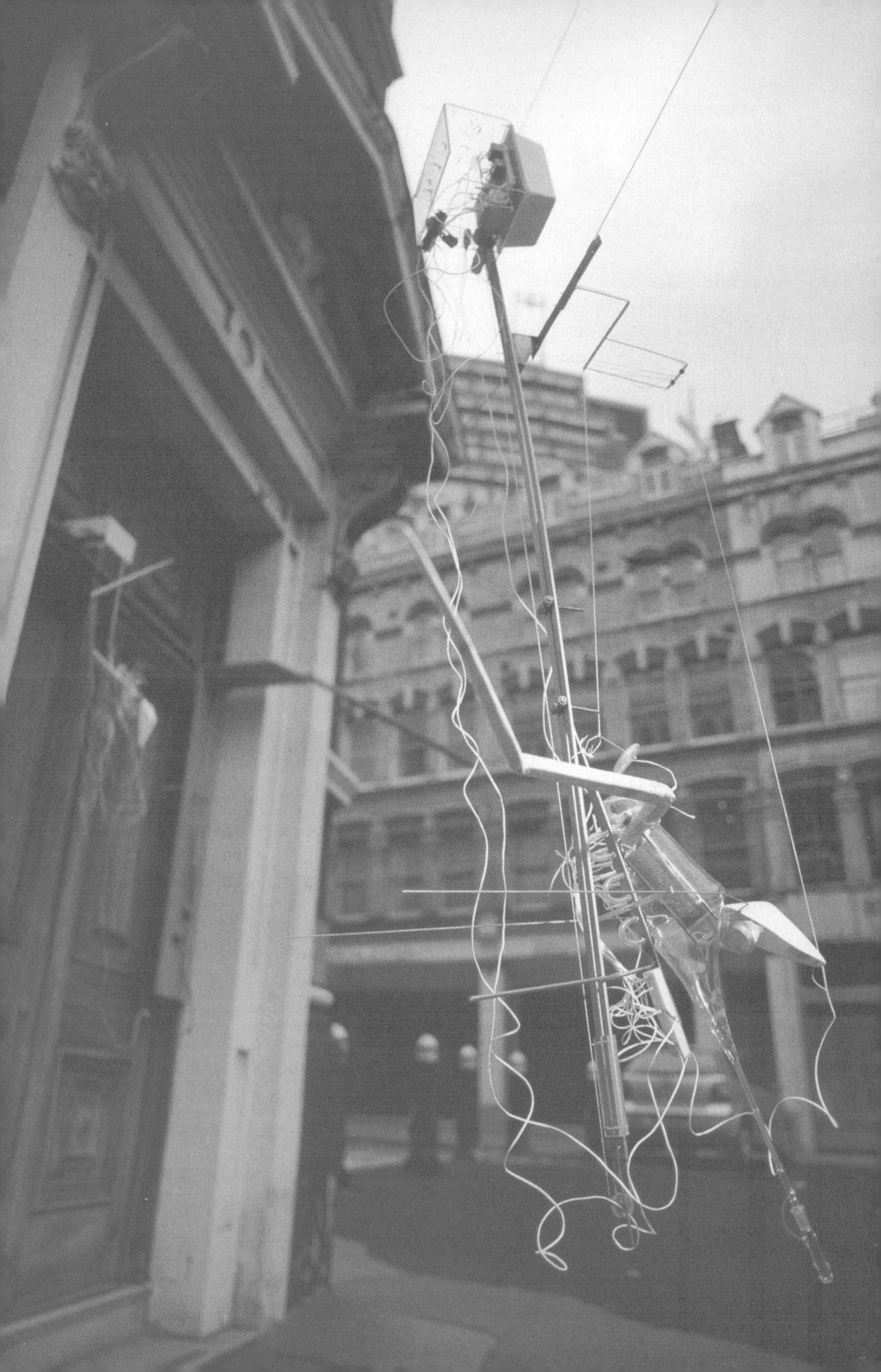

Designer: Joerg Majer

Device: Weekend Coat

Function: Enabling the flaneur to perform his daily tasks with class

Concept:
The street becomes a dwelling for the flaneur; he is as much at home among the facades of houses as a citizen is in his four walls. To him the shiny, enamelled signs of businesses are at least as good a wall ornament as an oil painting is to the bourgeois in his salon. The walls are the desk against which he presses his notebooks; news-stands are his libraries and the terraces of cafés are the balconies from which he looks down on his household after his work is done.

Walter Benjamin, The Arcades Project, 1938

The coat gives the opportunity to become an urban enthusiast for a weekend. Multiple layers of the garment contain hidden functions and the opportunity to accessorise.

On the inside, the coat provides the flaneur with facilities to maintain his immaculate image for a few days: shower, sleeping, laundry, etc. The setup of each individual function will depend on the urban situation given: water can be extracted from the public system or his sleeping place can be attached on the facade of a building.

The exterior however presents the image of a loafing gentleman, who wears the disguising shell to cover up his real identity. The coat acts as his veneer: a slick outside with a parasitic core.

Dimensions: 1600 x 400mm (varies)

Fabrication time: 3 weeks

Assembly time: 5 seconds

Materials:
Felt
Cotton
Polyester
Plastic
Photographic paper

Aluminium
Cotton thread
Velcro
Rubber

Fabrication:
- Choose your size according to your chest measurement.
- Cut out the pattern pieces along the marked lines. When sewing, fabrics should be facing right sides.
- Stitch pattern pieces 1cm from edge and secure ends.
- Trim seam allowances if necessary, turn and press open.
- Bend aluminium plates to suit body shape and sew into coat.
- Cut and bend aluminium rods to fit body.
- Mill the connecting elements from block of aluminium and join rods together.
- Screw rods to aluminium body plates to form exoskeleton and connect with fabric of coat.

Assembly:
- Put on coat.
- Attach accessories using the buttons provided.
- Coat connects to urban fabric through ropes or exoskeleton.

Additional notes:
- Do not tumble-dry.

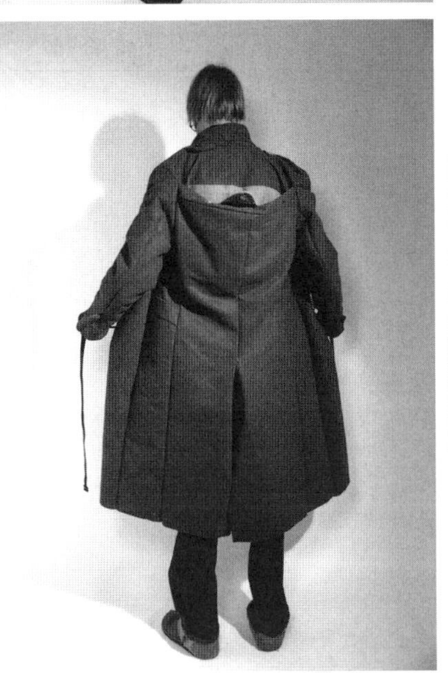

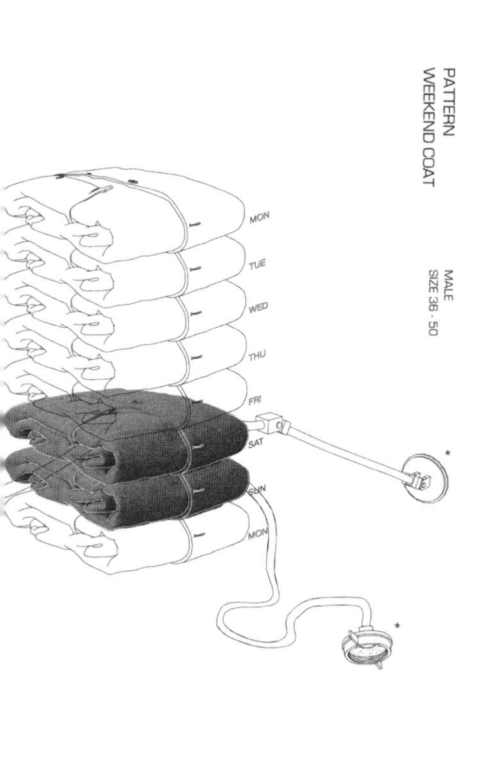

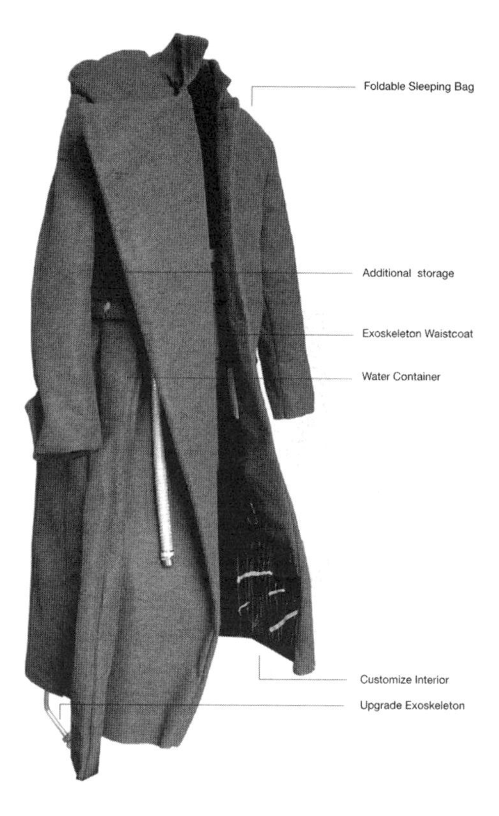

ACCESSORIES

1 Folding Sleeping Bag
2 Water Container

PATTERN
WEEKEND COAT
MALE
SIZE 36 - 50

*not included, please order accessory separately

1

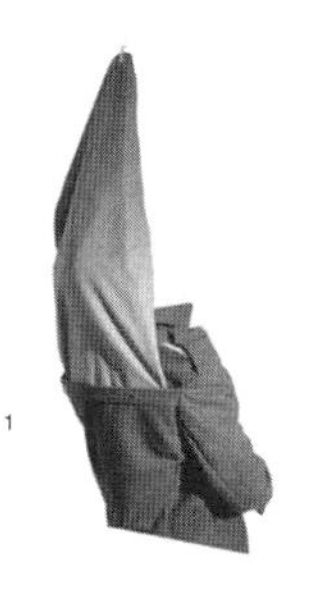

2

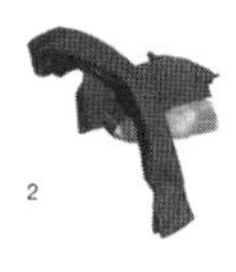

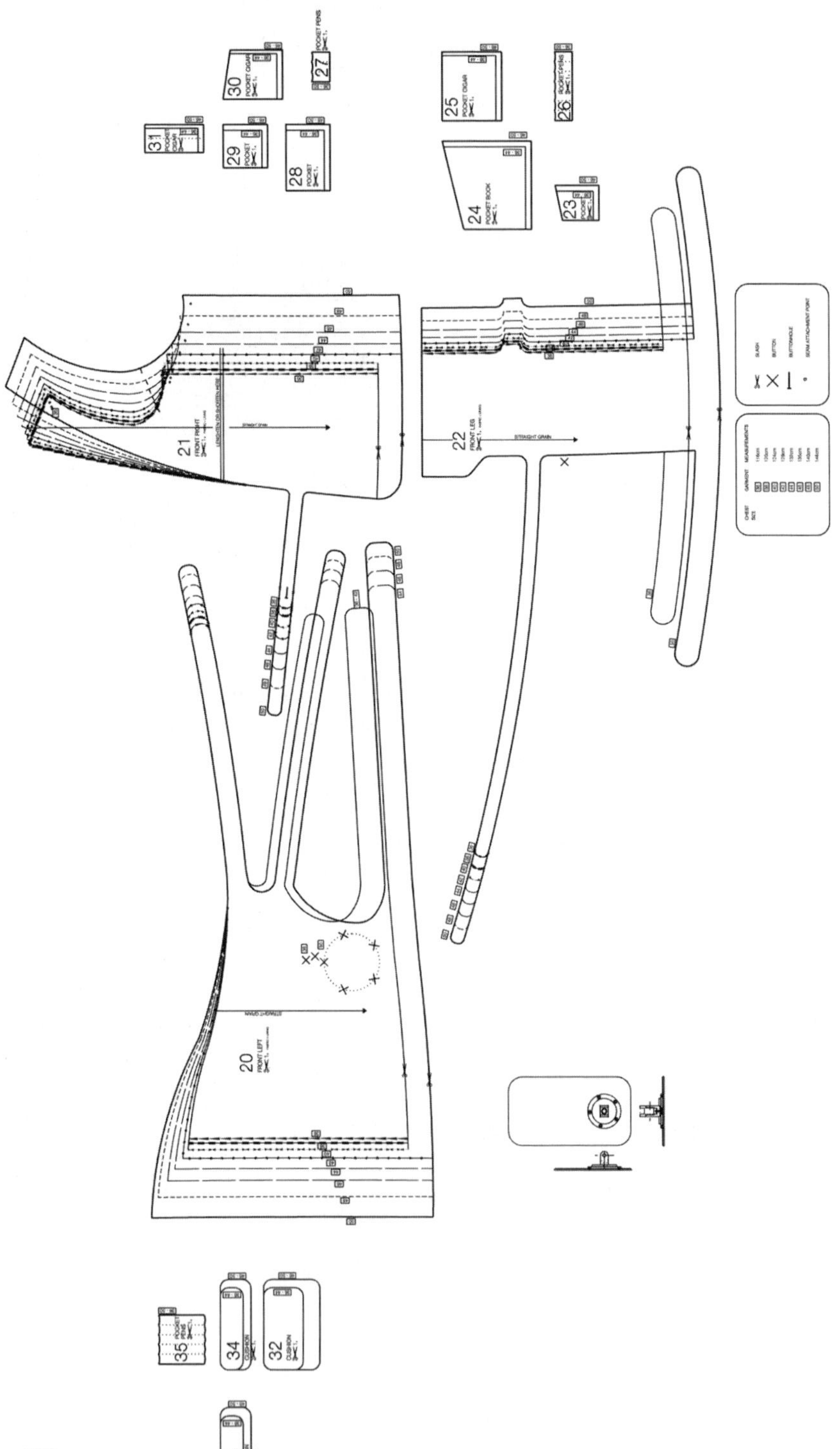
20 FRONT LEFT
21 FRONT RIGHT
22 FRONT LEG
23 POCKET
24 POCKET BOOK
25 POCKET CIGAR
26 POCKET PENS
27 POCKET PENS
28 POCKET
29 POCKET
30 POCKET CIGAR
31 POCKET CIGAR
32 CUSHION
33 CUSHION
34 CUSHION
35 POCKET PENS
STRAIGHT GRAIN
SLASH
BUTTON
BUTTONHOLE
SEAM ATTACHMENT POINT
CHEST SIZE
GARMENT
MEASUREMENTS

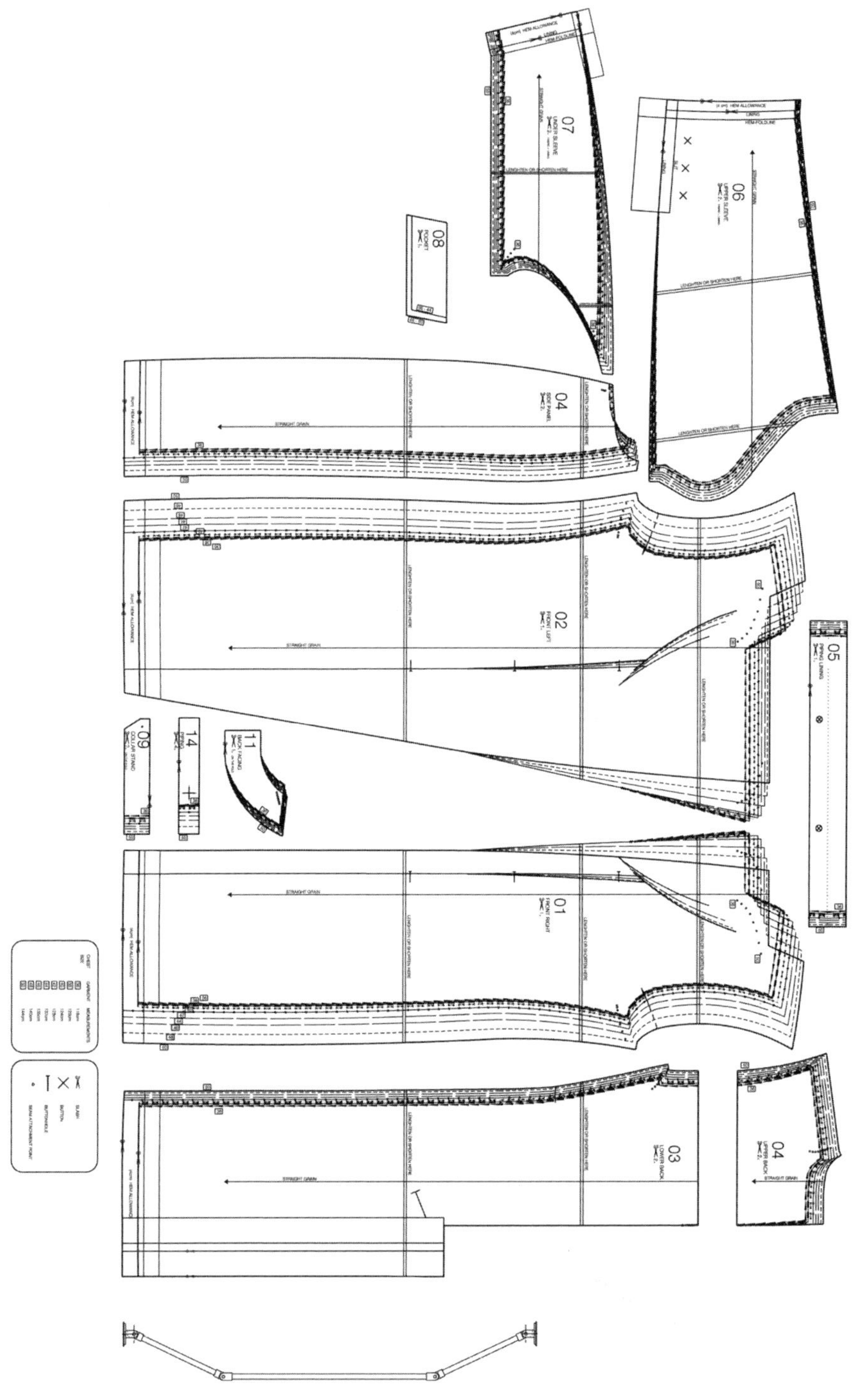

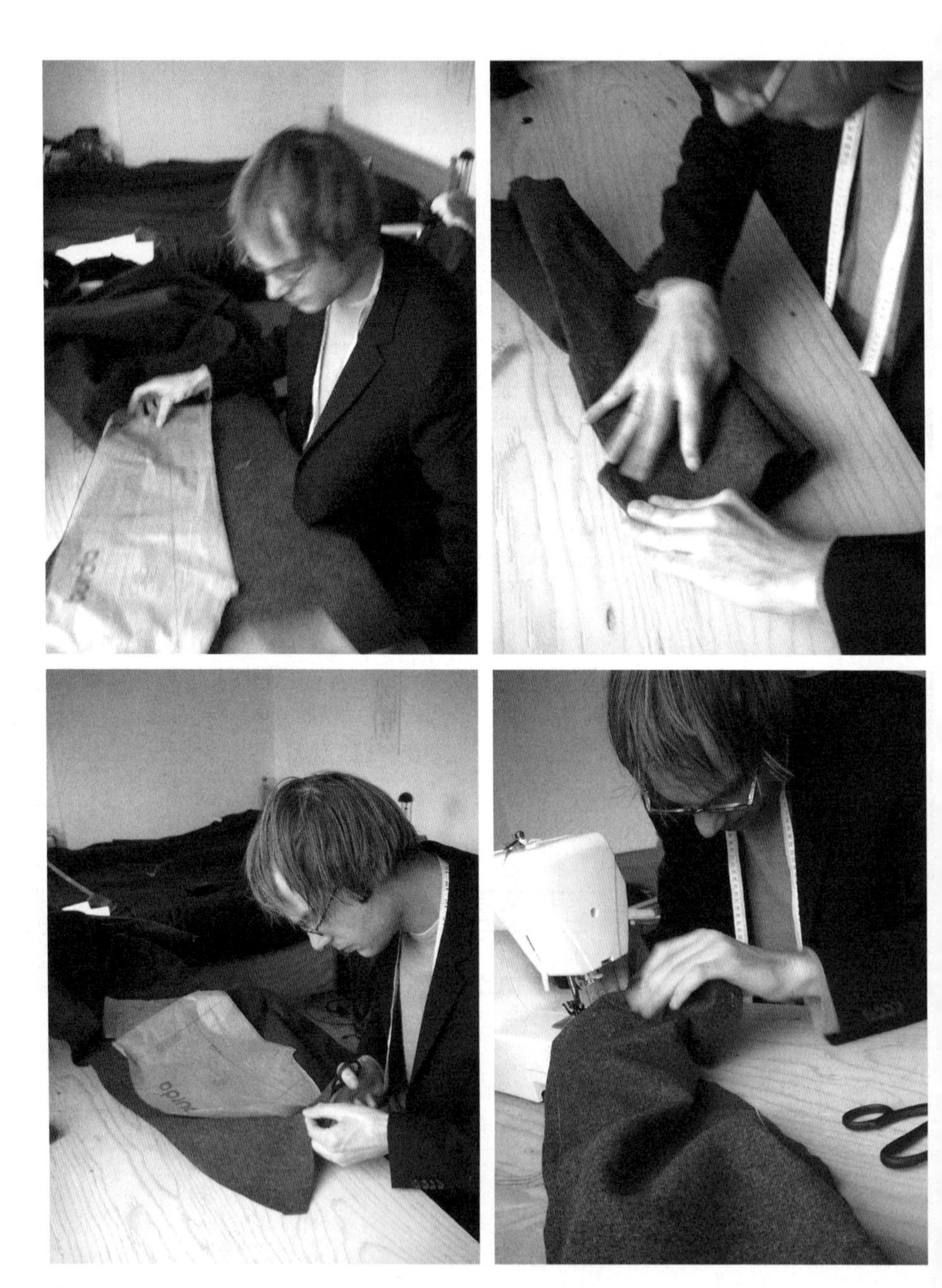

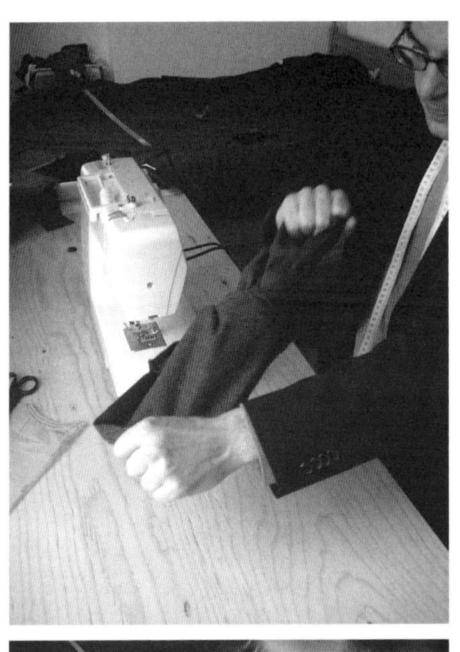

Designer: Nat Chard

Device: Wet Bog Camera

Function: Developing an understanding of JP Wilson's perspectival projection techniques

Concept:
The Cold Bog diorama has a curved background painting (behind some birds, bushes and a rabbit) with a view up a small valley representing a sphagnum moss bog in Connecticut. JP Wilson made many of the finest natural history dioramas at the American Museum of Natural History in New York as well as some very fine later examples at the Yale Peabody. He had trained at Columbia as an architect and then became a diorama painter, bringing with him a rigour learned from making precise measured perspectives of buildings.

Each camera has a film plane that is curved as an exact (upside-down) scale model of the diorama shell. To allow the necessary depth of field for such a film plane the cameras use a pinhole instead of a lens. This is located at the ideal viewing position for the scale diorama shell, and when photographing the existing diorama, located in this full-scale position. The camera uses 120 roll film that can be wound on so that the cameras can take several shots without reloading. The original survey of the Bog site was made on the 17th of June 1949. Wilson used stereoscopic photography when making his surveys.

The application of the Wet Bog Camera is to photograph the Cold Bog diorama at the Yale Peabody Museum of Natural History by Wilson. This is to unfold the picture plane and to photograph the original site for that diorama to construct the ideal perspectival projection for its diorama shell.

The camera took photographs of that site on June 17th 2001, and of the diorama on the following day. There are three Bog cameras, two to make stereoscopic photographs and one as a back-up. The width of the cameras allows normal eye separation between two cameras when photographing the diorama (when on the site a larger separation is used). When looking at stereoscopic photographs of the diorama taken with a normal camera the curvature of the painted background is apparent. When looking at a pair of stereoscopic photographs from the bog camera the background appears completely flat (with the three-dimensional elements in the foreground still in 3D), which provides a verification of the accuracy of the camera.

Dimensions: 65 x 75 x 120mm

Fabrication time: 2 months

Assembly time:
It takes five minutes to load each camera in a darkroom before using. Setting up time on site depends on the co-operation of the sphagnum moss (have you ever tried to get three tripods level on a floating sphagnum moss bog?) – but about half an hour. This includes exposure tests using a pinhole camera with the same focal length as the bog cameras but with a Polaroid back for almost instant results.

Materials:
The patterns are made in Cibatool, a synthetic tool-making material. Silicone rubber moulds were made from these, and the parts cast in various plastics. The shells are vacuum formed over sacrificial plaster forms as they are straight sided and reusable forms would be hard to extract. When the plaster forms were cast too thin the vacuum-forming machine would implode them, a process that was very beautiful but equally infuriating given the looming deadline of a flight. The ancillary components are CNC machined in various plastics or turned in aluminium and brass.

Assembly:
All elements are manufactured and then bolted down to the main (horizontal) chassis. The last pieces are the shells that join at the chassis. Camera tape is used to cover the join to make sure it is light-tight.

Additional notes:
The exposure times in front of the diorama were three-quarters of an hour. On the site they ranged from one to nineteen seconds as the light fell. If I were to build it again I would use roller bearings instead of plastic runners on the inside of the curved film plane to make winding on easier.

KODAK E100VS
50
KODAK E100VS
49

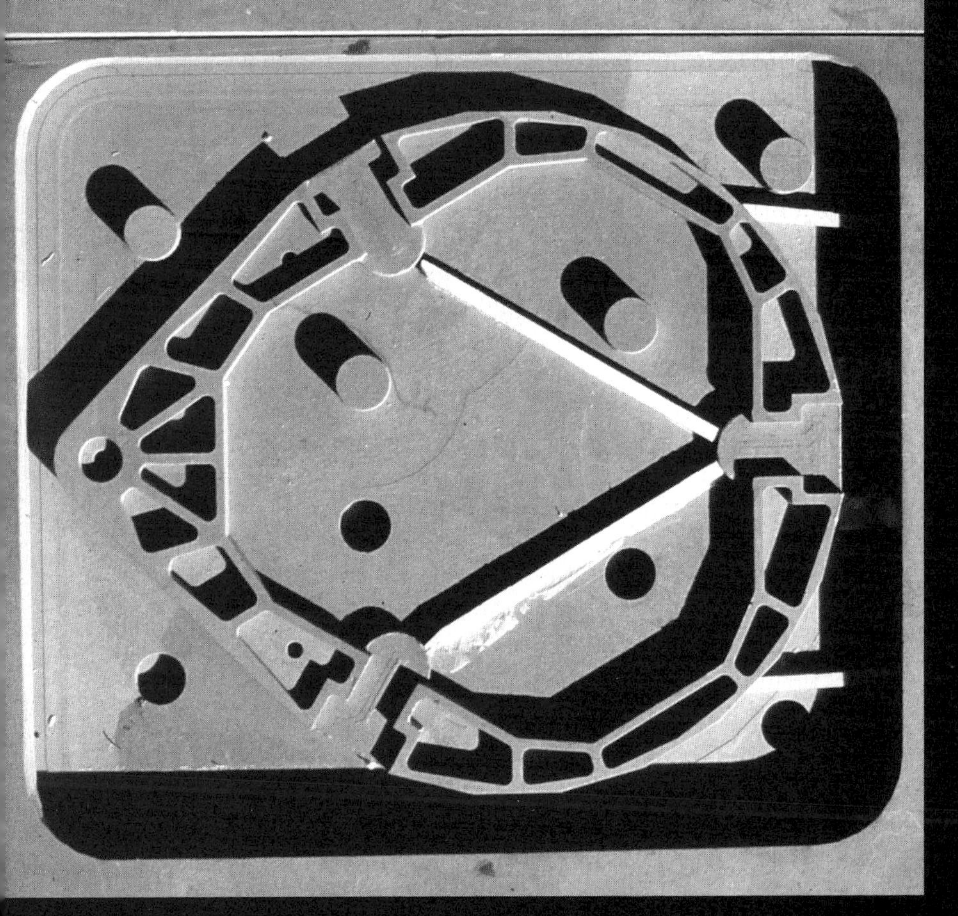

…and left to my own devices, I probably would…
Simon Chadwick, architect

…but at Hardwick not only the entrance front is symmetrical; the house is symmetrical on all four sides and its basic scheme of a rectangle surrounded by six towers, two to each long and one to each short side, is simple as an idea, but ingeniously complex in its results, for the towers assume an endless variety of groupings according to the angle from which they are looked at. Examples of this type of ingenuity were called 'devices' by the Elizabethans. They used the term over a wide range to cover, for instance, buildings of complex or original plan, acrostic or riddle poems, and the jewels incorporating a symbolic picture and matching motto which courtiers devised to sum up their approach to life and wore when jousting in front of the Queen.[1]

Hardwick Hall in Derbyshire is the ideal place to take your gran of a Bank Holiday Monday. It is as pleasant, culturally fulfilling and as inoffensive an experience as one could wish for. However, this place provides more than just an octogenarian exercise yard. As Mark Girouard's writings show, the genius of the design provides a vehicle for the greater understanding of 'devices', and an opportunity to observe an ideal example.

In addition to its use in the description of architectural problem solving, there are hints of cunning and mischief in the definition. There's also an enticing link to the distant social complexities of chivalry and the intricate world of medieval nobility. But with regard to the contemporary relevance of the word, do any of these notions remain?

Today the word 'devices' is attributed to little bits of electronic crap that, we are lead to believe, will make our lives effortless; that remind us of stuff we've forgotten. Little tiny plastic things that somehow store vast libraries of music, whether you've time to listen to any of it or not, and can you conceive of anything as useless as a phone that doesn't take pictures? In our modern world of function and utility is there room for a more romantic, theocratic device, or is it a term simply reduced to frivolous stocking fillers?

In exploring this question, I will source contemporary examples of the three strands delineated in Girouard's definition. The chosen subjects are programmatically very different, though the similarities between them are more than merely tentative. For me, they represent both aspiration and catharsis, and until writing this, I would have said I was comfortably familiar with them all, but critique has an interesting habit of revealing a little hidden extra, which, I suppose, is the point. Each example is a personal choice, and to quote Julie Andrews, as I often do, they constitute 'a few of my favourite things'.[2]

The phrase 'acrostic or riddle poems' hints at an element of the subject. To grasp at further references under this premise, it may be appropriate to look back to where this meander began, in the Elizabethan period. Christopher Marlowe's Doctor Faustus is a curious and darkly-loaded text. It has long been assumed that within Marlowe's writing, atheist and heretical beliefs were squirreled away, and he would playfully taunt his audiences with cleverly veiled subversive philosophies. He used the public performances of his plays as a cache in which his theories were secluded, multiple meanings and insinuation screening dangerous ideology. As a former spy, posted to northern France in the service of Elizabeth I, devices of subterfuge were familiar to Marlowe, and using this mechanism, he operated on the fringes of all things just and godly, in order to maintain both his extreme views and his freedom.

The director and designer Stewart Laing's most recent adaptation of Charles Gounod's *Faust*, based on the original play by Marlowe of 1592, displays a series of visual and dramatic devices, that contribute to, and further this ancient lineage. Certainly the most significant of these is the siting of the performance in the cheap surroundings of a modern commercial cinema auditorium.

The opening features the tired and wretched body of Faust, depressed and lonely. He is shown clawing at the upper reaches of middle age, mourning his lost youth and past love. As the credits have rolled and the room has been vacated, Mephistopheles moves slowly towards the audience, giving the cinema screen a vast and darkly supernatural cavernous depth. The drab, fabric-lined proscenium becomes the portal for the interaction and fusion of the natural and spirit worlds, as well as the oculus for the contrivance of the story.

When the bargain is set and the pact is made, rather than procure the transformation of Faust into the slim handsome figure of youth, Laing orchestrates the addition of Faust's youthful persona, played by the beautiful Pete Ashmore, into the world of the living. The cinema screen becomes the conduit for his arrival and frames the first tentative but powerfully charged contact between the two characters representing the young and old faces of the same man.

Throughout the performance the action flips from one side to the other of the screen's surface, emphasising the surreality of the premise of the plot. Each scene hovers on the edge of the real and the ethereal, dipping in and out of each world through the meniscus that separates the two.

The work harbours a plethora of devices to perpetuate the dramatic premise, but it is the setting that is the fulcrum. A familiar and universally accessible image, the cinema screen allows the creation of a stage within a stage, a well-wrought Elizabethan theatrical device, but in so doing separates, connects and emphasises the crossing of worlds. The solution to the problem provides what is necessary, but the device, in the true sense of the word, brings something more.

By the very virtue of its 'complex and original plan', the New Art Gallery, Walsall, retreats from two primary features of other supposedly regenerative architectural 'devices' of this part of post-industrial England. Making a confident, solid footprint on its hilltop site, the building's architects, Caruso St John, controversially present walls and windows to its surroundings, complementing and contributing to the unspecial streetscape. Elevations are crafted, forming an intellectual engagement with the issue of façade, and a complex strategy of analysis and subtle contextual commentary.

The building does not retreat behind ribbons of anonymous opaque glass screens, hinting at acres of flowing white space within. The massing carves a confident and proportionally astute form against the seasonal greys of the sky. The obligatory 'tin top' of so many recent buildings representing the lower end of the architectural spectrum, are openly taken on and humiliated by the gallery architect's stolid investment in a clear proportional strategy. The café's situation in a generous concrete cube, which culminates the route through the building, is an appropriately subtle and significant urban statement.

The formulation of a clear and distinct spatial sequence to the planning of the building shows an appreciation of, and a deep intellectual connection with, the great tradition of the design of fine country houses, and endeavours to orchestrate a series of rooms in which the proportion, lighting and exhibited work share significance with view and orientation through specific and sensitively cultivated fenestration.

The central suite of rooms displaying the Garman Ryan Collection makes reference to the planning devices of the villas of Adolf Loos, and is also redolent of some of the great civic galleries of the Victorian period, such as The City Art Gallery, Manchester, by Sir Charles Barry.

Fragments of Girouard's analysis are evident in this building, the plan's complexity and originality satisfying the Elizabethan usage of the word. Neither of these elements is essential to the function of the building, but their inclusion in its resolution provides a distinct difference. References are tentatively procured, but none obvious enough to be tripped over.

The intelligence behind the conception of the building makes a place to view art, but this is simply a means to an end. The broader connections and subtle references that the building makes add to the solution of the brief, but hint at a much greater agenda. This pursuit makes the building a 'device', and therefore puts it into the same category as Hardwick.

The final part of the Elizabethan definition describes 'jewels incorporating a symbolic picture and accompanying motto', which courtiers wore when 'jousting in front of the Queen'. For this analysis I turn to a fictional building, the home of Jay Gatsby as described by F. Scott Fitzgerald[3] in his novel. A clever and hopelessly romantic novel, this literary concoction holds one specific device, embodied in the life of the title character.

The young millionaire Gatsby builds an entire world of decadent parties and affluent and superficial friends around himself. The centrepiece of his elaborate fabrication is his palatial home at New York's wealthy suburb of West Egg on Long Island Sound. This vast 'wedding cake' of a house is described by Fitzgerald as 'a factual imitation of some Hotel de Ville in Normandy'.[4] The grounds of the mansion form the backdrop to Fitzgerald's depiction of the shallow, hedonistic world which envelops New York's nouveau riche, and which Gatsby seeks to manipulate.

There was music from my neighbour's house through the summer nights. In his blue gardens men and girls came and went like moths among the whisperings and the champagne and the stars […]. The lights grow brighter as the earth lurches away from the sun, and now the orchestra is playing yellow cocktail music, and the opera of voices pitches a key higher. Laughter is easier minute by minute, spilled with prodigality, tipped out at a cheerful word.[5]

Gatsby's mansion and all that takes place within it is meticulously designed as a gargantuan peacock plumage, with the sole purpose of attracting the attention of Daisy Buchanan, his quarry, and the object of his desire. The house becomes the centre of Gatsby's complex and excessive system of entrapment. Every tiny detail of his exuberant and indulgent lifestyle is designed to remotely seduce Daisy.

Whilst the house is the vessel, it is the society that Gatsby creates around himself that represents the device in this instance. The outlandish and exuberant parties constitute the jousting, the house is quite clearly the 'jewel', glittering across the water of Long Island Sound, its sole purpose is to attract a possibly wandering eye, that of Daisy, playing the role of the Queen. It is possible to conceive of this collective of elements as providing the 'motto', as a representation and communication of, Gatsby's approach to life.

Fitzgerald carves out his finest prose on his tragic character, illustrating in fine detail his desperate plight. But this is not the limit of his device. Jay Gatsby is tailored to represent a generation, the young and wealthy benefactors of the hungry child of capitalism. They arrived back to America 'restless' from the First World War, advancing technology stretching boundaries and possibilities, and ultimately beginning the shrinking of the world. Fitzgerald renders an image of a society with every decadent whim pandered to, but a total absence of soul. A vision of proud consumers, he ridicules the culturally baron, blind hedonism his characters represent.

Whilst significantly different, each example has a recurrent theme of multiplicity; each device indicated is versatile, performing a series of functions simultaneously. However, it is more complex still. Not only do these examples conform to the functional requirements of the pragmatic device, but each has an implication on an emotional, even romantic level. Walsall's spatial sequencing, the portal between earth and the spirit world in Stewart Laing's Faust, and Gatsby's purchase and manipulation of a piece of society, all provide a means to an end, but each also delivers something more than just the necessary. Whether it manifests itself in cunning, or cleverness, a slightly humorous element, or even a lean to the sinister, it seems that a little extra is essential to qualify.

Despite its envelopment into the world of cream teas and sensitive preservation, there is something hidden within the estate of Hardwick Hall. Although the house is now animated only by the shuffling sound of one thousand Dr Scholl sandals, the genius of its conception relates directly to this subject. Could it be that the Elizabethan definition describes a world free of the confines of machines, and therefore ignorant of the distinction our society may insist upon between the pragmatic and the poetic? Is it possible that they were regarded as one and the same thing?

In addition to its basic problem solving capability, a device is granted the term because it comprises an illusive ingredient which allows it to transcend the mundane and procure appreciation within a higher sphere of consciousness. A sure sign is when a device displays the necessary drop of cunning, or even the gleam of genius that makes you glad you encountered the problem that cultivated its existence. The list that makes up this category is not easy to write. It can be excessively subjective, and cover a vast area, but whether it's an oyster repetitively wrapping a grain of sand, or a barman dropping a slice of lime into your gin and tonic, you know when you see it.

[1]Mark Girouard, *Hardwick Hall* (National Trust, 2002) p16

[2]'My Favorite Things', Richard Rodgers + Oscar Hammerstein II, The Sound of Music. Dir. Robert Wise. (20th Century Fox, 1965)

[3]F. Scott Fitzgerald, *The Great Gatsby* (Penguin Classics, 2000)

[4]p11; [5]pp41-42

Faust (1859), Charles Gounod. Stewart Laing, director + designer. Malmö Opera Och Musikteater, 2005

Devices as they appear to a Western Engineer
Matthew Wells, structural engineer

For an engineer, they are the mediation needed to intervene in natural processes. A 'nuclear device' - a disruptor of matter with which to release energy.

The notion of life as continual problem solving activity is a Roman idea. They were great builders of machines. Egyptians and Greeks had beautiful boats and buildings, seemingly almost grown out of their environment, at one with their surroundings. However it was the Romans who transformed Hellenism and took their coarse but clever devices across the known world.

The utilitarian engineering of the Augustan Age set aside aesthetics and in the process achieved a distinctive expression of its own. Aqueducts, to carry fresh water to the permanence of great cities, multiplied the purest of structural devices, the arch. Smaller tiers on top of larger brought the creeping and settling stonework to level and a timelessness came into being.

The West has been in the collapse of that Empire ever since. Our devices became more and more shoddy and contingent. In the development of artillery to make up for inadequate manpower structural design was truly born. The pivot pins of the ballista became the measure with which to proportion all the parts of the weapon, large or small. Structural design: a human device economising effort but with the potential to embody a kind of elegance otherwise accessible only in the contemplation of number theory.

The Cathedral builders divided structural devices into two types. The structural systems, vaults and buttresses needed for the drive towards St Augustine's flood of light, and cranes and levers, meta-systems to the building, needed to raise the stones. Study of the latter became an obsession in itself. Their close correspondence with military hardware, catapults and siege engines developed a common way of encoding and communicating their use. Sketches, supported by proportional rules, constructed and disseminated a canon of knowledge far and wide. This body of information improved in turn through its encounters with local vernaculars.

And within these documents there was room for misunderstanding and therefore potential for new discoveries, new forms of machine. Leonardo da Vinci's sketchbooks collect a wide variety of devices and set them alongside anatomy depicted as mechanism and natural processes illustrated as machinery. His copy work is littered with errors and together with the paratactic ordering of systems on the page creates a fertile space for the imagination to roam within.

The commercial or perhaps political value of structural devices colours their development. The first systematic treatise on structural forms was a product of Galileo Galilei specifically to enable him to move through a court patronage system. Scientific and technological discoveries were gifts to be offered alongside automata and astronomical models. Sir Christopher Wren gave the King a papier-mâché lunar globe and secured the commission for rebuilding St Paul's Cathedral.

Other engineers won their work with secret methodologies and arcane. Hard to be believe but Filippo Brunelleschi commenced the dome of Florence cathedral having lured his patrons with only vague allusions to a unique construction method. He fulfilled his promise to complete a shell without centring using an age-old device - rediscovered through observation of ruins on his travels in the East. Old masonry vaults suffer condensation and water ingress in their crowns, rotting out and collapsing from their centre like teeth. If the sides remained stable as the middle opened out then the process must be safely reversible. The best of Brunelleschi's devices here was not his great crane for lifting the lantern or the structural idea of tiered hoops of brickwork progressing up and inwards, but the experiments needed for his inventions.

Devices used in building embody their own attractions independent of the artefact itself. Cleverness seems to be an essential characteristic. Technical complexity marks early examples of any new technology, a kind of exuberance of making. As soon as the new materials of industrialisation appeared — iron, steel, aluminium, plate glass and then reinforced concrete (others are of minor importance), there was an outpouring of experimentation focussed on each over-attenuated frames, inordinately complicated junctions, and a general mannerism where the problems associated with the materials' use would be highlighted in their solution. This expression of construction fixed itself into a heroic age of engineering. Captain Nemo's submarine Nautilus with its rivets and filigree metalwork epitomises a received idea of Victorian engineering. In more modern times the technological excessiveness of gadgetry, the loading process of a Sony camera, finds its counterpoint in the anthropometric minimalism of the control interfaces of *iPods* and *Bang + Olufsen* decks.

The English have always added a quixotic romanticism to mechanical engineering. The speculations of William Heath Robinson only match the reality of Barnes Wallace's bouncing bomb. The completeness of that idea is so appealing that the earlier setbacks of the R101 design and the system's subsequent irrelevance did nothing to dent the inventor's reputation. It is a masterstroke of storytelling by Elleston Trevor in his book *The Flight of the Phoenix* to make the technician dreamer a German.

All our domestic apparatus is fetishised. I have worked for the largest part of my career in the fag end of the English high tech. This attitude to buildings required heroic displays of tectonic-materials brought together in ways to display their assembly, together with sizes and shapes that reflected the characteristics of the materials being used. These materials were carefully selected for a particular expression. Timber and ceramic might be working in the upper eighties or nineties of percentage stress. They might be assembled into the most sophisticated devices, triremes and two-engined bombers, but they weren't high tech. To be high tech they had to be capable of illustration with a cutaway drawing, John Batchelor's pen and ink renderings for *Flight* or Leslie Ashwells paintings for *Eagle* comic. There would be lots of joints and junctions defining surfaces and articulating forms. Now that interest has moved to seamless free forms, blobs and shells of continuous concrete involving no engineering beyond the yes or no of the computer, interest wanes.

And it is with that final device, the computer, that the magic of mechanism tumbles down. For what can it offer next to a bonded pencil? There appears to be an inverse law of usefulness according to the degree of differentiation of a device. The less specific the tool the greater it's potential for misuse and for the incursion of hope for the future. We've spent a long time trying to understand all types of systems and devices and struggling to improve those used in our field of expertise. Perhaps we will preserve our remaining effort to maintaining the simpler tools, swamped rather than superseded by proliferating complexity and polysemy.

Suppliers

Accessories for models
www.smallworldproducts.com

Art + graphics materials
www.londongraphics.co.uk

Automatic weather station equipment
www.oregonscientific.co.uk

Balloons + kites
www.balloonandkite.com

BASIC Stamps + animatronics components
www.milinst.com

BASIC Stamps + development modules
www.parallax.com

Beads, wires + chains
www.beadworks.co.uk

Builders' merchant
www.travisperkins.co.uk

Camera + photographic accessories
www.jessops.com

Communications + 'iButton' devices
www.maxim-ic.com

Craft + modelling tools
www.proopsbrothers.com

Digital-to-analog converter components
www.linear.com

Electrical equipment
www.mkelectric.co.uk

Electronics
www.cricklewoodelectronics.com

Electronic + mechanical components
www.maplin.co.uk

Electronic + mechanical components
rswww.com

Embedded microprocessors for PIC devices
www.microchip.com

Ethernet hub
www.3com.com

Fabrics, zips + buttons
www.macculloch-wallis.co.uk

Fasteners + fixings manufacture
www.hafele.co.uk

Foam, rubber + latex
www.pentonvillerubber.co.uk

Glass blowing
www.columbia-glass.co.uk

Glass merchant
www.rankinsglass.co.uk

Graphics card
www.nvidia.com

Hardware products + hand tools
www.buckandryan.co.uk

High-Level BASIC compilers for PIC devices
www.melabs.com

High-performance IR beam-break sensors
www.sick.de

Infrared web camera
www.logitech.com

Kites accessories
www.kiteshop.co.uk

Leather
www.almahome.co.uk

Lenses
www.instrumentglasses.com

Medical tools
www.porternash.co.uk

Metal suppliers
www.industrialmetal.co.uk

MicroChip PIC microprocessors
www.crownhill.co.uk

Microelectronics
www.cibasc.com

MicroCode Studio Software Development IDE
www.mechanique.co.uk

Model-making materials + tools
www.modelshop.co.uk

Neoprene
www.tiscali.co.uk

Paint + hand tools
www.robertdyas.co.uk

Paint + power tools
www.homebase.co.uk

Piano-wire + radio control models
www.hobbystores.co.uk

Plaster + silicone for casting + mould-making
www.tiranti.co.uk

Plastics (industrial + engineering)
www.amariplastics.com

Plastics moulding + welding
www.vacuumpackaging.co.uk

Pneumatic cylinders, solenoid valves + sensors
www.electroquip.co.uk

Polarised filters and glasses
www.prolinx.co.uk

Pyranometer + metrological instruments
www.skyeinstruments.com

RC servo-motor actuators
www.futaba-rc.com

Resin
www.axson.com

Sequence controller + semiconductors
www.mitsubishichips.com

Shotgun microphone
www.sennheiser.com

Springs manufacturer
www.uksma.org.uk/alliance_spring

Stereoscopic screen
www.harknesshall.com

Surgical instruments
www.downs-surgical.co.uk

Telescope parts + lenses
www.telescopehouse.co.uk

UV paints + lighting
www.glowshop.com

Velcro, needles + thread
www.johnlewis.com

Veneers
www.tdveneers.co.uk

Miscellaneous
Local: Charity shop, Markets + supermarket,
Chemistry laboratories, Skips, Scrapyards